TEIKYO WESTMAR UNIV.

W9-AFS-304

The Teacher's Voice

Studies in Curriculum History Series

General Editor: **Professor Ivor Goodson**, Faculty of Education, University of Western Ontario, London, Canada N6G 1G7

The Teacher's Voice:
A Social History of Teaching
In Twentieth-century America

Edited by

Richard J. Altenbaugh

To Marianne,
the consummate mate,
friend, and teacher

92-1225

The Falmer Press

(A member of the Taylor & Francis Group)
London • Washington, D.C.

USA   The Falmer Press, Taylor & Francis Inc., 1900 Frost Road, Suite 101,
      Bristol, PA 19007
UK   The Falmer Press, 4 John St, London WC1N 2ET

© Selection and editorial material copyright
R. Altenbaugh, 1992

*All rights reserved. No part of this publication may be reproduced, stored in a
retrieval system, or transmitted, in any form or by any means, electronic,
mechanical, photocopying, recording or otherwise, without permission in writing from the Publisher.*

First published 1992

British Library Cataloguing in Publication Data
The teacher's voice: A history of teaching in 20th Century America.
  I. Altenbaugh, Richard J.
  371.100973

  ISBN 1–85000–960–0
  ISBN 1–85000–961–9 pbk

Library of Congress Cataloging-in-Publication Data
The Teacher's voice: a history of teaching in twentieth-century
  America / edited by Richard J. Altenbaugh.
      p.   cm.
    Includes bibliographical references and index.
  ISBN 1–85000–960–0—ISBN   1–85000–961–9 (pbk.)
    1. Teachers—United States—History—20th century.   2. Women
  teachers—United States—History—20th century.   3. Teachers—
  Social conditions—United States.   4. Education—Social aspects—
  United States—History—20th century.   I. Altenbaugh, Richard J.
  LB 1775.2.T44   1991
  371.1′00973—dc20   91–27672
                                                         CIP

Jacket design by Caroline Archer
The cover photograph has been kindly supplied by the Archives of the
Pittsburgh Board of Public Education. It remains the property of the
Pittsburgh Board of Public Education, and is used with their
permission.

Typeset in 10/11½pt Garamond by
Graphicraft Typesetters Ltd., Hong Kong

Printed in Great Britain by Burgess Science Press, Basingstoke on
paper which has a specified pH value on final paper manufacture of
not less than 7.5 and is therefore 'acid free'.

Table of Contents

Table of Contents

ACKNOWLEDGMENTS

Chapter 2, 'Having a Purpose in Life: Western Women Teachers in the Twentieth Century' by Courtney Ann Vaughn-Roberson, from *Great Plains Quarterly* 5 (Spring, 1985): 107–124. Reprinted by permission of the editor.

Chapter 10, 'The Complex Vision of Female Teachers and the Failure of Unionization in the 1930s: An Oral History' by Richard A. Quantz, from *History of Education Quarterly* 25 (Winter 1985): 439–458. Reprinted by permission of the editor.

Chapter 11, 'Teachers and the Workplace' by Richard Altenbaugh, from *Urban Education* 21 (January 1987): 365–389. Reprinted by permission of the editor.

Preface

This book claims seemingly obscure roots, reflecting my professional odyssey. Career decisions appeared to dominate my junior high school years during the early 1960s. My classmates and I spent countless hours in the school's library with the guidance counselor, taking aptitude tests, researching job requirements, and pouring over college catalogues. These career goals, some of us soon discovered, shaped our high school programs of study, with counselors sorting us into different academic tracks. I, alone among my peers, dreamed of becoming an architect, quickly consuming the biography of Frank Lloyd Wright, proudly brandishing my slide rule, and constantly fondling the expensive drafting instruments, which my father had purchased for me, not so much to contribute towards my career quest, but as a way to silence my compulsive nagging. Everyone, it seemed, knew about my exotic career plans.

I was surprised therefore when the assistant principal stopped me abruptly in the hallway one afternoon, and brusquely escorted me into his office for what I thought would be another in a long series of rule infractions. However, he nervously proceeded to convey to me that he thought I possessed all of the qualities necessary to become a fine teacher, but he never divulged these traits. I humored him, as usual, and quickly departed. I felt not only confused by this spontaneous outburst, but even worse, I was insulted by his preposterous suggestion. A teaching career had never entered my mind. Who wanted to be a teacher? No adolescent in his or her right mind would have openly expressed such a desire. To this day, I do not know what precipitated his action.

He proved to be prophetic, however, and serendipity played a role. An altercation with a high school geometry teacher resulted in a low grade, preventing me from qualifying for admission to a university renowned for its architecture program. I enrolled instead at the University of Pittsburgh and majored in history. But, as everyone seemed to ask, what can you 'do' with history? As I saw it, I had two choices: to teach it, or to study it more. I decided to pursue both, obtaining a secondary teaching certificate while earning a masters degree. I loved to teach, which added mystery as well as credence to that assistant principal's seemingly outrageous observation. Following four years of teaching at the junior and senior high school levels, I pursued my doctoral studies full-time, but continued to teach summers at a local high school.

While I found teaching to be fulfilling, I soon discovered its complexities and pitfalls. The state-mandated certification courses did not prepare me for the, at times, overwhelming classroom situations. I attempted to rectify this shortcoming when I eventually began to instruct teacher candidates in my history of education classes. Yet these sincere initiatives too often deteriorated into a 'war story' motif. This feeling of inadequacy sparked my interest in the history of teaching, which I reasoned would best convey the bittersweet experience of teaching to my students. I quickly became disappointed by what I found in the secondary literature, that is, a largely neglected area of research mired in an antiquated institutional approach.

I first stumbled on the potential offered by the oral history method while I served as a Visiting Assistant Professor at Indiana University during the 1980–81 academic year. B. Edward McClellan, in his usual gracious manner, encouraged me to pursue this research interest, which I did when I returned to the University of Pittsburgh. My chance encounters with Richard Quantz and Courtney Vaughn-Roberson at the 1981 History of Education Society meeting, held in Pittsburgh, further stimulated my enthusiasm for oral history as a way to capture a different perspective of the history of teaching. Discussions with both of them at the 1983 American Educational Studies Association conference, in Milwaukee, solidified the concept of this collection; it has since evolved and grown. I met the other contributors over the years, through chance encounters, word of mouth, and relentless pursuit, gaining commitments from each of them. They always appeared congenial, tolerating my over-exuberance for this work. They also excused my often excessive demands as an editor. I asked a great deal of them, and they responded. I grew because of my work on this project and through my association with these fine authors. I hope that it has been as rewarding for them.

The publishing process also proved to be pleasant. Ivor Goodson enthusiastically supported this study, inspiring its title. Malcolm Clarkson efficiently and professionally expedited the review and editing processes. They both proved to be surprisingly unobtrusive, which gave me free reign. Carol Saumarez facilitated the editing of this manuscript through her enthusiastic support for its substance and style. At Northern Illinois University, James Norris, Dean, Liberal Arts and Sciences, provided subvention resources necessary to complete this book. Cheryl Fuller's irrepressible congeniality and Ilga Janouskovec's unshakable patience eased the word processing stage. My dear friends Bruce Nelson, at Central Michigan University, Jane Flanders, at the University of Pittsburgh, and Michael Hickey, at Northern Illinois University, read drafts of the completed manuscript, offering stylistic and substantive comments.

Finally, I owe an invaluable debt to Marianne, Ian, Colin, and Buffy; I hope that this study reflects the precious time that I stole from each of you to work on it.

Richard J. Altenbaugh
DeKalb, Illiois

Chapter 1

Introduction

Richard J. Altenbaugh

History as human agency.

Montgomery (1981)

The recent 'crisis' in education has produced a flurry of policy studies in education (US Department of Education, 1983; Boyer, 1983; Holmes Group, 1986; Carnegie Forum on Education and the Economy, 1986; Goodlad, 1984; Sizer, 1984). They treat a broad range of topics, including educational goals, students, curricula, classroom routines, and have offered a multitude of recommendations for reforming the schools. Of course, each of these policy studies addresses the subject of the teacher — albeit some more than others.

In spite of the voluminous nature of these studies, the policy makers who prepared them failed to include a detailed, historical analysis of the actual conditions of teaching as experienced by the teachers themselves (Altenbaugh, 1989). Goodlad (1984), for example, relied in part upon the interviews of 1,350 teachers to assemble his data. But they were limited only to practicing teachers and their contemporary experiences and perceptions; no historical perspective was either injected or deemed necessary or appropriate. Commenting on the nagging presentism that often characterizes policy studies, Donald Warren (1978) argues that history 'can be useful in understanding the extent to which policy and policymaking are influenced by inertia, the weight of established practice, familiar ideas, and traditional approaches to problem solving' (p. 16).

Worse yet, most policy makers overlook the central actor in the educational process, the teacher (Clifford, 1975). The teacher occupies a strategic position in the schooling process. Students, and often administrators, are transient, but teachers are likely to remain in their classrooms and school buildings year after year, sometimes decade after decade. Too long ignored, or patronized, by policy makers, the teacher holds the key to a humanistic process of schooling as well as permanent school reform. For as Larry Cuban (1984) warns: 'There should be a page in the *Guiness Book of World Records* on failed classroom reforms, for few ever seem to have been incorporated into teachers' repertoires.... Most instructional reforms in the last century were

generated outside the school and were shoved downward into the classroom'
(p. 6).

Few historians stress the role of the classroom teacher in the development of public education in the United States. Although Willard Elsbree
noted this deficiency in his 1939 classic study, *The American Teacher*, historians have only recently turned their attention to the study and analysis of the
public schoolteacher. Geraldine Joncich Clifford (1975, pp. 262, 268) addresses this issue in an historiographic essay which calls for a 'people centered' approach to the study of the history of American education 'that deals,
in significant and sensitive ways, with students, parents, school board members, as well as teachers — warts and all.' Clifford (1978) later applies this
concept to her insightful study of conflict and cooperation between the family
and the school during the nineteenth century. Barbara Finkelstein (1974)
likewise emphasizes teachers in her approach to a selected bibliography of the
autobiographies of schooling and schoolteachers in the nineteenth century.
She categorizes the works regionally and divides them into student and
teacher experiences, and suggests that this kind of data might be used to
examine a variety of questions about educational history. John Gillis (1977)
similarly points to a departure from the traditional narrative of institutional
history and urges educational historians to focus on 'those who teach and
those who learn ... actors in their own right, irreducible to institutional
imperatives and systematic roles' (p. 92). While Clifford, Finkelstein, and
Gillis argue for the historical study of teaching as a means to a more humanistic approach to the history of education, Michael Apple (1983) contends that a
closer scrutiny of teaching will facilitate an analysis of political questions in
education such as the sociology of knowledge; gender, race, and social class
relations; and social, racial, and sexual divisions of labor.

A few historical anthologies and studies that underscore the experiences
and perspectives of teachers have appeared in recent years. Nancy Hoffman's
Woman's 'True' Profession (1981) appears to be the most significant of these
works. Relying upon diaries, letters, and other autobiographical sources,
Hoffman allows women to describe their own teaching experiences. However, like so many recent books about teachers (Jones, 1980; Dyer, 1981;
Kaufman, 1984; Finkelstein, 1989), Hoffman places hers largely within the
context of the nineteenth century. Although these works enrich our understanding of the history of education, few examine the twentieth-century
schoolteacher.

Some fine studies of twentieth-century teachers exist, of course, but they
appear to be limited either in scope or in historical analysis. Sociological
pieces, such as those of Willard Waller (1932), Howard Becker (1957), Dan
Lortie (1975), and Andrew Gitlin (1983), while occasionally relying upon
teachers' perceptions, are devoid of any historical treatment. Although William Eaton (1975) and Wayne Urban (1982) expand our understanding of the
historical development of teacher organizations, they largely ignore the views
of individual classroom teachers. Robert Reid (1982) focuses on the experiences and perceptions of Margaret A. Haley, one of the founders of the
American Federation of Teachers (AFT). While his account is valuable, it

remains too narrow to offer any historical generalizations about classroom teachers. Larry Cuban's (1984) historical examination of classroom pedagogy is important, because it relies heavily on qualitative methods and stresses the classroom teacher, but it fails to extensively use teachers' views themselves. In their efforts to investigate teachers, teacher organizations, and teaching methods during the twentieth century, these authors have tended to objectify the teacher.

The only exception of this trend seems to be Hoffman (1981). After illustrating the experiences and perceptions of teachers during the Common School Era and the Reconstruction Period, Hoffman turns her attention to the urban classroom teacher of the late nineteenth and early twentieth centuries and notes the paucity of diaries and letters by teachers. Hoffman overcomes this obstacle by utilizing student sketches and teacher interviews to recreate the work histories of some urban teachers during this period. She also appeals to oral historians to further reconstruct teachers' careers.

Alice Duffy Rinehart (1983) appears to have responded to Hoffman's rallying cry. Her compilation of oral interviews with thirty-eight teachers represents an important contribution from a narrative standpoint. Yet her wholly descriptive study lacks focus, both from a theoretical position and from the viewpoint of the narrators. Rinehart covers important topics, the reasons for entering teaching, family background, preparation, as well as the impact of major social, economic, and political events, but she avoids scrutinizing them within a theoretical context. Further, the cohort of teachers that she interviews includes males and females, elementary as well as secondary instructors, and varying years of experience. Still, these teachers do not represent a cohesive sample. Some are retired while others are still actively employed, and they all resided on the eastern seaboard. Thus, many questions remain: What generalizations can be made? How do the experiences of urban teachers compare and contrast with rural teachers? Small-town teachers? Unfortunately, the study leaves a significant and profound gap in the literature of the history of teaching.

As Hoffman and Rinehart illustrate, qualitative research methods in general and oral history in particular offer unique, personal insights into the schooling process. The school 'may have a clear-cut grading system, an organizational chart, a class schedule, a curriculum, and an official motto that suggests the primary goal of schooling'. Yet people do not always 'act' according to what the school is supposed to be, or what administrators say it is, but rather 'according to how they see it' (Bogdan and Biklen, 1982, p. 34). This is especially true with teachers. As Susan Moore Johnson (1984) found in her study of the impact of teachers' unions on the schools, teachers clearly exert their control in the classroom. But this transcends the classroom as well. Through field studies in six school districts and interviews of school administrators, union leaders, building principals, and classroom teachers, Johnson discovered the concept of 'covert insurrection', that is, teachers have always 'reserved certain important powers for themselves' (p. 143). Teachers have even manipulated their unions to protect their own needs and interests.

Johnson's analysis of teachers' attitudes and actions is substantiated with an historical perspective. Social historians like David Montgomery (1981) and E.P. Thompson (1963) view human agency as an important element in the making of history, and teachers as historical actors have demonstrated an uncanny, though often overlooked, ability to shape events. For instance, Jacqueline Jones' (1980) fine study on the Reconstruction period in the South reveals how female, Yankee teachers protested against unequal pay scales for male and female teachers, male-dominated supervisory positions, and certain policy decisions.

Oral history provides the vehicle for such a social history of twentieth-century schooling (Clifford, 1975; Bertaux, 1981; Bennett, 1983; Stearns, 1983). Paul Thompson (1978) outlines the broad and provocative applications of oral history methodology:

> While historians study the actors of history from a distance, their characterizations of their lives, views, and actions will always risk being misdescriptions, projections of the historian's own experience and imagination: a scholarly form of fiction. Oral evidence, by trans-forming the 'objects' of study into 'subjects', makes for a history which is not just richer, more vivid and heartrending, but *truer*. (p. 90)

However, as Hoffman (1981) points out, the oral histories of public school teachers have been rarely recorded or preserved, let alone analyzed within an historical context. Studs Terkel's highly acclaimed oral history, *Hard Times* (1970), includes the memoir of only one teacher, Elsa Ponselle. She recalls as tumultuous those Great Depression years as a Chicago schoolteacher. Teachers went unpaid and some starved while others marched and organized a union. Local newspapers occasionally published an interview with a teacher. For instance, Lillian Chapin, a Los Angeles teacher, made it into the news-paper as a human-interest story when she celebrated her hundredth birthday and eightieth year of teaching. She summarized her life as 'no big deal' ('No big deal', 1981). Finally, Donald Warren's more recent, comprehensive anthology of the history of teaching in the United States relies on some 'insiders' perspectives' (1989, p. 4), but none of the chapters depends solely on personal histories for its sources. He adds, 'the proposition that historians of education ought to consult teachers at all — past or present — has been revived only recently' (p. 1). Oral history enables educational historians to open the classroom door and investigate schooling from the perspective of one of its principal participants — the teacher. 'Oral history can be used to preserve feelings and attitudes, shedding light on the emotional atmosphere in which decisions were made or actions taken' (Cutler, 1983, p. 96).

This collection of essays tries to salvage and analyze the narratives of public employees who worked in one of the nation's largest and most vital social institutions. Their twentieth-century teaching careers are reconstructed, emphasizing the parts played by crucial social, economic, and political events and issues, the school organization, and people — students, parents, and others — in shaping the subjects' evolving definitions, or perceptions, of their role as a teacher in a particular community. It is multi-dimensional in scope, stressing qualitative research approaches, oral histories, autobiographies, and diaries, as sources, undergirded with in-depth analyses. This collection also focuses on a comparative examination of teachers' experiences and perceptions in different regions (Northeast, Midwest, West, and South) and in various settings (rural, small town, and urban). The contributions fall under three broad headings: 'Women's Work'; 'Teachers and Their Communities'; and 'Professionals or Workers?'. An introduction providing a contextual and conceptual texture precedes each section. In the final section, Richard Quantz's reflective historiographic article builds on Clifford's (1975) notions, emphasizing qualitative research methods as an approach to the study of the history of schooling. Quantz leads the reader through an intellectual odyssey of postmodernism/poststructuralism as a theoretical framework to better understand the significance of the teacher's voice. This collection ends with an essay, 'The History of Teaching: A Social History of Schooling', by Richard Altenbaugh, which attempts to bring unity and closure to the perspectives and issues raised in this volume.

Part I

Women's Work

She holds her commission from nature.

Horace Mann (1843)

Introduction

The closing chapter of Lotus Coffman's 1911 classic study, *The Social Composition of the Teaching Population*, addressed several 'problems' then facing the 'teaching force'; 'feminization' headed that list. He connoted this with low status, declining standards, and a general educational malaise: 'Feminization of the teaching force has been due in part to the changed character of the management of the public schools, to the specialization of labor within the schools, to the narrowing of the intellectual range or versatility required of teachers, and to the willingness of women to work for less than men' (p. 82).

Although male schoolmasters appeared common through the early nineteenth century, 'the feminization of teaching has a long history.' New England towns began to hire married women for teaching positions as early as 1700, but during the latter part of that century they employed single adolescent women as they completed their schooling. Towns preferred them to men because they lacked familial obligations and possessed more education. Nevertheless, school officials 'still considered women inferior to men teachers', usually assigning women to the summer sessions and men to the longer, more prestigious winter school periods (Preston, 1982, pp. 29, 138).

Nineteenth-century labor market conditions facilitated the feminization of teaching. Demand for instructors steadily rose due to population growth and the commitment to common school reform; traditional high turnover rates for teachers exacerbated this situation. A ready labor supply conveniently appeared with an increased number of educated women. Since other professions excluded them, women turned to the classroom as the only outlet for their talents. This oversupply depressed salaries, resulting in reduced district costs. The drive to maintain low, locally funded school budgets, in turn, induced the hiring of inexpensive female teachers (Preston, 1982; Melder, 1972; Strober and Tyack, 1980).

The cult of domesticity, extolling the inherent nurturance, innocence, and submission of women, ensured a favorable cultural environment for the entrance of females into teaching. Through her countless writings and speeches during the nineteenth century, Catherine Beecher essentially redefined the gender of the American teacher, envisioning it as a vocation 'dominated by — indeed, exclusively belonging to — women'. Teaching enabled women to enlighten society and to exert their moral influence, thus adding the schoolhouse to 'women's proper sphere' (Sklar, 1973, p. 97; Welter, 1966). As secretary of the first public school system in the country, Massachusetts' Horace Mann (1843, p. 28), officially promoted this notion, particularly in the case of young children:

> She [the female teacher] holds her commission from nature. In the well developed female character there is always a preponderance of affection over intellect. However powerful and brilliant her reflective faculties may be, they are considered a deformity in her character unless overbalanced and tempered by womanly affections. The dispositions of young children of both sexes correspond with this ordination of Providence.

Preston (1982, p. 55) adds an important caveat: 'The expansion of education, with the associated need to curtail costs, created a need to hire cheaper female teachers, but the adoption of a centralized, bureaucratized, school system with its hierarchical structure furnished a way to hire female teachers while retaining male control.' Further, neither Beecher nor Mann, or anyone else for that matter, intended teaching as a career, but rather as a 'procession into marriage'. 'Thus, Victorian ideology about women's place made positive use of sex-typing to encourage women to enter teaching as an occupation and appealed to employers not wanting to undermine the family but wishing cheap and efficient teachers' (Strober and Tyack, 1980, p. 496).

All of these factors culminated in a profound transformation. By 1888, women nationwide comprised 63 per cent of the teaching force while in cities they constituted 90 per cent. In Massachusetts, approximately one out of every five women had taught at some time in her life (Bernard and Vinovskis, 1977; Cremin, 1980, pp. 144–47; Kaestle and Vinovskis, 1980, p. 206; Rury, 1989, p. 27; Sklar, 1973, pp. xiv, 97, 172–73, 182). Teaching therefore represented a universally accepted occupation for women. Yet the feminization process proved to be more complex and uneven than these figures illustrate, revealing both regional variations and historical specificity (Preston, 1982). Economic and ideological preconditions were different in rural and urban labor markets, with women teachers generally less common in the former. The domestic service of a daughter appeared to be more critical to a farm family than to its city counterpart. Moreover, with few job opportunities for men in the countryside, male teachers tended to leave teaching at a slower rate than urban males. Isolated one-room schoolhouses also presented occasional discipline obstacles for women. City districts solved this problem through age-grading and by hiring male managers. 'Thus, as compared to urban labor markets, in rural areas the ratio of men to women available for teaching was higher and the wages of the two sexes were equal.' (Strober and Tyack, 1980, p. 497).

Iowa represented a case in point, as Thomas Morain (1980) points out. The pressure of Civil War enlistment quickly depleted the number of males available and willing to teach in that state. Only then were women teachers in the majority, amounting to 73 per cent by 1865. However, this figure should not imply that women simply replaced men, because this trend continued even after the conflict ended and many veterans returned. By 1900, women accounted for 83 per cent of Iowa's classroom instructors. Rather, men chose not to teach, and for two reasons. First, low salaries drove males away from teaching. In Iowa, as in Massachusetts, Horace Mann championed the employment of female teachers 'because of savings realized by their lower salary demands permitted scant budgets to go further' (Morain 1980, p. 165). Second, Iowa formalized teacher preparation after the war. A comprehensive school law required that every county offer a summer training institute, and mandated that teachers attend at their own expense. Male teachers balked at this, thus avoiding the twin burdens of tuition expenses and loss of income. They no longer saw teaching as a stepping stone to another career and now by-passed it completely, pursuing other, more lucrative occupations. Morain

(1980, pp. 169–70) summarizes the ironic outcome of Iowa's school reform efforts: 'The professionalization of medicine and law — formal educational requirements, examinations, state licensing laws, professional associations — had the effect of closing these pursuits to women. The professionalization of teaching had the opposite effect.' When teaching became a primary job instead of a secondary one, low wages and credentials made it less attractive to men than women in rural areas (Strober and Lanford, 1986; Strober and Tyack, 1980). In Iowa, as elsewhere, men had choices, women did not.

Teaching did liberate women to some extent, providing more diverse and complex lives for them than for their nonteaching peers. It soon became the 'aristocracy of women's labor' (Murphy, 1986, p. 58). 'Taking a school offered a respectable and sometimes pleasant alternative to young women who needed to work and found few alternatives except textile mills or domestic service.' (Melder, 1972, p. 25). Compared with other women, teachers earned superior wages, accrued pensions, enjoyed better working conditions, lived in comfortable surroundings, and achieved relatively high status. In Colorado, during the late nineteenth and early twentieth centuries, female teachers attended college, gained economic independence, traveled frequently, and married later. Single and married women, as well as separated, divorced, and widowed ones, reaped financial benefits (Clifford, 1989, p. 302; Underwood, 1986).

Limitations did exist, however. 'Teaching did not revolutionize women's lives; the decisions they made frequently were shaped by the social and familial context within which they lived' (Underwood, 1986, pp. 525, 530). Teaching had become 'women's high calling', but motherhood remained women's 'crowning glory' (Melder, 1972, p. 20). Thus, regardless of location and grade level, early twentieth-century female teachers taught a median of four years, with seven for their male colleagues (Coffman, 1911, pp. 25–30; Rury, 1986, pp. 222–24). Given the relatively short work life of a female teacher, it appears questionable whether this effort should be regarded as a career at all — at least in the same manner as a male perceived it. Teaching, instead, seemed more like a '"dead-end job", one reserved for youth without prospect of promotion' (Rury, 1986, p. 229). This partially explains why female salaries continued to lag behind those of male instructors. In 1905, the typical female high school teacher received 69 per cent of her male counterpart's pay, although many urban female instructors earned a higher income than rural male teachers (Fraser, 1989, p. 131). Yet, in the long run, women received less money because 'they left the teaching force much sooner than their male colleagues' (Rury, 1986, p. 215). They were helped along in many cases, since by 1930 77 per cent of some 1,473 school districts refused to hire married women, and 62 per cent compelled them to resign once they married. Because females taught for shorter periods than males, men tended to advance to school administrator posts (Strober and Tyack, 1980). This sexual division of labor encompassed teaching as well. Women comprised only 50 per cent of the high school instuctors by the turn of the century. School boards and administrators relegated them to elementary positions, both teaching and administrative. But even this had its shortcomings. While women accounted for 62 per cent of elementary principalships in 1905, this figure had deteriorated to 20 per cent by 1972. 'When women "took over" teaching in nineteenth-century New England, they "took over" the jobs but not the institution' (Preston, 1982, p. 70; Rury, 1989, p. 27; Strober and Best, 1979; Tyack and Hansot, 1982, p. 183). Preston (1982, p. 147) offers a compelling conclusion about this experience by pointing to a broader context, that is, the treatment of female labor, not just the teaching occupation: 'It has been argued that women are either hired for lower-paying jobs with poor working conditions or alternatively, the hiring of women causes the jobs to become low-wage, undesirable work. In the case of schoolteaching, neither occurred. As women were hired, they were offered low pay and the most undesirable positions because they were women.'

New research findings and theoretical frameworks address this issue in unique and challenging ways. Sari Biklen expands our understanding of this women's work by arguing for a revision of the concept of 'career.' The traditional notion has always been based on male terms and experience, that is, free from primary responsibility for the family. However, 'for women to put career commitment over family commitments, to set their professional priorities straight, so to speak, they must act against social norms' (Biklen, 1985, p. 217). Furthermore, advancement has been a moot question, especially since teaching always has been an occupation marked by horizontal, rather than vertical, mobility (Lortie, 1975). 'Looked at this way, teaching is at least a "semi-profession", at best a fringe profession' (Biklen, 1985, pp. 215, 216).

Biklen analyzes work obligations by stressing the 'internalized structuring of a career' (1985, p. 219). Although externally characterized by frequent work interruptions for maternal and domestic reasons, female instructors, whom Biklen interviewed, remained internally committed to teaching, even when not physically present in the classroom. Moreover, they maneuvered their return in ways that circumvented ideological battles with their husbands or challenges to social norms, utilizing substitute teaching, temporary assign- ments, and other gradual re-entry strategies. These women always thought of themselves as teachers, regardless of the circumstances: 'They valued their work identities as teachers and did not want to have to choose between work and family' (Biklen, 1985, pp. 220, 222–23). Hence, they perceived coherence in their lives, raising children and sustaining a family as well as maintaining a teaching 'career'. To avoid any cultural conflict over these goals, they approached their work idealistically, focusing on the children; they pur- posefully shunned the self-serving motives usually associated with careerism. One teacher saw her teaching career as a 'marriage' between her and her students. Therefore, when historians and policy makers analyze the occupa- tion of teaching, 'the concept of career must describe the patterns of women's lives as well as those of men's' (Biklen, 1985, pp. 226–27).

In a similar vein, Madeleine Grumet (1988), relying on a poststructuralist framework, posits that teaching, as women's work, has been sandwiched somewhere between the 'so-called private and public worlds' of women's lives, between the experiences of the classroom and domesticity. She (p. xv) points to the 'daily passage' women have made between their public and private lives, and the contradictions that they have encountered:

> The feminization of teaching and the cult of maternal nurturance did little to introduce the atmosphere of the home or the integrity and specificity of the mother/child relationship into the schools. Dominated by kits and dittos, increasingly mechanized and impersonal, most of our classrooms cannot sustain human relationships of sufficient intimacy to support the risks, the trust, and the expression that learning requires. (Grumet, 1988, p. 56)

Grumet (1988) celebrates the possibilities of overcoming the existing 'contradictions' between mothering and teaching, but this must unfold in an environment that touts patriarchy in form, knowledge, and values (pp. 56, 164, 185–86).

The articles that follow engage many of the issues surrounding this women's work. Courtney Vaughn-Roberson uses interviews of retired, rural southwestern teachers who taught from 1900 to 1950 to investigate how these women resolved the contradictions implicit in a domestic definition of teaching and a teaching career. We switch regions with Margaret Nelson's contribution, which taps interviews and focuses on Vermont during the first half of the twentieth century; she examines the schoolhouse as an extension of the family, noting the overlap of those two worlds. Patricia Carter's essay, which closes this section, relies on articles in women's journals and press reports to capture the teachers' voice; she analyzes the aggressive campaigns of New York City teachers between 1900 and 1917 for equal pay, the right to marry, and the freedom of having children of their own.

R.J.A.

Chapter 2

Having a Purpose in Life: Western Women Teachers in the Twentieth Century

Courtney Vaughn-Roberson

> Who ever heard of a man taking primary teaching courses or a woman majoring in engineering?
>
> > Letha Campbell
> > (former teacher)

Beginning late in the eighteenth century, social theorists planted seeds for an ideology of domesticity, maintaining that women's proper role lay in the care of children, the nurture of the husband, the physical maintenance of the domicile, and the guardianship of both home and social morality (Cott, 1977; Degler, 1980; Ryan, 1981; Sklar, 1973).[1] Although in the United States this ideology helped to propel European-American females into teaching, historians have not agreed on the impact of domestic ideology on women teachers and on the education profession itself. Some scholars conclude that women's easy access to teaching posts turned the classroom into a workshop for motherhood for the average female, perpetuating anti-intellectualism in education to the present day (Allmendinger, 1979; Bernard & Vinovskis, 1977; Conway, 1974; Wein, 1974; Melder, 1974; Sexton, 1974; Leggatt, 1970; Lorti, 1975). Linda Perkins (1983) maintains that during the nineteenth century female African-American teachers enjoyed an egalitarian relationship with male colleagues, also involved in 'racial uplift'. Yet, during the twentieth century, African-American women teachers' influence began to suffer under the influence of domestic ideology. Other research, focusing particularly on White women who dedicated themselves to teaching during the nineteenth and early twentieth centuries, portrays them as independent and highly professional (Kaufman, 1984; Jones, 1979; Scott, 1979; Hoffman, 1981; Underwood, 1986; Cordier, 1988). A few studies highlight both the professional opportunities and the behavioral restrictions that domestic ideology provided to both African-American and Anglo women teachers and perhaps to other women whose careers were and still are defined by the traditional women's role (Sklar, 1973; Kelley, 1979; Vaughn-Roberson, 1984; Clifford, 1989).

This chapter draws on the experiences of 547 women teachers, from the western US states, most of whom were born during the first decade of the twentieth century, who developed their own personal and professional variations on the traditional ideology of domesticity, an ideology that seemed to them to give their work meaning and purpose. Although changing social conditions and personal experiences encouraged them to emphasize varying interpretations of the domestic role during their lives, these teachers have remained firmly entrenched within the traditional female sphere, and it is from there that they have observed the world and judged themselves.

Description of Subjects

Because most published historical studies of female educators do not deal with the twentieth century, I began in 1980 to locate subjects for a study that would test earlier scholars' observations on the importance of the ideology that upheld the domestic ideal for women teachers by evaluating the paradoxical significance of domesticity in the lives of a new era of career-oriented women. If the traditional belief had survived as part of their vocational and personal value system, then its resilience as a social force would be documented well into the current century. Moreover, I could trace the historical and social reasons for its survival despite the contradictions inherent in using the ideal of domesticity to show women's increased involvement in gainful employment outside the home. Thus my search centered around professional associations and other organizations likely to include women who had taught for many years. My end product was a large body of reminiscences, letters, personal interviews, and biographical sketches of 547 women teachers from three western states — Oklahoma, Texas, and Colorado.

The Oklahoma Retired Teachers Association in the mid-1970s had written to its members asking each to 'tell her or his story' and had been rewarded with a wealth of material (Smallwood, 1976). From seven volumes of that correspondence I selected 214 women teachers of the appropriate age to form the nucleus of this study. They were all of predominantly White ancestry, although a few reported partial Native-American descent. Even those 'mixed-bloods', however, were patriotic Protestants who identified with the dominant society. I obtained additional information on forty-seven of the 214 teachers by writing to them myself. Their responses contained such demographic information as degrees held, marital status, and place of birth. Respondents also explained why they had selected careers in education, what constituted their own educations, how supportive their families had been, and what they held to be acceptable male and female behavior. I contacted another 104 teachers by mail and interviewed three more, having obtained all of their names from fellow teachers. In Oklahoma I also located twenty-five African-American teachers, and three full-blood Native-American educators, but because many professional groups (my major source of contacts) initially excluded minority members, my sample size for the tri-state region was so small that I omitted any separate analysis of those teachers (Vaughn-Roberson, 1984).

In Texas, a state contiguous to, but more southern in character than Oklahoma, I contacted sixty-three women teachers, most of whose names I found on the membership lists of Delta Kappa Gamma, an organization of women educators founded in 1929. *Personalities*, a work of paraphrased interviews with selected state members published in 1980 by the Texas Iota chapter of Delta Kappa Gamma, contributed twenty-seven more subjects. A series about notable Texas women, run in the *Amarillo Daily News*, added another seven teachers; citations from these articles led to the work of more female educators, among them Laura Hamner, who wrote *Light 'n' Hitch*. Finally, I conducted one personal interview. The entire list totalled ninety-nine Texas teachers.

In an attempt to maintain some geographical consistency, while obtaining subjects from a more liberally oriented western state, I contacted forty-three Colorado women teachers, again gleaning names from the Delta Kappa Gamma rolls. *Torchbearers*, a 1967 publication about key women teachers in that organization, contained an additional forty-eight Colorado women appropriate for this study, and manuscript material originally gathered for the book, but not published, offered information on eleven more. I found the remainder of my Colorado teachers among the subjects of oral history interviews conducted largely by the state's county library personnel and catalogued at the Denver Public Library Western History Collection. One more I found through an article in *Colorado Magazine*, and one I interviewed.

My final sample, then, consisted of professionally minded women teachers from three states who had spent twenty to twenty-five years on the job. Moreover, 85 per cent of them hailed from small towns or rural areas, pervaded with traditional American values, including conservative views of women's roles. These women felt a sense of consistency and purpose despite the complexity involved in trying to reconcile the contradictory messages of domestic ideology.

Domestic Ideology, and Women Teachers

The rich heritage of the ideal of domesticity for women in American educational thought makes perfectly understandable its persistence well into the twentieth century. During the American Revolution, progressive social theorists first popularized the notion that the new nation's mothers had a patriotic duty to rear morally sound and literate children. Advocates of women's education such as Benjamin Rush and Sarah Pierce reasoned that the new country's women should be molded for Republican Motherhood — the rearing of patriotic, ethical, and knowledgeable children (Kerber, 1980; Fitts, 1979; Norton, 1980). As the self-sufficient rural household gave way to an urban ideal of consumption, women's productive role declined, and their claims to influence rested ever more on their alleged ethical, emotional, and spiritual superiority (Ryan, 1981). For the early nineteenth-century woman, economically displaced by the em .gence first of a commercial market and then by an urban-industrial economy, caring for children and shaping their morals became the woman's paramount duty, sanctified by the domestic ideology. In the midst of growing class antagonism, urban disorder, and changes in the division of labor, a new generation of educators such as Catharine Beecher, Horace Mann, and Mary Lyon hoped women's pious and quiet influence over men and children would cure the ever-increasing social unrest. In their ideal society, gender, rooted in biology and hence unalterable, would be the only division (Sklar, 1973; Green, 1979; Woody, 1980). The celebration of male and female spheres had arrived but not without feminist opponents such as Margaret Fuller, who confided that after leaving teaching in 1838, 'she now hoped to do something for women' (Cross, 1965, p. 109). Despite such opponents, the 'culture of professionalism' flourished, although with very different implications for males and females. A separate set of careers were offered to men and women, based on the assumption that males were mandated to manage and females to nurture (Bledstein, 1976).

Female teachers, nurses, social workers, and volunteers, laboring in both sparsely populated and urban settings, greatly influenced the building of communities in the United States (Hoffman, 1982; Blair, 1980; Freedman, 1979; Cook, 1979). Women followed the frontier across the North American continent, and helped create new settlements, erecting churches and schools or staffing social service agencies. Though a few historians emphasize the role of the domestic ideology in subordinating female pioneers to male authority, other scholars highlight the power and influence that western women gained as community builders (Faragher, 1979; Schlissel, 1982; Goldman, 1981). Julie Roy Jeffrey (1979), in an analysis of the trans-Mississippi frontier from 1840 to 1880, and Mary Ryan (1981), in a depiction of Oneida County, New York, from 1780 to 1865, explain that women formed social institutions that were the agents of morality in the community. Although, according to Ryan, later generations of the more urbanized Oneida women spent more time within the newly privatized home, the female sphere had already been extended and formalized beyond the domicile. Despite the many ways in which women's interests extended into the community, however, the school remained the primary institution for single women's professional gainful employment because dedicated teachers were always needed 'to facilitate the passage of children out of the home and into society and the economy' (Ryan, 1981, p. 234).

More and more females responded to this need, until by 1888, 63 per cent of the nation's teachers were women (Sklar, 1973). Western settlers seemed to show a special appreciation for women's roles in establishing and running schools. In 1838, Kentucky, then a frontier state, initiated a novel experiment, granting women the right to vote in elections that concerned education. It was twenty-three years before another jurisdiction, Kansas, would grant the same right to its adult females. This ignited a trend in the trans-Mississippi West, where thirteen other states and territories had implemented the measure by 1890 (Kraditor, 1981). In 1893, North Dakota became the first state to elect a female state superintendent of schools. By

1922, nine western states had placed women in the educational chief executive's seat, the only females in the country to hold such positions (Tyack and Hansot, 1982).

Colorado women involved themselves in educational policy-making during and after Reconstruction. With statehood in 1876, they won suffrage in school elections. Seventeen years later, marking a period of Populist ascendancy, Colorado males became the third group of voters in the country to approve the full franchise for adult females (Faherty, 1956; Jensen, 1964; Jensen, 1973). Beginning in 1895, after J.F. Murray's term ended as Colorado state superintendent, the expanded state electorate consistently designated women for the position until 1952. Many of these administrators became known and respected in national education circles. Helen Grenfell, who held the post from 1898 to 1904, in 1903 was elected the country's first female vice-president of the National Education Association (NEA), founded in 1857 (Grenfell, 1939; Delta Kappa Gamma, 1967; Burstyn, 1980). In 1909, the organization named Ella Flagg Young, Chicago city school superintendent, as its first woman president (Tyack and Hansot, 1982). Mary C.C. Bradford, a regional promoter for the national suffrage campaign, served as Colorado state superintendent from 1913 to 1921 and again from 1923 to 1927 (Delta Kappa Gamma, 1967). Willing to stretch the limits of domestic ideology in her day, neither Coloradan accepted the common notion that marriage and motherhood demanded that she relinquish her professional position. As Grenfell (1939) reasoned, education was part of the female domain, an 'outgrowth of the home or . . . the family's way of working out the best interests of the child' (pp. 17, 19).

Like their colleagues to the northwest, Oklahoma women educators actively reached for the political power to shape their social environment. In 1895 Oklahoma Territory sixth-grade teacher Margaret Rees founded the Oklahoma Equal Suffrage Association, and when Oklahoma and Indian territories joined to become the state of Oklahoma in 1907, women obtained the vote in school-related elections (James, 1982; 1979). Nevertheless, four years later, a newly appointed state board of education put a ceiling on women's involvement in running schools, decreeing that 'no person was eligible to the office [of state superintendent] except a male . . . of more than 30 years of age' (Lambert; and Rankin, 1969, p. 979). Until the Nineteenth Amendment was ratified in 1920, White racism helped defeat the full suffrage issue in Oklahoma because many White citizens feared the potential for African-American power if that race of women could vote (James, 1979).

Despite restrictions, Oklahoma women educators, such as Indian Territory's Alice Robertson, eventually gained state and nationwide recognition. Like hundreds of other nineteenth-century teachers, Robertson was an ardent Christian who sought to impart moral values and practical knowledge to both Native-American and White children. She became a founder of the Indian Territory Teachers Association in 1884, and sixteen years later federal officials selected her superintendent of education for the Creek Nation. In 1905, two years after Grenfell had made history, Robertson became the NEA's next vice-president. By 1920 the Oklahoma Republican educator's popularity helped make her the country's second woman to serve as representative to the United States Congress (Stanley, 1967; Hubbell, 1982). Though she had opposed woman suffrage, while serving Oklahoma in Washington, D.C., Robertson challenged her newly enfranchised sisters to continue spreading domestic values: 'The American women, instead of standing aside and drawing their skirts about them piously, must now pitch in and work for the reforms they have been demanding. Women suffrage is like an automobile ride. When something goes wrong with the flivver and the man gets out to fix it, the woman in the back seat ought to either get out and help him or keep her mouth shut.' (Alice Robertson Collection).

Texas women also sought to broaden their social influence. The Texas Equal Rights Association was established in 1893 and reorganized twenty years later as the Texas Woman Suffrage Association. Hampered by racism, it accomplished only the partial enfranchisement of women in 1918, when Texas males finally granted women suffrage in primary elections. A year later Texas suffragists supported Annie Webb Blanton, the only woman in the state ever to hold that position in her successful bid for state superintendent of education (Taylor, 1951).

Blanton held a doctorate from Cornell University and, as superintendent, worked to improve the credentials of all Texas teachers, but especially of women. In return for her demands on female educators, she lobbied for their equitable treatment on the job and for a non-gender-based pay scale throughout the state (Blanton, 1923). In addition to being state superintendent from 1919 to 1923, Blanton served as president of the Texas State Teachers Association, founded in 1879, and was elected vice-president of the NEA on three separate occasions (Lynn, 1960). In 1929, in Austin, she and a handful of others founded Delta Kappa Gamma. Created initially for White female educators with impeccable credentials, its purpose was to provide money and encouragement for capable women teachers to work toward advanced degrees and to claim places as administrators in local schools. A few years later Oklahoma and Colorado formed their own chapters of Delta Kappa Gamma, which is today an integrated international society. Despite advances in female solidarity, neither Blanton, nor most of her more labor-oriented sisters who were founding teachers' unions to the northeast, overtly challenged the concept of separate spheres, using domesticity instead to argue for women's paramount position within the education profession (Delta Kappa Gamma 1979). For example, in 1910 Grace Strachan, head of the New York Interborough Association of Women Teachers executive committee wrote, 'I am firmly convinced that while teaching is a natural vocation for most women, it is rarely the true vocation of a man' (Hoffman, 1982, p. 298).

Teacher Socialization and Education

Although notable women educators were role models for girls coming of age during the early twentieth century, the women in this study were more strongly influenced in their initial career decisions by their own families and their own teachers. As a child, Coloradan Minnie Schroter strove to be like Marion, the schoolteacher next door, whom her parents greatly admired. 'That girl is very intelligent', Schroter's father had said, and Minnie's mother had reiterated, 'Indeed, she is, and what's more, she is very pretty.' (Delta Kappa Gamma, 1967, p. 21). Christine Kirkpatrick's parents concurred with the Schroters that 'teaching was the highest profession a young woman could pursue' (Dickey, 1980, p. 46), while Opal Scales (1976) recounted that she and her sisters 'became teachers because at that time teaching was considered the most desirable occupation for a young girl'. Presenting a dramatic example of a parent's commitment to education, Allie Collin's mother pleaded with her father-in-law from her deathbed, 'Pa, promise me that my children will get an education.' For Allie such schooling led to a teaching career ('Allie Smith Collins: Wife, mother, teacher', 1982, p. 4-B).

To some parents, preparing a daughter for teaching was an act of almost religious importance. Eleanor Reser (1976) remembers her father's admonitions: to 'sincerely commit myself to the child, community, and school and [to remember] that each individual child's future education depends on the foundation I could instill within him or her'. Zelma Farris (1976) received the same encouragement, which led to her goal of 'instill[ing] in the minds of our young Americans the art of living an honest and upright life that they might be able to take their place in this fast changing world as useful and law-abiding citizens'. Ada Faus was one of dozens who felt that during her years of service she had become a minister of sorts, reckoning that she had helped to produce countless 'substantial citizens' (Delta Kappa Gamma, 1967, pp. 109–110).

In preparation for future duties as educators, little girls constantly played the role of 'teacher' in imaginative games (Delta Kappa Gamma, 1967, p. 166). Sally Reeves wrote that she wrapped corncobs with paper and pretended to teach them words from a *Blue Backed Spelling Book* (Delta Kappa Gamma, 1967). Charlotte McGinnis exclaimed, 'How I loved to ... order my imaginary pupils around and tap a bell to assist them to march!' (McGinnis, 1954). As teenagers, these future teachers often had the chance to live out their fantasies, for country educators, faced with large ungraded classes, called on the better female students to instruct the younger children (Wheeler and Wheeler, 1978). The experience gained in such cases, added to the relative ease of obtaining teaching certificates, encouraged a number of the women to begin their careers on or before their eighteenth birthday.

A sense of professional pride drove all of the women in this study including those who entered the classroom at an early age, to complete a baccalaureate degree years before Texas, Oklahoma, or Colorado required it for teacher certification (Stinnett, 1969). Moreover, 68.6 per cent of the eighty-three Texans, half of the 308 Oklahomans, and 48.9 per cent of the ninety-eight Coloradans earned at least a master's degree, while eighteen from the three states went on to obtain a doctorate. Such achievements appear to be higher than the regional norm. By the 1940s, many of the women depicted here had completed their undergraduate training or were working on an advanced degree. In 1942, in Colorado, however, 32.8 per cent of that state's teachers, both male and female, lacked a four-year degree. In 1946, in Oklahoma, 29.3 per cent of the teachers had not acquired a bachelor's degree, and even by 1948, 18.6 per cent of Texas teachers lacked that credential (State Dept. of Colorado, 1943; State Dept. of Oklahoma, 1948; Evans, 1955).

Alone, this impersonal data about degrees could tell a somewhat erroneous story; for, not all the teachers discussed here initially complied with their families' and teachers' prodding. A few girls were afraid to leave home at all. Jewel Peterson (1981) remembered praying, 'Lord, I wish I didn't have the intelligence to know that I need to go to college, but I do.' Others who were eager to continue their education aspired to professions other than teaching, but they, too, eventually enrolled in the pedagogical course of study. Mary Carden explained, 'I wanted to become an artist, but since I had the opportunity [to go to East Texas State Teachers College] I became a teacher' (Ingram, 1980a, p. 8). Reenacting what was for many others an almost unconscious career choice, Letha Campbell (1981) wrote rhetorically, 'Who ever heard of a man taking primary teaching courses or a woman majoring in engineering?' Similar testimony came from Ruth Marshall (Ingram, 1980b), who confessed, 'In those days I did not know that [a woman] went to college for any other purpose except to become a teacher' (p. 57).

Thus, though they may have been confined to the teaching profession, female education students did not believe that they were negatively stigmatized; rather, they felt honored and expected respect. That only six teachers with whom I corresponded identified any gender discrimination in their higher educational experience evidences how swiftly the domestic ideology appeared to resolve any conflict involving career choices and to complete the assimilation of the young women into the education field. Professors, counselors, and college administrators consciously manipulated the ideology, channeling women toward their accepted role as teachers (Anonymous, 1981). One woman identified the subtle manner in which women were 'cooled out' of traditional male program areas, explaining that her Ph.D. mentor at a Texas university advised her, '"not to take this man's course [as she] didn't need it".' 'I went ahead, though,' she continued, 'and did not earn but was given a 'C' in the course.' In her mind, she had merited an 'A'. J. Smith (1981) reported another case involving a friend enrolled at the University of Oklahoma 'who practically fought her way into Geology School.... The Dean did everything he could to stop her,' Smith recounted, 'but she persisted, although he made her life miserable.' Similarly, Texan Frances Watkins (1981) remembered, 'The Dean of Women was horrified that I would ... post 'As' in difficult math courses and only 'Bs' in English.... [In] her words,' Watkins repeated, '"you may major in math, but no one will hire a woman to teach math."'

In 1981, Vernice Sellman (1981) looked back and tried to explain why as young college students she and her counterparts had accepted the job of teacher as their only professional alternative. 'During most of my college years there was no ERA to make us conscious of any difference,' Sellman recollected. Such a statement illustrates that at the time, or even today, she and many of her colleagues were unaware that an Equal Rights Amendment had been proposed in 1923 and that it was debated in the United States Congress almost every year thereafter (Degler, 1980; Cott, 1984.) Given the importance of domestic ideology to a woman's teacher-training experience, however, it is understandable that as a young adult Sellman's frame of reference would have excluded a concept that threatened to dissolve the traditional social importance of the woman's role. In fact, some of the female educators defined sex discrimination in college as male disregard for their separate but hallowed station. Edna Frederick (1981) wrote with perhaps unconscious irony that she 'was aware of no discrimination whatsoever,' because 'the men students treated us [women] with a certain gallantry.'

As new teachers, these women entered the classroom fairly rooted in a world view that embraced separate male and female spheres, and they expected to be rewarded and acknowledged for acting out the most conservative interpretation of nineteenth-century femininity, emanating from the 'cult of true womanhood' (Welter, 1966). We considered it our 'duty,' explained one teacher (1976), 'to conform to [these] social ideals.' When asked to wear a girdle, dry their underwear on the line in a pillowcase, stay in town at all times, go to church, teach Sunday School, say prayers over the dead, and refrain from drinking, smoking, dancing, or card playing, they usually complied, 'accept[ing] and question[ing] little' (Moore, 1976; Witever, 1981).

Because of the dearth of detailed information on how the women actually conducted their classes, it is difficult to say whether the teachers consciously perpetuated gender stereotypes among their students. Ruby McKenna (1981), a junior high school mathematics teacher, did channel her male and female pupils into two different directions, 'A woman mathematics teacher was best teaching in the junior high school,' she stated. 'Here', McKenna continued, 'you could encourage girls to work in the field of mathematics and a man in the high school mathematics department could give the boys a more practical outlook on the subject.' Gladys Hubbard also revealed her bias, writing, 'I'm afraid I must admit to being just a little bit partial to the boys in my classes. Perhaps it was because they seemed more honest in their attitude toward their teachers — if they didn't like you ... you always knew it.' (Delta Kappa Gamma, 1967, pp. 95–96). Conversely, the remarks of Coloradan Bertha Hume (1981) suggest that on-the-job experiences convinced some teachers to focus more on women's abilities and rights and less on their social duties. Hume reasoned that girls had just as much, if not more, forthrightness as boys and consequently helped a girl named Darle become student body president. Hume worked for Darle even though an administrative official asked her to talk the girl out of running. 'I chuckle now at our temerity,' Hume later wrote, 'for Darle was elected student president and made the headlines of *The Greeley Tribune*.'

The Struggle for Professional Recognition

During the decades following the passage of the Nineteenth Amendment, continued discrimination against women encouraged many teachers to become as assertive as Hume, without abandoning their belief in separate gender spheres. Because most school boards throughout the nineteenth and early twentieth centuries refused to hire married women, many females refused to marry in order to keep their jobs (Degler, 1980; Tyack and Strober, 1981). Mima Williams (1981) succinctly explained, 'I never found a man I couldn't live without.' In fact, available data show that 45.5 per cent of the 121 Coloradans, 16.8 per cent of the 273 Oklahomans, and 36.8 per cent of the ninety-five Texans in the study remained single throughout their lives. At least two widows and five divorcees from the three states reentered the classroom after a stint as housewives and never married again. In addition, a number of teachers deferred matrimony until they were 30, 40, or even 50 years of age and purposely limited their family size so that they could maintain an uninterrupted career. On the other hand, many married women indicated that their holding a job, especially during the lean years of the 1930s, significantly altered gender stereotypes in their homes, as men and women juggled roles to keep their families together. Ora Mason (1979) explained, 'I went outside [the house] and worked ... and [my husband] always helped take care of the children.' Similarly, Eunice Salomonson (1981) remarked, 'We had no time to consider specific roles. We were a family aiming at mutual goals, and this included our two sons.'

At work and even in some homes, however, gender conflicts persisted, exacerbated by Depression-Era poverty and Dust-Bowl devastation. Married women teachers who had been able to override the longstanding ban on their employment were fired by school boards acting on the assumption that women, especially married ones, had someone to take care of them, but that in hard times men needed work to support themselves and their families. In addition, many of the teachers, women and men, who managed to keep a teaching job during the depression often worked for discounted paychecks or, at times, literally for nothing.

During the Second World War, when men were in short supply, many women teachers advanced professionally. Often they were asked to assume a male administrator's post. Mary Roberson (1981) became superintendent of the Hartley County, Texas, school system, a responsibility and a doubling of her work load for which, however, she received no increase in pay. Nonetheless, she liked her new position, but after the war Roberson, and many others like her, lost their jobs. As school systems grew, administrative salaries and managerial responsibilities increased, making educational leadership positions attractive to more and more men (Button and Provenzo, 1983). Subsequently, officials phased out many county superintendencies and teaching principalships, often held by women, or males took charge of the new consolidated rural or expanding urban institutions. This trend reached its logical conclusion in Colorado in 1952 when the state's last elected state superintendent, a woman, stepped down to be replaced by the first in a series of appointed male commissioners of education (Hardiman, 1981). At mid-century, throughout the entire country, men began reclaiming high school teaching posts as well, and by 1983 they constituted a bare majority of secondary classroom instructors. Women, on the other hand, still held almost all of the less prestigious elementary and special education positions (Feistritzer, 1983; Payne, 1976; Rosenberg, 1983). Estelle Faulconer (1981) recorded her reaction to such evolutionary developments in Oklahoma, charging, 'Men were given a title so they could get more money.' Donna Van Hoove (1976) responded even more vehemently, claiming that during her career, she had found 'but a handful of principals ... who were not egotistical, had a bad case of master/slave syndrome, expected women to be subservient, and generally had poor organizational skills.' In a more general context, Fleta Hill also complained, 'It's been my experience that many times women do the work and men get the credit!'

Even the traditionally acquiescent female teachers, however, had a history of struggle against such discrimination. In 1914, Althea Barr Taft disrupted a meeting of the Oklahoma Education Association (OEA), exclaiming, 'I want to warn you men that women teachers will not participate in another convention without being active in it and without learning for themselves what is going on' (Hubbell, 1982, p. 151). Twenty-six years later many of her professional progeny joined Texas, Oklahoma, or Colorado branches of the Department of Classroom Teachers Association (DCT), founded in 1913 as an affiliate of the NEA. In 1933, Muskogee teacher Kate Frank reorganized the DCT and served as president for four years, beginning in 1934. Three years later Frank became president of the OEA, going on to serve on the NEA Board of Directors and eventually holding that organization's vice-presidency. Her aggressive leadership won her a broad following and so frightened the Muskogee school board that she was fired in 1943. Frank and the OEA fought the decision, and she was reinstated in 1945 (Hubbell, 1982; Frank, 1974).

During the 1930s, women members of ACTA from Denver successfully threatened resignations if the city's school board did not institute an equal pay scale for men and women (Bullesel, 1981; Springer, 1981; Hardiman, 1981; Krig, 1981). In addition, the women teachers joined other activist groups formed earlier, such as the American Association of University Women (AAUW), founded in 1881 exclusively by and for women. In Colorado, Beatrice Young (1981) supported AAUW because it promised to work for the installation of more female professors at the University of Denver. Many who joined Delta Kappa Gamma attested to their organization's consciousness-raising effects. According to Christine Kirkpatrick, the association 'contributed to the well being of women teachers and enhanced their own feelings of worth ... [which] provided impetus for ... self improvement' (Dickey, 1980). The exchange of ideas 'with other top professional educators,' Joe Johnston added, 'proved to be challenging and rewarding and encouraged intellectual achievement as well as recognition of academic excellence' (Lucas, 1980).

Postwar Challenges to the Traditional Role

Dramatic social changes devaluing the traditional female role came in the quarter century following the Second World War. Afraid that their profession's philosophical base was in jeopardy, teachers held fast to their support of women's separate sphere, even as they struggled for professional recognition and status. As early as the late 1940s, Colorado teacher-educator Edith Beechel (1946) voiced concern about the diminishing numbers of young women who aspired to be teachers. She noted that many girls were attracted, not to education, but to the more glamorous vocations of 'secretary or air stewardess'. Beginning in the 1960s, modern feminists and scholars, some of whom intended to 'liberate' women from what they perceived as the age-old domestic prison, furthered the decline in the popularity of the teaching profession by casting aspersions on all occupations associated with the maternal role (Friedan, 1963; Bardwick and Douvan, 1972; Horner, 1970; Epstein, 1970; Feulner, 1979). Both single and married women teachers observed this decline with great regret, striking back with comments such as 'The home and especially children have suffered from women not staying where they should', and 'The liberation movement is destroying the family unit.' (Hamilton, 1981). Revealing her solution to this problem, Wilma Scott (1981) proposed: 'If it is necessary for mothers to work, they [should] plan their work hours so that their children are not cheated.... I still believe one of the most honorable stations in life is being a good mother. Both parents must be equally interested in the education of their child, but a mother's influence is vital.'

Interestingly enough, organizations such as Delta Kappa Gamma have in recent years supported measures like the Equal Rights Amendment, which could eliminate the legitimacy of gender-linked occupations or social roles (Hardiman, 1981). Of all the women with whom I corresponded, however, only about one-third could agree with the policy, and most of them had strong reservations concerning their choice. In keeping with other national associations representing women in the traditionally domestic career fields, Delta Kappa Gamma's national leadership has been more willing than the everyday practitioner to discard domestic ideology, which had been the heart of the nineteenth- and twentieth-century community-building experience (Melosh, 1982). For instance, Louise Holler (1981) insisted, 'God in His wisdom chose to make me a woman, [and] it is my choice to continue to think, behave, and react as a woman and be treated as a woman.' Eunice Salomonson (1981) agreed, charging: By wanting to be mannish instead of feminine ... women have written their own ticket to defeat. Never in the history of mankind has esteem for women been so lacking.... Women are not, at the present time, proving that they can fulfill the two roles of career and home — consequently there are too many broken homes and unsuccessful career[s].' Selma Long (1981) had similar difficulties advocating a feminism that would lead to the dissolution of gender spheres, because, like her contemporaries, she fretted over the diminishing status of domesticity. 'My husband [has] treated me as a partner besides being my protector; it never occurred to me that there was a need for an Equal Rights Amendment,' she wrote. Only a few women teachers agreed with Annie Joy (1981), who admitted somewhat sadly that freedom from gender-role stereotypes 'takes some things away, but ... it provides a great deal more than it takes'.

Unlike Joy, the vast majority of the women in this study will never repudiate the ideology of domesticity. Their belief that women are essentially homemakers and nurturers, who also have a right to put their talents to use outside the home, has unquestionably caused conflict for these women, particularly for those few, who as children dreamed of careers in art or engineering, or who left their parents' homes with trepidation. But the ideology that first marked out teaching as an appropriate profession for them has also irrevocably shaped their understanding of their profession and the meaning of their own lives (Geertz, 1964). Their jobs did, after all, gain for them social approval both in the work place and in the home. More important, these teachers, like their predecessors, capitalized on the social support that the rhetoric of domesticity granted them to demand recognition for their professional achievements and their role as community builders. On the other hand, this generation of teachers is also bound to some extent by the rhetoric that served them. Accepting the core assumption of domesticity, that women are responsible for the maintenance of familial and social morality, they identify today's feminism with narcissism and loss of values rather than self-respect and a demand for equality. Although younger feminists may view the educators in this study only as symbols of the past, these women, in their retirement, view what they perceive as the tragedies of contemporary society with a renewed belief that their own lives, securely nestled within the ideology of domesticity, have been full of purpose.

Note

1 I would like to thank Robert Griswold and Glenda Riley for their insights and support.

Chapter 3

The Intersection of Home and Work: Rural Vermont Schoolteachers, 1915–1950

Margaret K. Nelson

> I didn't teach for several years and I was very
> lonesome. I was almost willing to go into a school
> and say I'll pay you to let me teach....
>
> Vermont Schoolteacher

The century-old assumption that teaching was an ideal 'feminine' occupation guided scores of young women to the front of the class. Yet throughout the early twentieth century, few stopped along the way to consider whether schools actually functioned as work environments that could meet the 'particular' needs of women. This question is a critical one; it is also difficult to answer. It suggests that we not only be able to describe the work lives and careers of schoolteachers during a specific time period, but that we be able to evaluate those conditions as well.

The first task appears difficult enough, involving non-objective processes: what we notice for the purpose of description is clearly going to be shaped by our own preconceived ideas about what is important. The second task proves to be an even greater stumbling block. What kind of criteria do we want to use to evaluate work settings for women? Do we want to see if women and men have the same work environments and, if so, call them 'fair'? Do we want to evaluate the work conditions according to the extent to which they allow for our own personal ideologies of liberation and autonomy? Suppose the women under consideration do not recognize these same goals or concerns? Can we apply contemporary standards in retrospect? Whose criteria should be used?

One solution to this impasse is to take a problem which, given a basically non-egalitarian society, always confronts women who work — the problem known as the double burden or the double day. We can then evaluate work settings with respect to the extent to which they exacerbate or ease this problem. This represents the major route I have selected for a consideration of the work settings of teachers in rural Vermont during the first half of the twentieth century. I argue essentially that there existed multiple intersections of home and work, and that these intersections provided solutions to the double burden on female teachers.

In what follows, I first describe the methods by which the information for this chapter, and chapter 6, was acquired. I then offer a description of what I have referred to as the 'multiple intersections of home and work'. Next I reconfront the issue of evaluation and consider the description from the perspective of the solutions it offered for easing the double burden. In the conclusion, I suggest reasons why these solutions existed and raise questions about the implications of my findings for the lives of teachers today.

Methods and Setting

This chapter is based on information gathered from taped interviews with forty women whose teaching careers included some time in schools in Addison County, Vermont, prior to (though often continuing beyond) 1950. I obtained names of many of the subjects at a Retired Teachers' Association meeting where I described my research interests and asked for volunteers. Other names were suggested by the subjects themselves, taken from school records, and offered by individuals in the community who were familiar with my project. The sample is not random. The limits imposed on the kind of individuals to be interviewed derive from both my research interest — women's work — and my effort to keep the study feasible by confining it to a single county and a narrow time period.

I used an interview schedule designed to obtain a total life history into which more detailed information about occupational involvement could be placed. As a starting point, I relied quite heavily on the life history schedule developed by Sherna Gluck (1977) and the interview schedule developed by the Project at the University of Michigan (1977) for work on women in trade unions. I designed the interviews to be free-flowing and open-ended, to allow the interviewees to tell their stories in their own words; I directed the interviews only as necessary to cover specific areas. I interviewed most of the subjects at least twice.

The interviewed women were born between 1894 and 1921, nine of them before 1900, seventeen between 1900 and 1910, twelve between 1910 and 1920, and two in 1921.[1] They started teaching between 1910 and 1939. Three of the women started teaching directly out of high school; eighteen of them had a one or two year Teacher Training Class attached to a local high school, twelve attended a Normal School for one or two years, and seven were college graduates. All of the teachers began their teaching careers in elementary schools; only two women subsequently taught in high schools and only one woman became an administrator. All except four of the women had been married at least once by the time they were interviewed, and twenty-nine of the forty taught for some period of time after marriage. The majority of the teachers had careers of between ten and thirty years, often with interruptions which lasted anywhere from six months to twenty-three years.

One of the teachers only taught for a single year; several taught for over forty years.

Addison County, bounded by Lake Champlain on the West and by the Green Mountains on the East, and although adjacent to cities both to the north (Burlington) and the south (Rutland), is primarily a rural community. In 1910, Addison County claimed a population of slightly over 20,000 of which only 14 per cent lived in towns with populations over 2,500 (US Bureau of the Census 1910, p. 580). The county experienced some population loss between 1910 and 1940, but by 1950 the population, at 19,442 inhabitants, was at about the same level it had been forty years before (US Bureau of the Census, 1950). Addison County also remained rural: in 1950 only 19 per cent of the inhabitants lived in 'urban' areas and almost half (46 per cent) of the rural inhabitants lived on farms. At the beginning of the century, most schooling took place in one- or two-room schoolhouses: In 1910 Addison County had 179 different schools (of which twenty-six were graded) and 318 teachers serving a school population of 935 students (Vermont State Board of Education, 1910). By 1950, most of the schooling occurred in graded buildings although, as elsewhere in the state, many towns in Addison county continued to operate more than a single elementary school (Vermont State Board of Education, 1950).

Multiple Intersections

Structure

While it is commonplace to note that women have traditionally entered those occupations perceived as having a rough resemblance to the tasks they performed at home, such as nursing and teaching, we rarely ask whether the women themselves saw the work in the same manner as those who stood outside their occupations, and if so, whether such an analogy had positive or negative connotations for them. Many of the teachers spontaneously drew a comparison between family life and school life.[2] For example, one woman distinguished her experiences in the one-room schoolhouse, in which she began her teaching career from her later experience in a graded school: 'In my first school we were all very happy and busy. The older children helped the younger ones and everybody worked together. We were just like a big happy family in there.' Not only did this teacher delineate a specific way in which the school was like a family, but she offered this similarity as proof that the school was a pleasurable and satisfying environment. Moreover, she later suggested that she chose to intensify this similarity by making family-like rules for behavior within her school. When she fed the school children the hot lunch provided by parents in the community, she required that all children, 'take three bites of everything whether they liked it or not'.

Even when the teachers failed to draw explicit similarities between home and school, the language they used revealed that these identities underlay their thinking. Many of the teachers referred to the individual in charge of hiring and firing them as 'My Superintendent'. This use of the possessive 'my' in reference to a superintendent is much like the 'my' used by people to refer to other family members: my husband, my sister, my father. And, in fact, the structure of authority relations between a teacher and 'her' superintendent seemed very much like the relations between a wife and her husband. On a daily basis, a teacher (like a wife) had a great deal of autonomy: she made innumerable decisions about how to handle ongoing activities. But major decisions, or decisions about extraordinary events, she would leave to the superintendent's approval. For instance, when one teacher wanted to allow a child to participate in daily activities, even though he was under the official age for school entry, she spoke to the superintendent about her plan; a teacher who wanted to take the children in her school skating down the river at the noon hour to visit a friend who was teaching in another school asked for permission in advance.

Skills

The teachers also implicitly drew an analogy between home and school in the manner in which they discussed the skills required for their jobs. First, the major reason teachers offered for having entered the occupation (after noting that there were few other options) was that they liked to work with children. Only a few of the college-educated women expressed an initial interest in teaching because they liked a particular subject matter. The vast majority of them, like Mrs. Winter, said, 'I always knew that I wanted to be a teacher because I always loved to be with children.'

Second, once having embarked on teaching, they attributed their successes and failures to their ability to relate to children. Some of them traced these traits to their own family experiences. One woman commented that she always worked better with boys than with girls: 'because I grew up in a house full of brothers.' This assumption that family life and school life required the same, or highly similar, skills was made explicit by those teachers who noted that they were better at their *jobs*: 'after I had children of my own,' or that they were better *parents*: 'because I had taught all those years and understood children.'

Demands

Not only did teaching appear to require the same skills as mothering, but the same kinds of demands appeared to be placed on both teachers and mothers. Community members expected that the schoolteacher would meet the needs of all the children in the community, whether or not they were enrolled in the school. One teacher recalled, 'They expected the teacher to do everything and know everything. If there's a child was sick, they'd send word down, want to know what to do. They'd send down the bottle of castor oil if they couldn't make the kid take it and wanted the teacher to make her take it.' Another teacher mentioned that her school was often used as a drop-off day care center by at least one mother in the community: 'I had a family in that school, and the mother used to come down with a carriage and she'd have three babies in it — one tiny baby and another that was just beginning to walk around and the other was a little older — and she went downtown shopping which was almost the whole day and she'd leave those three babies for me to take care of.'

But just as these 'outsiders' brought their families into the schoolhouses and asked the teacher to take over, so did the teacher willingly enter the families of students. This appeared true in both the literal sense of visiting the homes and becoming acquainted with parents and siblings, but also in the figurative sense that the teachers saw themselves as being responsible for helping to make up the deficits of the home. The manner in which the teacher in one school perceived the need for a hot lunch program demonstrates this in a particularly poignant way:

> I can see that pretty little girl now with her golden curls — she was one — a member of a large family — she was very good as a rule in math — and at that time the Maltex Company in Burlington were sending out big posters to school: 'Eat a good breakfast, you'll get 100 per cent in math' and so on and so on as an advertisement. We had some of those on the wall and so, well, anyway, I said something I always regretted saying. I said uh, 'What's the matter, Lorraine, this morning? You don't seem to be doing as well as usual in math. I guess you didn't eat that breakfast.' She straightened up and looked at me as if she wanted to hit me and she said 'It wasn't my morning to eat!' ... As a result of that, I thought we better have one warm meal.... I got together the mothers and said can't we have one hot dish furnished for hot lunch?

Another teacher similarly noted that she let a child sleep during school hours, because his family lacked enough beds in his home, and he was tired on the days following 'his night to sleep in a chair.' Many of the teachers interviewed had much the same kind of empathy towards the physical and emotional needs of their charges. The teacher, quoted earlier as saying that she taught because she loved children, described the orientation that she and others had for their work:

> And the older teachers taught for themselves and for the children and for the community and the parents. I know one teacher taught down in Cornwall for years, her father had a farm — raised potatoes, raised crops — and she gave them all away to the parents that she taught their children because they were poor. And a lot of the teachers did that. I don't think today you'd find a teacher buying clothes for children or giving them food. I don't say they aren't as good teachers

— they're probably better because they're very educated — in books — but there's something in the human touch there that's missing.

Personnel

Home life and school life thus appeared similar for these teachers because the two had the same general structure, required the same skills, and allowed them to meet the same demands. They also, significantly, overlapped in terms of personnel.

The schoolteachers I interviewed either felt no impulse to keep their home lives and their work lives separate or they seemed unable to do so. Whatever the cause (and I believe it was usually the former), the two worlds slipped and slid into one another. Family members and close friends of teachers were brought into the life of the schools in a variety of ways. Some teachers brought their own children to school with them before the children were old enough to be enrolled in school, because there was no other reliable babysitting arrangement. Others remembered teaching their own children as well as a variety of other relatives. Mothers and daughters also helped each other out in school life. Several women noted that, when they became pregnant and had to leave teaching, their own mothers or their close friends took over for them. One woman noted that, when her daughter broke her leg and had to stay away from work for a time, she took over for her. Another woman said that her daughter came in to assist when her regular aide was absent.[3] Some of these teachers brought their husbands in to help with field trips and other special school events:

My husband was so good with the kids at school. He did more for them than any of the fathers ever did! Like Christmas time he'd always go out on Sunday with some of the bigger boys, and some of these big boys would get the Christmas tree, and they'd come back and set it up. He did this every year.... He liked the kids. He was always playing with the kids and talking with them.... I remember when I used to teach in Charlotte, we used to go out to Ethan Allen Park rollerskating. Of course, you'd take the kids in those days because they couldn't get there. Charles would take the day off from where he was working and we'd take the kids.

This intermingling of home and school worked in the other direction as well. Teachers often shared apartments or lived with the superintendent's family. One teacher relied on the wife of her principal as her babysitter for her son. And at times teachers brought students into their homes for afternoon visits or even long periods (as in the case of a teacher who adopted one of her students).

Time

Finally, the intersection of home and work occurred on a temporal level as well. The teacher's work life punctuated domestic life and vice versa. Mrs. Cook's description of her normal routine would be familiar to teachers today:

> I left for school at eight o'clock in the morning ... and I was home between five and six at night.... I put the school behind me when I left and spent that time cooking, cleaning, taking care of my family, talking ... whatever until bedtime. And then of course there were always papers. In the morning we were always early risers and we had a couple of hours in the morning for our family. And when I left to go to school I left my family behind and faced my day working.

But she did not always leave family behind: when her child was three he started to come to school with her and he continued to do so until he was old enough to go on to high school.

The interview with Mrs. Fredricks indicated a similar integration of home and work life. She left her child to be cared for by a woman who lived in a house adjacent to the school. Looking out of her classroom window she could watch her child playing, and if she spotted trouble, she would ask the teacher (her best friend) in the other classroom to watch her students for a time, while she ran out to talk to her child, comfort him, or just make momentary contact. When that same child first entered school, he was in the class right next to hers and could (and did) come in periodically during the day to say hello. In later years he was in her class.

Despite such idyllic descriptions, the two worlds of the female teachers did not always appear so well interwoven. Marriage interrupted many teaching careers. Several of the teachers quit their jobs upon marriage, noting in retrospect that it was expected of them, or that it was what their particular husbands wanted. But some of the teachers soon convinced their husbands that they would be happier having work to do. Mrs. Staples recalled this time:

> I didn't resent [being asked by my husband to give up my job] though I was very lonesome for teaching. I didn't teach for several years and I was very lonesome. I was almost willing to go into a school and say I'll pay you to let me teach.... And after a while I said [to my husband], 'I don't like this, why don't I go back to teaching,' and he said, 'Okay if you really want to.'

Other teachers, like Mrs. Cook, noted that, during the Great Depression at least, they had few choices:

> Q: Did you think you'd have to give up teaching when you got married?
> A: Oh, yes, it was just taken for granted in this town that, if you married, you were no longer eligible for teaching.

Q: So why did you continue teaching?
A: Because we needed the money. I needed the money. My husband's family had lost a farm and a home in the depression. And he could not find work.... [My teaching] wasn't anything we wanted. It was just like living from day to day. It's something that you faced and made your choice and did. Not the way it is today — me first. Nothing of that sort. No open end with your fingers crossed. Nothing of that sort. It was just the way the times were.

But family emergencies could arise at any time. Several women spoke about returning to teaching after they had dropped out to raise their own children, because of crises, such as accidents which left their husbands disabled, or the loss of the major source of family income through farm failures.

Since for much of the period between 1900 and 1950, Vermont had a teacher shortage (to be discussed below), re-entry posed little problem. An informal network spread information about a teacher looking for a job to the appropriate superintendent, or information about a superintendent in need of a teacher to the appropriate woman. Mrs. Staples, once she had convinced her husband that she really wanted to resume teaching, found it easy to find a new job: 'So I wrote to my old superintendent and he gave me a job.'

Childbearing served as another reason for a temporary interruption. The interviews revealed surprisingly modern-seeming attitudes towards work during pregnancy. Mrs. Fredricks remained in her teaching position until six weeks before her second son was born. When questioned about the attitude of her supervisor she recalled,

I taught until February, and nobody knew I was pregnant, and then came February Vacation, and I sent [my superintendent] a note and said he better look for somebody quick. He and the school nurse came to see me during February Vacation, and asked me how I was, and what the doctor said, and so forth. And I said [the doctor] said I'm fine, and [my superintendent] said, 'as long as you're all right, you go right along.' And so I did.

With respect to the attitudes of other members of the community, it is clear that only in instances where the parent had other causes to be angry at the teacher was the pregnancy raised as an objection. Mrs. Staples recalled trying to convince a little boy to take off his sweater on a hot day and the boy's guardian coming into the school saying, 'I was not to tell her kid what to do and all that, and anyway it was time for me to stop teaching when I was as big as I was.' But most teachers spoke of support. One teacher described the baby shower that parents gave her at the end of the school year to celebrate the impending birth of her child; another teacher testified also to community acceptance: 'When I was pregnant I was down in East Middlebury and I finished right up until June.... There was no comment at all that I ever heard of.... There was another teacher there and we both of us wore smocks, she did as well as I did, and it seemed to work out all right. I never heard any repercussions.'

Given the common assumption that teachers were not even allowed to teach while married (Tyack and Hansot, 1982; Tyack and Strober, 1981), much less while pregnant, these community attitudes require some explanation. The teacher shortage mentioned above might have had something to do with the eagerness of a community to retain a teacher, regardless of what might, at other times, have been regarded as impropriety. The general pressures of the depression might also have been a variable, as suggested by Mrs. Cook, quoted above as having said that she returned to teaching following her marriage, in spite of not wishing to do so:

Q: You were mentioning about how it was frowned upon to teach and to be married. How did others feel about your teaching then?

A: I don't really know. I think that probably people were so taken up with their own affairs and their own mortgages collapsing, financial distress and difficulties that anybody's personal affairs were not looked upon. It wasn't that sort of time.

For some of the women childrearing (as differentiated from childbearing) served as the cause of career interruption. In those cases, where the period away from work was short, re-entry followed the same patterns indicated before: the informal network spread the word until the appropriate contacts were made, or the woman simply called her superintendent and said she was ready to teach again.

Longer career interruptions presented somewhat more difficult reentry problems. In 1910, when the first teacher in this study began teaching, a high school education seemed more than sufficient preparation for receiving a teaching certificate; by 1950 a college degree had become the preferred minimum (Vermont School Reports 1910, 1950). Throughout this period (and especially during the Second World War), permits were granted to teachers who did not adequately meet the certification requirements — if no more fully qualified person was available — but they had to work towards appropriate certification. Teachers described taking courses on Saturdays and at night, or enrolling in intensive teacher training programs during the summer. Acquiring additional education could thus be a major burden in an already busy life. Still, it often appeared easy to obtain a job itself. Mrs. Bright, for example, spent thirteen years out of the classroom while raising her children. She remembered how she obtained a job after that period: 'The second time around I remember right the day [a couple of members of the school board] came. I was up in our barn floor making apple boxes, I came down and they said, "would you be interested in filling such a job?" and I took it for the fall term.'

Evaluation

I have chosen to emphasize these intersections of home and work, because they help to clarify some of the difficult issues surrounding the evaluation of work environments for women that I raised in the beginning of this chapter. This work existed within a context which made very traditional assumptions about the nature of women and their associated roles (see Quantz, chapter 10) — assumptions which many might find difficult to accept today. Clearly the members of the community assumed that women loved children, that they were willing to make enormous sacrifices for these children, and that they would nurture them beyond the boundaries established by the schoolhouse itself. There was also a generalized expectation of altruism: that women placed the needs of others first, that women's priorities were organized around others rather than themselves, that when there was a perceived need — in a family or a community — women would be glad to respond. Thus I found examples, in addition to those reported before, that illustrate this point: women abandoned their *occupational* lives, because a member of the extended family was sick and needed tending, because a brother's wife had died and he needed a housekeeper, because a husband's occupation required her assistance or relocation. The reverse was true as well: women were asked to abandon their *domestic* lives, because they were needed by the schools. A woman recalled that when she was home with her new-born child her superintendent, 'during Christmas vacation of that same year', expressed his desire that she return to school in these terms: ' "You want to leave that little baby at home? Up in Starksboro they need you in a big school up there".' Another woman, when asked why she had transferred to a school, even though it was farther from her home than the one in which she had been teaching, responded simply, 'I was needed there.'

Finally, these teachers' comments suggest a high degree of paternalistic control on the part of the superintendents and school board members (see Abbott, 1986). If close and personal relationships with supervisors could work to the advantage of the teacher, they could also work to their detriment. One teacher reported that following a conflict with her superintendent she was told that she would 'never get another job in [his] district'. And, she said, 'I never did.'

Schoolteachers in rural Vermont, then, did not carry out their professional lives within the framework of liberated notions about the equality of men and women or the nature of women's roles. But, as I suggested in the beginning, other ways of evaluating the same evidence exist. First, and most important, is the issue of how the women themselves viewed the set of assumptions within which they operated. In fact, the evidence strongly suggests that the women shared the expectations of self-sacrifice. To a great extent, the value of their work, and the pride that they took in doing it, emerged from their sense that they were fully and appropriately engaged in fulfilling a woman's mission. To discredit their work by saying that it exploited them would be to impose an inappropriate set of criteria which they could not understand. Similarly, it would be inappropriate to argue that these women qualified as incipient feminists, because they worked full-time even after they married and assumed responsibility for young children, carried on in their careers through pregnancies, and reaped enormous satisfaction from their professional activities. The women themselves did not see their careers in the terms of personal liberation: many of these women worked either because they had to or because they were needed; even those, who returned to, or continued in, their occupations because they wanted to do so, explained their actions in terms of needs, albeit in this case their own needs, rather than in terms of the rights of all women. And most of the women spoke contemptuously about 'modern girls', who think only of themselves, without stopping to consider how they are affecting those around them.

Having warned against the retrospective application of evaluative criteria, I want to return to the issue of the double burden which I suggested earlier. These narratives by rural schoolteachers revealed rich evidence that the multiple intersections of home and work provided solutions to the double burden — solutions which appear unavailable to women today. First, as noted in the descriptions of the lives of some of these teachers, the community allowed these women to bring their small children to school with them, thus simply resolving the ongoing problem of what to do with children during working hours. Second, friends and relatives brought in during absences created through illness or maternity, assured these women that their jobs would still be available if and when they chose to return to work: a mother would give way to a daughter, a friend to a friend. Thus these intersections not only provided the solution for the immediate problem of 'who can be trusted to take over my school?' but for the longer term problem of 'will my job still be there when I get back?' Third, the intersections at a temporal level provide us with ample evidence that women of the past could move in and out of their careers in response to domestic needs.

Finally, women who work outside the home today often find that their children and their spouses are unwilling to assume a portion of the domestic burdens (Ferree, 1987). But some of the women that I interviewed noted that they received such help. Mrs. O'Malley commented that the division of labor was very flexible in her house during her work years: 'My husband almost always got home from work first and started the supper; but if I got home before him, then I did things like starting the fire.' Mrs. Harrington, also, in a matter-of-fact way, noted that her husband cooked dinner 'because he was home earlier than I was.' Another teacher said that her husband, who was a carpenter, took care of their young child until she could take him to school with her. Other teachers noted that their children were a great help and eased the burdens for them considerably. Perhaps because the domestic and work lives of these women overlapped and intersected, they were able to make visible the former to members of their own families in ways that are unavailable when work and family are more clearly differentiated. Moreover, because they were so often working 'out of need' the women did not have to justify the sacrifices demanded by their occupational roles: to have *not* worked would have entailed greater family sacrifice.

Conclusion

In the descriptive portion of this chapter I noted that schoolteaching for the women I interviewed seemed to be almost an extension of their normal domestic activities: it had the same structure, required the same kinds of skills, and incorporated the same kinds of demands. Moreover, this notion of the schoolhouse as an extension of the family appeared to be reinforced by the fact that the two worlds overlapped in terms of both personnel and time. In the evaluative section, I noted that these intersections of home and school existed within a context of very traditional assumptions about women and women's roles, but that the teachers shared these assumptions, and that within this context the pressures of the double burden were lightened in ways not always available to women who work today.

Some of the accommodations to the double burden I have described might have been unique to Vermont, such as the willingness of the community to allow a teacher to continue in her occupation while married and even pregnant (Tyack and Strober 1981). Why was the situation so flexible and accommodating? I suggest two possible explanations, both of which I have alluded to already. First, this period included two world wars and the Great Depression. Each of these events required extraordinary behavior from citizens: during the wars women were sought explicitly to take over men's jobs; during the depression people had to make a variety of adjustments in order to ensure survival. Gendered expectations about proper behavior for men and women adapted to meet these contingencies (Milkman, 1979). The stories that these teachers recounted about accepting attitudes on the part of their families, supervisors and communities, may simply have been the only response possible when the situation demanded flexibility. If this were the only reason, however, more historians might have noted this kind of accommodation. Yet this has not emerged from the research.

Vermont also faced a second, and unique, situation which might have made such flexibility particularly likely. During most of the first half of the twentieth century, as suggested at various points earlier, a desperate shortage of teachers existed in the state. In 1910, Vermont's Superintendent of Education wrote: 'In the administration of the public school system there are two stubborn and unavoidable facts: first, the dearth of teachers; second, the dearth of trained teachers.... Almost anyone who can earn a certificate or permit is employed for the reason that none others are available.' (Vermont State Board of Education, 1910). In 1918, the Superintendent still lamented about the teacher shortage:

> The scarcity of teachers presents a very grave problem. A careful census of the teachers needed in Vermont ... showed that there were lacking six high school principals, thirty high school teachers, eight teachers of special subjects, and more than one hundred fifty rural teachers.... During the existence of the war many former teachers were willing as patriotic duty to leave their homes and serve in our

schools. This condition will not exist in times of peace. We must therefore prepare ourselves to deal with a most serious shortage of teachers during the coming year. (Vermont State Board of Education 1918, p. 13)

This situation continued into the 1920s, in spite of the implementation of training programs designed to make the occupation easier to enter. During the depression, when women lost teaching jobs in most places, Vermont's state superintendent observed:

At the present time most states have a large oversupply of teachers. It is surprising to learn that Vermont's only real oversupply is for high school positions. The fact is that there is actually a dearth of well-qualified teachers for the elementary school positions. As the depression lifts, many who have now gone back to teaching in order to supplement the family income, will again take up their duties as home makers. The enrollment in the normal schools must then increase to meet the increased demand for teachers. (Vermont State Board of Education 1934:11–12)

Just prior to the Second World War, the superintendent still complained, 'There remains a shortage of teachers though less acute than in the past several years.' (Vermont State Board of Education, 1940). The war certainly brought no relief for this dilemma.

Scarce labor is often powerful labor. The teachers I interviewed show no conscious realization that they occupied a strong position. And in many ways they were not powerful. They repeatedly lost in their struggles for better pay, and they remained subject to extremely personalized and paternalistic control. But it is possible that they did, in fact, use their advantageous position as scarce labor (whether consciously or unconsciously) and the community-wide awareness of those 'extraordinary times' to win concessions which facilitated their handling of the double burden in the ways that I have described above.

Today we still have the analogy between school life and domestic life as noted by the teachers of the past. But in some ways the occupation has undergone enormous change: teachers today have a more complete professional identity, higher salaries and other kinds of fringe benefits, and membership in unions to protect them from arbitrary and paternalistic control. However, the flexible arrangements for handling the double burden have been lost in the transition from the one-room schoolhouse to the graded school. Teachers today, like other women who work outside the home, struggle to balance the obligations of work and family life. Perhaps it is time to institute a new set of arrangements that ensure the flexibility that early twentieth-century schoolteachers enjoyed.

Notes

1 The names used in this research are all pseudonyms.
2 For a similar finding, see Quantz, chapter 10.
3 A similar phenomenon has been described by Tamara K. Haraven as occurring among workers in the Amoskeag Mills during the period 1880–1936: 'Relatives took turns running machinery and taking breaks, and substituting for each other during illness, childbirth, or trips to Canada.' (Haraven, 1987, p. 70).

Chapter 4

Becoming the 'New Women': The Equal Rights Campaigns of New York City Schoolteachers, 1900–1920

Patricia Carter

When spinsters can support themselves with more physical comfort and larger leisure than they would as wives; when married women may prefer the money they earn end excitement they find in outside employment to bearing and rearing children, when they can conveniently leave their husbands should it suit their fancy — the conditions are clearly unfavorable to marriage and the family.... This vast horde of female teachers in the United States tends to subvert both the schools and the family.

J. Cattell, 1909 (p. 91)

This epigraph reveals an editorial commitment to defend the patriarchal order from the attempts by female teachers to address workplace discrimination. Popular beliefs about female teachers' rejection of their traditional roles as wives and mothers surfaced in the new century. These concerns received heightened attention in the first two decades of the twentieth century when female public school teachers in New York City undertook several campaigns in an effort to expand their rights as workers, including equal pay for equal work, the right to teach regardless of their marital status, and the right to maternity leave and reinstatement after leave. This chapter focuses on these three campaigns and illustrates how local women's organizations and feminist ideology, with the help of the press, provided an impetus in the drive for equal rights.

In these efforts, female teachers became prominent members of the controversial population, 'the new women'. This concept, reflecting the changing morals and manners of urban middle-class women, emerged between 1910 and the First World War (McGovern, 1987). The history of the teachers' campaigns helps to document changing attitudes and shifting discourses as to the effect of reforms, such as women's economic freedom and family planning, on American family life (Chafe, 1972; Gordon, 1976; O'Neill, 1973; Tax, 1980). The ideological shift in societal thinking about the feminine sphere contributed to positive attainments for women such as suffrage, better educational and career opportunities, marriage and divorce rights, as well as media distortions as illustrated by the hedonistic 'flapper' image which began to appear at the end of this period (Freedman, 1974; Smith-Rosenberg, 1982).

Women's clubs and urban organizations, central in achieving many of the reforms, sought publicity for their causes through the press. By 1900 the women's page of local city newspapers had become an essential element in communicating the progress, problems, and occasionally some titillating news about women in the community. However, the publishers of local presses, sometimes conservative and aligned with community business interests, moved slowly in providing in-depth or balanced coverage of feminist events. As a result, women formed their own presses for which they acted as the editors, reporters, writers, and the newsmakers.

The self-described 'voice of the women's movement', was the *Woman's Journal*, a weekly suffrage newspaper with a national readership, published by Lucy Stone and her daughter, Alice Stone Blackwell, between 1869 and 1920 (Blodgett, 1971; Filler, 1971). Stone, a former teacher, often editorialized and reported on events affecting women educators. She drew parallels between women's lack of suffrage and their devalued position within the profession, a concept illustrated by the *Journal* (1911) political cartoon (see figure 1). (Blackwell, A.S., 1910; Blackwell, H.B., 1905; K.G., 1902).

In the absence of a national women's teachers' organization, the *Journal* became a critical informant of educational reform activities across the country. For instance, while some educational journals ignored or offered only scathing evaluations on the campaign to elect Ella Flagg Young as the first female president of the NEA, the *Journal's* coverage was complete and sympathetic. Other women's publications which covered the New York City teachers' campaigns included Charlotte Perkins Gilman's the *Forerunner* and the New York suffragist paper, the *Woman Voter*. Gilman's monthly magazine (1909–1916) provided several thoughtful and theoretical pieces on the situation regarding teacher-mothers (Gilman, 1913, 1915, 1916). The *Woman Voter* documented the work of New York City teachers registering to give talks to vacationers at the upstate summer resorts and criss-crossing the countryside in their 'Franchise Fords' (Blake, 1915; 'Teachers to the front,' 1915). Though generally sympathetic to the teachers, the *Woman Voter* lashed out at the Interborough Association of Women Teachers (IAWT), when the *Voter's* editors grew weary of the IAWT's equivocal stand on suffrage ('Schoolteachers and suffrage,' 1912).

Figure 1

An unequal footing! (1911). *The Womans Journal* **42**, 4 March p. 1.

The Origins of the Teachers and Clubwomen's Coalitions

The early twentieth century saw a virtual explosion of membership in women's clubs and organizations as middle- and upper-class women rushed into reform and suffrage activities (Ryan, 1975, p. 174; Blair, 1980). New York City served as the headquarters for many large women's groups, including the National American Suffrage Association, the Woman's Suffrage Party, the East Side Equal Rights League, the Equality League of Self-Supporting Women, the United Suffragettes of America, the Equal Franchise League, the Political Equality League, the New York Women's Suffrage Association, and the National Women's College League ('Directory of Women's Suffrage Headquarters in NYC', 1910). Women teachers joined these organizations as well as formed their own. In fact, by 1910, 50 per cent of all US cities (with populations over 30,000) had at least one organization representing women teachers. Some of these groups aggressively brought issues of workplace discrimination before their schoolboards and the public.

Club women's interest in teachers resulted, in part, from their work in progressive school reforms such as student health programs, playground beautification, open air classrooms, and art and music programs. Also, protective labor legislation, though focused primarily on female factory workers and domestics, helped to heighten club women's awareness about the plight of teachers as breadwinners. It quickly became evident that the institutional changes most strongly supported by the male-dominated school leadership were not the work place issues of women teachers (Biklen, 1978).

Women's increasingly marginalized position within the teaching profession necessitated their interdependence with outside women's groups. With school administration, school boards, professional organizations and journals virtually closed to women, teachers had no choice but to request club-women's involvement in their fight. Female teachers, during the nineteenth century, had tried effecting change by building their own professional networks. In cities across the country, teachers' reading and social groups metamorphosed into organizations which actively campaigned for issues such as equal pay and female principalships. Their work met with extremely limited success. Furthermore, in joining these groups, teachers risked being fired, denied promotion, or being ostracized by colleagues (Berkeley, 1984; Clifford, 1978; Koehler, 1984; Collins, 1976). Thus, coalitions between teachers and outside women's groups can be recognized as effective twentieth-century strategy for pressuring school boards and elevating public attention to the sexist hiring practices of American schools, while protecting individual teachers from administrative retribution.

Equal Pay for Equal Work

As early as 1853, Susan B. Anthony predicted feminist activism for teachers' rights in the workplace, when she spoke at the New York Teachers convention. In responding to the discussion about the lack of respect accorded the profession, Anthony pointed out that it was a sex-segregated job market that suppressed wages and lowered the general status of teachers. She asked, 'Do you not see that so long as society says woman is incompetent to be a lawyer, minister, or doctor but has ample ability to be a teacher, every man of you who chooses the profession tacitly acknowledges that he has no more brains than a woman? ... Would you exalt your profession, exalt those who labor with you ... increase the salary of women engaged in the noble work of educating our future Presidents, Senators, and Congressmen?' (Lerner, 1977). Two years later the *Woman's Advocate*, a Philadelphia periodical, advocated the concept of equal pay for women teachers: 'We can imagine no valid reason why a woman, who had spent time and money in acquiring an education, and who is engaged to teach as many hours, as many pupils, and as correctly and thoroughly, should not receive as large a salary [as a man]' ('Compensation of male and female teachers', pp. 94–95). The most commonly suggested reason for the failure to pay the same salaries to women and men was that women teachers did not need as much money as their male colleagues. Men, responsible for supporting families, required a family wage while women should be supported by parents or a husband. This argument ignored those women who were the sole support of children, siblings or elderly parents. And, as Charlotte Perkins Gilman suggested in her classic text, *Women and Economics* (1899), the argument was irrelevant. Gilman felt that woman's salary should have no bearing on her marital status or economic need; indeed, a woman's economic dependence upon man 'perverted society', Elizabeth Cady Stanton (Stanton, T. and Blatch H.S., 1922) agreed that female economic independence was indispensable to achieving female liberation. This concern for economic justice for women appeared inherent in the three campaigns of the New York City female teachers, but most significantly in the equal pay for equal rights fight.

The campaign for equal pay for equal work began in response to the wage schedule set by the New York State Davis Law in 1900 (Hammack, 1982). The law brought the school districts of the five boroughs of Richmond (Staten Island), Brooklyn, the Bronx, Manhattan, and Queens under a single Board of Education, a move initially supported by women teachers; the new salary schedule, however, surprised many of these same supporters. The annual minimum salary for male teachers, for instance, began at $900, but was only $600 for women. Furthermore, after sixteen years of service, female elementary schoolteachers reached a maximum of $1,240, though men earned $2,160 after only ten years of service. Female principals, too, earned less than male principals. In high schools female salaries ranged from $1,100 to $2,500 while men's started at $1,300 and capped at $3,000 a year (Maxwell, 1903; 'The Davis salary schedule', 1900). Despite the fact that New York City teachers' salaries were among the highest in the nation, the issue of salary equalization incited action, especially by Brooklyn teachers, who previous to the Davis law received equal pay for equal work.

In November 1904, the New York City Federation of Women's Clubs held a debate titled 'The Equalization of the Salaries of Public School Teachers'. Alida S. Williams, principal of Public School (PS) 33, was scheduled to speak in favor of equal pay and Dr. B. Crowson, principal of PS 125, against it. When Williams did not appear, Crowson faced the audience alone. Among his arguments against equal pay were: that women were mentally and physically inferior to men; that teaching was only a temporary position for a woman but a long-term career for a man; and that a woman teacher spent her salary only on herself, while a man required it to support a family. Alice Blackwell, reporting for the *Woman's Journal*, stated that Crowson 'made his audience so indignant . . . that almost all the women there seemed to wish to get up and speak on the other side' ('Should women teachers have equal pay?', 1904). Consequently, the issue became increasingly polarized, and male principals and teachers were seen as adversaries to equal pay for women. For many men, in a profession increasingly dominated by women, salary differentials symbolized the value of their masculine presence. Furthermore, many men contended that salary equalization would not increase women's wages but lower their own (Chancellor, 1906; 'Men teachers reply', 1909; 'New turn in equal pay fight', 1908; Strachan, 1910a; 'Tell men teachers they shan't meddle,' 1909; 'Women teachers challenge. . .', 1908).

Differences over gender issues led to the fragmentation of the New York Class Teachers' Association (NYCTA), an organization representing nearly

2,000 members. In April 1905, a group within that organization began to circulate a flyer that declared:

> The time is ripe to establish the principle of equal work. Why should a woman's minimum annual salary be $300 less than a man's and why should her maximum be $900 less than a man's? The women teachers do the same work, are exempt from no rules or duties, and most of them have fathers, mothers, sisters or brothers dependent upon them.... Why, then, should women not receive the same salaries? ('Schoolma'ams want men teachers' pay', 1905, p. 1).

The circular further suggested that the best way to begin this effort was to depose the current president, George Cottrell, and replace him with 'a womanly woman, one loyal, faithful, [and] conscientious' ('Teachers' election fight', p. 12:2). The *New York Times* monitored the meetings of the organization and on May 7, 1905, reported that 'the anti-suffrage members' had organized to keep Cottrell as president ('Teacher's election fight', 1905). At the next NYCTA meeting Cottrell's supporters, conscious of the circular's attack, read resolutions commending him for the work that he had done. The equal pay advocates interrupted with boos and hisses. One of the leaders of the anti-Cottrell contingent, Augusta Black, took the floor and asked the audience: 'How many of you have ever signed a payroll and seen upon it the name of a man who is doing the same work as you are, but who is receiving double your salary?' The listeners cheered and applauded her statement. She continued, 'Haven't you felt humiliated?' She urged those in support of equal pay to elect a woman president of the organization ('Class teachers war over equality plan', 1905).

Though the suggestion seemed like an instant remedy, the tactic backfired, losing more votes than it gained. Fearful that any attempt to equalize the salaries of men and women teachers in the elementary schools would result in a general reduction, the Brooklyn teachers reluctantly defeated the female presidency ('Defeated by their own sex', 1905). As a result, several hundred equal pay proponents decided to withdraw and form their own group, the Women Teachers' Organization (WTO) ('City's women teachers demand pay of men', 1906). As its first action, the group presented an equal pay proposal to the City Board of Education, which turned it down without a hearing. After much discussion, the WTO made plans to appeal their case to the state legislature ('Board rules against the women teachers', 1906).

By September, the WTO, now called the Interborough Association of Women Teachers (IAWT), had 4,000 members. Within two years the membership grew to 14,000 under the leadership of Grace Strachan, a Brooklyn school district Superintendent (Strachan, 1910b). The change in leadership is noteworthy, because it marked the beginning of a united coalition between the IAWT and outside local women's groups. Strachan, who may have emerged as the IAWT president in deference to her unusually high position with the school system, had a history of developing feminist coalitions. In 1903, women's groups from throughout the community, including the

International Sunshine Society, the Chiropean Club, the Women's Principals' Association of the Borough of Brooklyn, the Clio Club of Harlem, and the New York Equal Suffrage League championed her unsuccessful bid for associate superintendent of schools ('Marriage under bar', 1903). The likelihood of continuing support from these groups certainly made Strachan an attractive candidate for the IAWT presidency. During the equal pay campaign notable suffragists, including Carrie Chapman Catt, Harriot Stanton Blatch, Lillie Devereaux Blake, Beatrice Forbes Robertson, and Ida Husted Harper, accepted appointments as honorary vice-presidents of the IAWT. Organizations including the New York Federation of Women's Clubs, the National General Federation of Women's Clubs, and the City Club of New York passed resolutions in support of the Equal Pay Bill (Strachan, 1910a).

Strachan, born in 1863 in Buffalo, New York, received her early education in parochial schools, and graduated from the State Normal School at age sixteen. After teaching three years at Buffalo High School, she took an appointment at PS 11 in Brooklyn. A year later, she served two years at the Training School for Teachers before advancing to principal at PS 42 and Evening School 85. During this time, she also became vice-president of the Brooklyn Teachers' Association, and one of the organizers of the Branch Principals' Association. Her fast-track career continued with her appointment as district Superintendent of Schools in 1900, at which point she seems to have hit the glass ceiling. Though she made two bids for Associate Superintendent of the New York City schools, in 1903 and 1914, it was not until one year before her death in 1922 that she gained the position ('Mrs. Grace Strachan Forsythe, 1922). In 1914, the Mayor claimed that Strachan's political past made her an inappropriate candidate. The *New York Times* editors agreed, noting that the Mayor's was a 'sober and moderate but candid expression of an opinion shared by a great body of well-informed persons who have at heart the best interests of the schools' ('Not the most eligible', p. 12:3). The political activity to which they refer was the equal pay campaign.

On other issues, even suffrage and labor unions, areas from which the IAWT received its largest support, Strachan remained noncommittal throughout the equal pay battle. She walked a razor's edge of political opinion, encouraging support from whatever organization would consider it. What she promised in return remains unclear. The uneasiness of her position, especially in regard to the suffrage movement, is evoked in her 1911 statement: 'We ourselves do not want the ballot, but our rights, and our best friends in the Legislature do not want women to have the ballot' (Doherty, 1979; 'Equal pay meeting', 1909). She could not afford to offend those friends in the Legislature who did not agree with a woman's right to vote. One could assume that suffragists understood this statement was made for the benefit of those 'friends' and did not express Strachan's personal opposition to suffrage. Why would suffragists continue to support the equal pay campaign so tirelessly? One indicator of Strachan's support for the ballot is illustrated by her active involvement in suffrage after her equal pay victory when she taught at a New York 'suffrage school' ('Miss Strachan's denial', 1913; Strachan, 1913; 'Suffrage school well attended', 1913). Her suffrage work took on an even more public role after her 1914 defeat for the Associate Superintendent position, when she became the chairwoman of the Teachers' Branch of the Empire State Campaign for Suffrage (Strachan, 1915; 'Teacher suffragists organize', 1915; 'Teachers to enter soapbox campaign', 1915).

Between 1907 and her death Strachan remained president of the IAWT. As her first act, she led over 600 women teachers into the halls of the Albany legislature to attend the hearing on the equal pay bill. The *Woman's Journal* noted that the local press had been vituperative in its coverage of the teacher's efforts: 'We are told that the teachers pervaded the capitol building and overflowed the rooms and corridors, that all the Senators were besieged by rings of teachers three deep, plying them with arguments' ('Teachers ask equal pay', 1907, p. 1). Although the bill passed quickly through both houses, it was defeated by a veto by the New York City Mayor, as was permitted on issues affecting the city ('Equalization of salaries', 1907). Despite the loss, the IAWT's lobbying efforts had increased public visibility for the issue of equal pay. Newspapers and educational and popular journals editorialized regularly, often negatively, about the issue. For instance, the *Journal of Education* prophesied that equal pay would result in a net loss of jobs for women ('New York women teachers', 1906). The *New York Herald* agreed, claiming that the concept of equal pay 'may be right in theory but wrong in practice' ('Equal pay or equal work', 1906, p. 212). An editorial in *Outlook* suggested that rather than equal pay, the schools needed more male teachers, 'because for example, the average boy, if he is taught only by women, comes to regard scholarship as a purely feminine accomplishment and look upon it with something like contempt' ('Equalization of salaries', pp. 594–95).

Many of the arguments, pro and con, used this separate spheres concept — that women and men were fundamentally different and made different contributions to society. Dr. William H. Maxwell (1908), school superintendent, cited Herbert Spencer's *Study of Sociology* (1899) as the source for his contention that 'the intellectual and emotional characteristics of men and women are different' and his rather ironic conclusion 'that women respond more readily to the appeals of pity and men to appeals of equity'. The *New York Times* agreed with Maxwell's position and commented in an editorial that the superintendent 'does not slight the conflicting claims of the men and women teachers, but seeks rather to reconcile them to the needs of the public' ('Dr. Maxwell', 1903, p. 6:2). Following the same separate spheres logic, the *Outlook* reasoned: 'A woman is not a man in petticoat; a man is not a woman in trousers. Their work is essentially and inevitably different' ('Justice to teachers', 1908). On the other hand, Edward Forrester in writing for the *Bookman*, used this same concept to arrive at the opposite conclusion that 'both men and women should stand upon an equal footing in the schools, in order that our public education should be well-rounded, harmonious and complete' (Forrester 1907, pp. 177–79).

As might be expected from such gender-bound thinking, a second source of opposition to the IAWT's equal pay bill emerged in the form of the Association of Men Teachers and Principals of the City of New York (AMTP.) This organization formed in March 1907, on the heels of the

IAWT's trip to the New York State Assembly. The group of 600–700 men represented members from the Brooklyn Teachers' Association, the Bronx Principals' Association, the Principals Association of New York, the Assistant and Junior High School Teachers Association, the Schoolmen of New York, the Schoolmen of Queens and the Male Teachers' Association. Taking a cue from the IAWT's lobbying tactics, the AMTP quickly released a lengthy circular which attacked the latest equal pay proposal. Among their arguments against equal pay were: that women did not require the same standard of living as men; that women did not deserve equal pay, since they were intellectually inferior to men; and that equal pay would result in more women avoiding marriage in favor of work (Association of Men, 1907).

Such opinions, deemed 'unchivalrous' and 'uncolleagial' in the *Woman's Journal*, failed to bring about the desired community response and resulted in a number of converts to the equal pay cause. *The New York Evening Sun* called the male teachers 'self-seeking male persons opposed ... [to] a simple act of justice' ('Teachers' equal pay bill', 1907, p. 82). To make matters worse, the male teachers lacked the more subtle and persuasive qualities of the IAWT lobbyists. The *Woman's Journal* reported on an indignant Assemblyman Hoey, after a run-in with one representative from the men's organization. He accused the male teacher of 'insulting and threatening [him] because [he] dared vote for this bill' ('Teachers' equal pay bill', 1907, p. 82). Carrie Chapman Catt, president of the National Suffrage Association, excoriated the men's association, claiming the circular contained '24 excuses ... not ... 24 reasons against equal pay' (Strachan, 1910a, p. 398).

Despite continuing success in ushering the Equal Pay bill through the legislature, vetoes, first by the New York City Mayor and then by the Governor, frustrated the IAWT's efforts. As an alternative strategy the IAWT actively pursued pledges for the equal pay bill from mayoral and gubernatorial candidates during the 1910 election year. The IAWT saw the election of new people to these key positions as crucial in overcoming the two major stumbling blocks to the passage of equal pay. Since the incumbents were both Republicans, and the equal pay bill's strongest advocates Democrats, the IAWT urged teachers to campaign for the Democratic party ('Censure teachers for campaign work', 1911, p. 20:1). In autumn of 1911, with no hesitation, the legislature, and the two newly elected Democrats, Governor John Alden Dix and Mayor George B. Gaynor, signed into law Chapter 902 of the 1911 Laws of New York. It specified that teacher salaries were to be regulated only by merit, length and degree of experience and grade level taught ('Recommends equal pay', 1910).

The Rights of Married Teachers

A concern for the moral development of students provided school boards with the rationale for a controlling interest in both the private and public activities of teachers. This argument became recognized by the theme 'women's peril to education' and was documented in popular magazines such as the *Independent, Survey, Good Housekeeping* and *Popular Science* as well as professional journals, including *School and Society, Education Review, Journal of Education,* and *School Review*. Between 1890 and 1915 dozens of articles with titles such as 'Are there too many women teachers?' (1904), 'Celibate female teachers' (1903), 'The monopolizing woman teacher' (1912), and 'Shall biological failures be our teachers?' (1915) underscored many popular concerns about the changing roles of women, and how, in stepping outside their accepted feminine roles, teachers contributed to a general decline in the schools and the moral fabric of society. For instance, F.E. Chadwick advocated this line of thinking, claiming that: 'For generations the American boy . . . has been under the women tutelage. The effect of such procedure has had no evil an effect upon the manhood of the country, on the qualities that go for making the masculine character, that it is more than full time to consider . . . this great and vital question.' (p. 109).

Some articles held women teachers almost singularly responsible for the 'race suicide' of the native-born White US citizen, as evidenced by a rapidly increasing divorce rate, the growing numbers of women in the labor force, and the later marriages and fewer children in the families of the White middle- and upper-classes. Theodore Roosevelt contributed to this concept as he wrote and spoke widely about the dangers of 'selfish' women, who refused marriage in favor of employment, or those who limited their procreation to one or two children (Silverman, 1975). As did many other proponents of the 'race suicide theory', Roosevelt felt that the duty of White middle- and upper-class women was to bear at least four children and thereby save the United States from being overpopulated by immigrants of 'inferior' nationalities (Roosevelt, 1924).

Other articles relied on ideas derived from the sciences of eugenics, sociology, biology, psychology, and industrial management; still others on traditional religious or cultural beliefs. At times, they seemed to contradict each other. For example, one group castigated women teachers who never married, claiming that they presented an aberrant lifestyle to impressionable young students, which might eventually result in the extinction of the race. Others argued that married women teachers also cast the wrong image of 'true womanhood', for they championed the love of the dollar over the love of the family. In 'The monopolizing woman teacher', Charles Bardeen (1912) expressed alarm that the biological functions of women, such as menstruation and menopause, were destroying American education: 'Women's chief disadvantage is the fact that in every month there are one or more days when she ought to be in bed, yet when she must be in her place.' Furthermore, he reasoned, that twenty-eight should be the maximum age for women teachers and six the total years she be allowed to work. After that, he opined, 'they develop a pessimism, a contempt for mankind that is not healthful and that boards of education shrink from'. And woe to the unsuspecting school that allows women to teach during menopause, a time, he warned, that 'renders the best of women . . . impossible.' Misogyny provided the foundation for many such 'scientific' arguments.

In essence, the women's 'peril to education argument' made several claims:

1) that the presence of so many women in education feminized the institution and emasculated male students, resulting in a weak nation;
2) that women teachers threatened to subvert men's dominant role, both in the work place and in the home;
3) that women were biologically and intellectually unsuited to long-term careers in teaching;
4) that women teachers contributed to the race suicide of the native-born and educated White population in the United States.

A few of these articles were written in response to the New York City teachers' efforts to gain equal pay and the right to keep their jobs after marriage, and during and after pregnancy. The question of married women teachers and the right to work became a public issue in New York City as early as 1903, when the Board of Education instituted a regulation which formally prevented married women from holding positions in the schools. The ban was in response to a lawsuit filed against the School Board by Kate M. Murphy, a teacher who was fired when she married. Murphy contended that the practice of dismissing women teachers upon marriage had been unevenly applied and that there were many married women teachers employed by the Board of Education (Murphy v. Maxwell, 1902). When she pursued the case in court, local women's groups began to take notice. Feminists variously upheld married women's right to teach, both on the grounds that women were equal to men and should be treated accordingly, and that women's 'differentness' made married women 'superior' to men as instructors of children. But all opposed the Board's decision to exclude married women from teaching. The *Woman's Journal* commented contemptuously on the situation: 'It is not a very deadly matter, only one more instance showing our general conviction that a married woman belongs solely to her husband, that her work must be domestic, and that if a mother she can not be anything else' ('Married teacher's victory', 1904, p. 98).

As public debate on the New York City married teacher's campaign increased, so did the pressure on the Board to modify their initial position. At their 22 April 1903 meeting, several Board members proposed what they considered to be a more sympathetic rule: 'No married woman shall be appointed to any teaching or supervising position in the day schools unless her husband is incapacitated from physical or mental disease ... or has consecutively abandoned her for no less than three years prior to the date of her appointment' (Gilman, 1904). This, they reasoned, would provide for those few married women teachers who needed their income to support their families. But it hardly spoke to the argument that women should be allowed to work regardless of financial need and that the School Board had no right to pry into the private lives of women teachers. The situation was parodied by feminist author, Alice Duer Miller, in a piece, 'The Ideal Candidates,' printed in the *New York Tribune*:

Characters:
Board of Education
Three women candidates

Chorus by the Board:
Now please don't waste your time and ours,
By pleas all based on mental powers.
She seems to us the proper stuff
who has a husband bad enough.
All other please appear to us excessively superfluous.

1st Teacher: My husband's really not that bad ...
Board: How very sad, how very sad!
1st Teacher: He's good, but hear my one excuse ...
Board: Oh, what's the use, oh, what's the use?
1st Teacher:
Last winter in a railroad wreck,
he lost an arm and broke his neck.
He's doomed but lingers day by day.
Board: Her husband's doomed hurray, hurray!

2nd Teacher:
My husband's kind and healthy, too...
Board: Why then, of course, you will not do!
2nd Teacher: Just hear me out. You'll find you're wrong.
It's true his body's good and strong;
But, ah, his wits are all astray.
Board: Her husband's mad, hip, hip hurray!

3rd Teacher: My husband's wise and well — the creature!
Board: Then you can never be a teacher!
3rd Teacher: Wait. For I have lead such a life;
He could not stand me as a wife;
Last Michaelmas, he ran away.
Board: Her husband hates her hip hurray!

Chorus by Board:
Now we have found without a doubt,
By process sound and well thought out,
Each candidate is fit and truth,
to educate the mind of youth.
No teacher need apply to us,
whose married life is harmonious. (Miller, 1915)

Despite biting satire and the scandalous married woman teacher controversy, the School Board remained firm in its position. In December, Jennie L.

Vandewater, a newly married teacher, made it public that she would refuse to resign her position, in order to make a test case. Kate Murphy had just lost her case and a local women's rights group, the New York Legislative League, appeared anxious to see the issue tried again. The *New York Tribune* explained: 'Many women teachers have been waiting for some such test, putting off marriage to men they are engaged to or keeping their marriages secret to retain their positions in the schools' ('May make it a test case,' 1903, p. 6:1). Vandewater was suspended a short time later, and the League, whose membership included such feminist notables as Elsie Clews Parson, Lillie Devereaux Blake, and Josephine Shaw Lowell, held a community forum on the issue (Will permit women teachers marry, 1904, p. 16). The organization developed a resolution in support of Vandewater, which was printed in its entirety in the *New York Tribune*:

> Resolved, That we would respectfully remind the Board of Education
> that it nowhere appears in any section of the criminal code that it is a
> crime to be a woman, nor do any of our statutes enact that it is
> reprehensible or in violation of any law for a woman to marry, . . .
> ('Not a crime', 1903, 7.5)

In March 1904 the New York Court of Appeals rendered a new verdict in favor of Murphy, noting that the School Board had been authorized to dismiss teachers only on grounds of gross conduct, insubordination, neglect of duty or general inefficiency ('Married teacher's victory', 1904). Marriage did not constitute grounds for dismissal. The press reaction to the Appeals Court verdict was generally positive. The *New York Globe and Commercial Advertiser* commented that the court's decision was 'along the line of enlightenment' ('Married teachers victory', 1904). The *Independent* noted that 'The decision ought to have a good effect on school boards in other places who have a prejudice against married women teachers' ('Teachers May', 1904, p. 1044). When asked to comment on the court's decision, School Board member M. Dwight Collier replied, 'We are tired of fighting over this matter in the courts, and the public is in favor of retaining married teachers.' But he warned, 'I think the public will regret that married women are permitted to teach' (Collier, 1904).

The Board's clear disagreement with public opinion became an even more sharply defined point in what came to be seen as an issue separating an old-fashioned Board and a new-thinking public. As a result of the court's verdict in the Murphy Case, Mary L. Grendon, who resigned when she married in July 1903, asked to be reinstated in her teaching position. The Board refused and the case went to court. In July 1906 the court decided against her, with the court finding that the School Board had used no duress or coercion in order to induce her to resign ('Grendon v. Board of Education of the city of New York', 1906). The School Board immediately reopened the debate: should married women teachers be retained? The *New York Post* noted that 'several hundred' of the district's 12,000 women elementary school teachers were married and that in the previous summer alone seventy-four more were wed ('Married women as teachers', 1906, p. 168). The Board decided to study the question of whether these married women lowered the standards of the teaching profession, starting with a review of the individual employee records. In the end, the study did little but to serve notice to married teachers that they would be closely scrutinized for any infraction of the rules for which they could legally be dismissed. In the meantime, local women's groups turned their attention to suffrage and city improvement and the press found other issues on which to focus. Without a clear guarantee of their rights, teachers found a less public means to protest discrimination against married women. Some chose to enter 'secret marriages' in which they hid their new status from the public, and more importantly from school administrators. Close friends and teaching colleagues took a collective vow of silence to protect these women from dismissal. There were others, as well, who succeeded in keeping their marriages secret only to have an untimely pregnancy expose their deception.

The Fight for Maternity Leave

A regulation against those who became known as the 'teacher-mothers' developed as a natural consequence of the New York City School Board's failure to prevent married women from teaching. The 1911 by-law declared: 'A married woman's sphere is the home, if she has a family. A woman who has infant children to rear has no business trying to take care of these and at the same time teach school.' Just hours before this announcement the Elementary Schools committee of the Board formally suspended four young mothers on the charge of chronic absenteeism. When asked by a *New York Times* reporter whether a teacher could return to her position after her child had grown, Stern (a School Board member) stated: 'Yes, if she resigned and later came up to the regular requirements imposed on former teachers who returned to work.' 'However,' he warned, 'if she were discharged for cause it is improbable that she could ever be reinstated' ('Bar out teachers with small babies', 1911, p. 13:1). But when Catherine Campbell Edgell, physical culture teacher at Erasmus High in Brooklyn, applied for a maternity leave, her request was promptly denied ('Lost job as teacher for bearing child...', 1913).

This reflected the national attitude, since schoolboards in other cities created similar regulations. In May 1908, the Chicago Board of Education formally adopted a rule which stated: 'No mother with a child two years of age shall be appointed to a position as teacher' ('Duties of teachers', 1908). In Indianapolis, teachers could be reinstated after their children were grown but had to start at the bottom of the pay scale ('Minutes of the Board of Education for Dec. 30, 1914', 1914b). A 1914 survey of forty-eight US cities with populations over 100,000 found that only three, Cincinnati, Los Angeles, and Milwaukee, had a policy of granting maternity leaves ('Progressive Cincinnati', 1914).

However, Edgell's dismissal and the subsequent suspensions of other teacher-mothers caused feminist notables, such as Charlotte Perkins Gilman, Harriot Stanton Blatch, Henrietta Rodman, Alice Stone Blackwell, Reverend Anna Howard Shaw, and Fola La Follette, to lend their names, influence, and active participation to the *cause célèbre* ('New fight to save teacher-mothers...', 1914). Henrietta Rodman, an English teacher at Wadleigh High School in New York City, the secretary of the League for Civic Service of Women and a founding member of the New York City Feminist Alliance, served as a prominent leader in the campaign for teacher maternity rights ('Aided Mrs. Edgell, married herself', 1913). Rodman's strategies included forming a coalition of groups in support of maternity rights, encompassing the City Mothers Club, Woman Suffrage party, and the Woman's Political Union. These groups held debates and periodic press conferences in reaction to each new teacher-mother case that came before the Board of Education ('Won't act against teachers...', 1913; 'Motherhood held as civic service...', 1913).

A key case was that of Bridgett Peixotto, who had taken a leave for a nose and ear infection. However, her supervisor learned from an 'anonymous writer' that the reason for her absence was childbirth. She was suspended in April 1913, two weeks after she gave birth. The press gave a great deal of coverage to the Peixotto case, including photographs of her with her infant child. Several editorial cartoons appeared in New York City newspapers, including the *Tribune* and the *Evening Sun*; reprints appeared in national magazines and newspapers, such as the *Woman's Journal* (see figures 2, 3, and 4). What is particularly intriguing about the cartoons is that in each case the board is shown as a small group of men, despite the fact that five female members sat on the twenty-eight member body. Little attention was paid to the fact that the two single women on the board favored the teacher-mothers while the married women did not. However, the press did begin a call to reorganize the board.

The *World* suggested fewer board members 'with greater executive and general powers and less scope of interference in administrative details'. To which a warning was added: 'In public service whom the gods destroy they sometimes first make ridiculous' ('The crime of motherhood', 1913, p. 802). In general, the press became an increasingly vigilant voice in favor of maternity leaves for the teachers and critic of the board. Even the *Journal of Education* admitted: 'It does seem criminally silly for a body of able-bodied men to leave real problems in order to try to frighten 19,998 women so that they will never bear a child unless they are willing to sacrifice their salary' ('Should mothers teach?', 1913, p. 432). *Outlook* agreed: 'The duty of the Board is not to direct or modify social forces; it is to see that the schools are conducted with efficiency' ('Motherhood and Teaching', 1913, p. 462). The *New York Tribune* reported caustically: 'Having been so successful in ferreting out criminals among our married teachers who actually had the brazen immorality to have children, our Board now seeks other fields to conquer.' ('The crime of motherhood', 1913, p. 802). Rose Young, in *Good Housekeeping*, accused the Board of being out of step with public opinion:

Figure 2

Board of Education — 'You may marry, but you must not have children'. —
Robinson in the New York *Tribune*. Reprinted (1913) *Literary Digest*, Nov. 1, p. 802.

Bearing twelve children and burying ten of them in infancy cannot be
accepted today as evidence of upright living that it was once supposed
to be. The waste of women in the old-fashioned way was so merciless
that it often took four wives to bring up one man's family. Sen-
timental reliance upon an old-fashioned phrase like the old-fashioned
home is an indefensible way in which to belittle the home of today.
(Young, 1914, pp. 31–32)

The *Independent* pointed out the inconsistency in the board's policies: 'The
board is willing enough to grant leaves of absence to teachers for recreation,
recuperation, travel, and study, yet it is blind to the fact that the experience of
maternity is far more important than any of these' ('Penalizing motherhood',
1913, p. 605).

The League for Civic Service for Women hoped to embarrass members
of the Board of Education, who had publicly stated that a pregnant woman
was incapable of teaching, and generated quite a bit of press coverage with the
announcement that a pregnant teacher had agreed to remain in her classroom
until 'the last possible moment'. The teacher wrote anonymously to her

Figure 3

Reprinted (1914) *The Woman Voter* **45**, (December) p. 12.

district Superintendent, stating, in part: 'I do not want any annoyance or notoriety, but I am willing to do my share to make a place for mothers in the public schools of New York' ('A married teacher's ruse...', 14, 18:2). Her anonymity appeared short-lived, however. A couple of weeks later, Lora Wagner gave birth only thirteen hours after she left her classroom ('Teacher becomes mother...', 1914). While still hospitalized, Wagner sent an appeal to the New York City Mayor, to which he responded: 'I am chary of interfering with the Board of Education.' ('Teacher-mother appeal to mayor', 1914; 'Teacher-mother to mayor', 1914, p. 11:4). On hearing this, several league members made an appointment to meet with the Mayor personally. The profit of their dialogue was evident in a letter that Mayor Mitchell sent to the Board of Education several days later, requesting a rationale for the policy on mother-teachers. He asked: 'Would not a simple rule providing for leave of absence in this case for a suitable period put an end to all this discussion, and instead of working injury to the schools be likely to do them a great deal of good?' (Minutes of the Board of Education, November 11, 1914, 1914a, p. 2354). The Mayor held a press conference the next day at which the *New York Times* reported that he felt the School Board would soon adopt a 'reasonable, rational policy' on the teacher-mother matter ('Teachers to get maternity leave', 1914, p. 8:4). A month later the Board established a

Figure 4

SHOO!

Courtesy The Evening Sun. Reprinted (1914) *The Woman Voter.* **45**, (December) p. 14.

compromise ruling which allowed maternity leave, but required it to be taken as a two-year absence without pay (Minutes of the Board of Education, December 30, 1914, 1914c, p. 2649).

In January and February 1915, the Commissioner of Education announced the disposition of the teacher-mothers cases, which had been appealed to him. He ruled Peixotto's dismissal illegal and ordered her reinstatement and paid in arrears ('Teacher-mothers case', 1914; 'Teacher-mothers win final verdict', 1915). He reinstated another teacher but denied all other cases before him. Though there were several attempts to mitigate the deposition of these cases, as well as the harsh terms of the new maternity leave policy, none succeeded. Henrietta Rodman endeavored to decrease the amount of required leave to that which was decided appropriate by the woman and her physician. There were also attempts to get those teachers, who had voluntarily resigned upon marriage, reinstated, but to no avail. For their obedience to authority, they received nothing ('Mrs. Gamse asks clubwomen' aid', 1914). The Board reasoned that it did not hire married women as teachers ('For opportunity classes', 1915). The whole issue seemed intractable until the First World War when dire teacher shortages necessitated reevaluation of the policies against married women teachers. This irony was not lost on feminists ('Married teachers', 1918).

Summary

The campaigns for equal pay and the rights of married teachers and teacher-mothers tested many traditional concepts about middle-class womanhood in America. Could women perform equally to their male colleagues in the work place? Should married women work outside the home? Did mothers make less effective workers? Between 1900 and 1920 public attitudes about these questions shifted significantly in favor of the woman's right to choose her own lifestyle. The press was essential in communicating this shift in thinking about women's roles. The city newspapers, the national magazines, the women's newspapers and magazines, and the educational journals covered the campaigns of the New York City women teachers, and in doing so helped to break the stereotype of the submissive and apolitical woman teacher, while challenging readers to face facts about sex discrimination in the labor market.

The coalitions formed between teachers and outside women's groups throughout the three campaigns can be recognized as an effective twentieth-century strategy for creating work place reforms for women within the education profession as well as other sectors of the economy. Throughout this period these groups became increasingly sophisticated, utilizing litigation, regular press conferences, and meetings with the Mayor and other key political figures as a means to increasing pressure and publicity. The IAWT demonstrated the political impact of women who did not even have the vote, with sobering results for the few who lost their offices.

Furthermore, the feminist ideology which supported the coalitions helped teachers, as working women, to bridge the middle-class work-motherhood dichotomy by showing that both roles could be carried out simultaneously. In choosing the more socially acceptable issues of the right to marry and have children, 'new women' teachers and their advocates stretched, but did not threaten, the traditional boundaries of the family unit. In this way they maximized social cohesion and political effectiveness between teachers and outside women's rights activists as well as the public at large.

Part II

Teachers and Their Communities

There is simply no place in this commercial culture for
the teacher or the profession.

Waller (1932)

Introduction

In 1936, Howard K. Beale, in his pioneer nationwide study on academic freedom, *Are American Teachers Free?*, characterized the relationship between teachers and their communities as that of conformity, meaning that the community shaped racial perceptions, galvanized teachers' roles, and restricted religious values, among other social and political prescriptions. The school operated as a cultural repository while the teacher served as a 'paid agent of cultural diffusion' (Waller, 1932, p. 40). Thus, the teacher functioned neither as an autonomous professional nor as an enlightened intellectual, both in the classroom and out of it. Social norms, more than credentials, county exams, and state certification codes, regulated the teacher's professional career and private life.

Communities appeared to be so pervasive and effective in their influence over teachers that Beale encountered almost insurmountable problems in merely collecting data for his study. He summarized his obstacles as teachers' fears and administrators' reticence, as he asked questions about 'ideas', like the League of Nations, socialism, income taxes, social and political equality for 'Negroes', as well as 'personal conduct', such as attending the theater, smoking, dancing and union membership (Beale, 1936, pp. 785–791). Classroom instructors generally seemed to be intimidated, if not downright frightened, choosing to remain silent. 'The multiplicity of examples of fears of teachers about supplying facts is in itself eloquent testimony to the lack of freedom in the schools' (Beale, 1936, p. xvi). In some cases, a surprised Beale (p. xiv) found that many teachers expressed intolerance of their colleagues' nonconformities, and identified instead with their communities. In still other instances, a frustrated Beale (p. x, xi) pointed to the fact that too many teachers lacked a cosmopolitan perspective, thus failing to realize that their communities' conventional ideas, values, and routines inhibited their freedoms: 'Thousands of teachers are utterly uninformed and unaware of anything outside of the textbooks and minutiae of small-town life.' A universal, hierarchical bureaucratic structure reinforced provincialism. Beale (1936, pp. xii–xiii) discovered blatant authoritarianism on the part of many school administrators: 'They are not interested in freedom. One characteristic of the successful administrator is skill in avoiding trouble.... In general, superintendents and school board members seem to feel ... that it is impudent for any one to question or enquire into their motives.'

Historical tradition, ideology, patriotism, personal relationships, and racism all trespassed on teachers' rights, Beale discovered. Although the nineteenth-century's legacy regarding academic freedom failed to be spotless, conformity assumed an even more ominous tone during the early years of this century, with such provocative biological theories as evolution, questioning religious dogma; political ideologies like communism, challenging capitalist beliefs; and profound social change like pluralism, overwhelming people in the once relatively homogeneous nation with ethnic, religious, and racial diversity. Pressure groups, including religious, business, and patriotic associations, stubbornly clung to the status quo. Less than legitimate organizations, like the Ku Klux Klan (KKK), spearheaded attacks on teachers and curricula. Although teachers achieved modest progress towards academic freedom, Elsbree lamented as late as 1939 (p. 543): 'Even today, however, the freedom which teachers enjoy in many communities depends to a large degree upon their intelligence, information, and tact.'

Religion represented a particularly touchy subject. Beale (1936) noted that Americans despised irreligion. Largely Protestant, they saw religious education as moral and civic imperatives as well as an integral part of American culture and tradition. Thus, in 1926, eleven (mostly southern) states required Bible reading in the schools, with stringent enforcement. Delaware designated fines and dismissal for teachers who violated the 1925 law. Although schools used the King James version of the Bible, most Protestants failed to see this choice as a sectarian act. Catholic, Jewish, and agnostic parents felt otherwise. As a result of their protests and legal actions, schools, especially those in heterogeneous communities like large cities, often excused children from these services. Yet teachers, unlike their students, faced coercion, that is, 'the alternative of the exclusion from teaching or else going through the motions of religious forms that are to him a mockery' (Beale, 1936, pp. 211, 218). In more homogeneous, and particularly fundamentalist religious settings, attitudes appeared to be more intense and rigid, while Catholic teachers served as special targets: 'In 1915 about one hundred Catholic teachers were dismissed in Denver, Colorado. In 1913 two women were dropped from the schools of Charlotte, North Carolina, because of the Catholic issue' (Beale, 1936, p. 223). During the 1920s, the KKK included Catholic teachers in its southern campaigns of prejudice and harassment.

Community constraints shadowed teachers outside of the classroom as well, occasionally assuming more abstract and subtle forms. Teachers had to maintain impeccable moral lives, as defined by the values of a particular locale. After the First World War, big city school districts appeared to be the most tolerant, yet in many states school buildings hosted temperance meetings, often led by teachers. Small towns and rural areas expected teachers to devote personal time to church attendance, Sunday-school instruction, and other such wholesome activities. While these communities presupposed that their classroom instructors be civic minded, they frowned on teachers' participation in political campaigns, especially those that confronted local customs. Teacher protests, as we saw in chapter 4, and tenure laws, passed by different states during the 1930s, alleviated some of these restrictions, but failed to eradicate them (Elsbree, 1939, p. 535).

Ironically, such exemplary behavior acted to isolate the classroom instructor: 'The community can never know what the teacher is really like because the community does not offer the teacher opportunities for normal social intercourse.' For Waller (pp. 49, 50), writing in 1932, this dilemma assumed gender and racial manifestations: 'It has been said that no woman and no negro is ever fully admitted to the white man's world. Possibly we should add men teachers to the list of the excluded' (Waller, p. 50). Why did these communities spurn their classroom instructors? First, they saw female teachers as sacrificing their adulthood and male teachers their masculinity through their association with children and devotion to a feminized occupation (Hofstadter, 1963, p. 320). Second, community residents perceived teaching as a 'failure belt'. Waller (1932, p. 61) cited a popular saying in this regard: 'Teaching was the refuge of unsalable men and unmarriageable women.' The old and persistent labels 'Ichabods' and 'Schoolmarms' hinted at a deep-seated American tradition of anti-intellectualism as well as the relegation of teaching to a quasi-caste occupation (Clifford, 1989, pp. 311–319; Hofstadter, 1963, pp. 309–22).

This especially applied to female and African-American instructors. On the one hand, teaching represented a respected occupation among such low status groups. On the other hand, community orthodoxy resulted in their lives being socially circumscribed rather than intellectually liberated. As we saw in Part I, the stereotyped female teacher's role, well into the twentieth century, adhered to rigid contracts governing such personal matters as religious activities, recreation, hygiene, relationships with males, and marriage (Eaton, 1975, p. 23; Waller, 1932, p. 43).

Race presented an equally formidable problem. Schooling represented the primary vehicle for race improvement, and African-American teachers traditionally symbolized 'knowledge, culture, and intellectual and moral authority — all attributes that society had routinely denied blacks' (Perkins, 1989, 347). The White community felt differently. In the antebellum North, African-American instructors who could find positions — usually in segregated schools — often earned half of the salary of White teachers, 'without reference to qualifications or the size of class' (Litwack, 1966, p. 133). Matters failed to improve dramatically during Reconstruction, when White missionary associations reluctantly sent African-American teachers to the South. Moreover, the American Missionary Association, although nondiscriminatory, clearly 'limited' the number of southern African-American teachers who applied for 'commissions'. Most taught in the country, 'where the societies had little interest in sending Yankee teachers' (Jones, 1980, pp. 65, 69). This situation existed in spite of the fact that African-American parents 'preferred black teachers to whites not only because of racism and indifference often apparent in the white teaching staff, but also because they recognized that black teachers were an inspiration to the children' (Perkins, 1989, p. 348). While southern Blacks fought for more and better schools, in the late 1800s, northern Blacks sought integrated schools, but their teachers paid the price with their jobs. 'Thus, it was not uncommon for blacks to argue for separate schools.' (Perkins, 1989, p. 349).

During the early twentieth century, the rural South attracted the least prepared teachers. Its underfunded, segregated schools, with abbreviated academic calendars, overcrowded classrooms, and poor pay, offered little incentive. The opposite occurred in cities, which hired African-American instructors with outstanding credentials from the leading colleges and universities. Beale (p. 439), writing in 1936, found that some city districts claimed 'complete equality, where curricula, texts, and salaries are usually the same. Often they have sufficient political power to safeguard their rights.... They mingle professionally with white teachers.' However, Proctor (1979) points to a wretched experience in Pittsburgh. Here the district only hired its first African-American instructor in the late 1930s, and until the 1950s, relegated African-Americans to stereotyped subjects, like music and physical education.

Homel (1984, pp. 6, 28, 187) presents yet another, more complex, experience in Chicago, where African-American teachers enjoyed relatively unrestricted opportunities. The Board of Education hired African-American instructors on an integrated basis as early as the 1880s, their number growing from thirteen in 1901 to forty-one in 1917; nor were they necessarily confined to schools with substantial African-American enrollments. Eight of the fifteen instructors in 1905 worked at schools with few or no African-American children. School administrators quickly dismissed protests from White parents and students, defending these teachers. The Great Migration changed all of this. Between 1915 and 1940, Chicago's schools underwent a profound transformation. African-American students became more numerous and segregated, and African-American instructors experienced the same fate. In 1917, 60 per cent of them worked at schools with at least 90 per cent White enrollment, but by 1930 only 9 per cent taught in such institutions. Much of the racial segregation that took shape during the 1920s and 1930s remains intact.

Nationwide public school desegregation during the 1950s often resulted, as it did earlier, in the elimination of jobs for African-American teachers. The subsequent Civil Rights Movement expanded opportunities for African Americans, replicating the women's experience in many ways. Educated African Americans chose more lucrative and prestigious careers: 'As the number of black professionals grows in other fields, teachers lose significance. In addition, because society evaluates one's worth and status according to income, low salaries have contributed to the decline in teacher status within the black community as it assimilates the values of the larger society' (Perkins, 1989, p. 363). In 1986, African Americans comprised less than 7 per cent of the nation's teachers; this figure is expected to decline further.

Finally, White teachers who taught African-American children, until recently, faced rejection from the White community. In the antebellum North, and in light of the shortage of trained African-American teachers, school boards frequently hired White instructors to teach minority-group students. They not only received less than meager salaries, 'but in some communities faced insults and social ostracism. In Providence, a white teacher threatened to punish any of his Negro students who dared to greet him in public' (Litwack, 1966, p. 133). A hundred years later, Beale (1936) found southern White teachers who taught African-American children likewise banished or ignored by the White community. In Chicago, during the 1920s and 1930s, White teachers, like their earlier counterparts in Providence, generally maintained racist attitudes towards their ghetto students (Homel, 1984, pp. 108–109).

Therefore, American teachers have experienced an ambivalent relationship with their communities in the twentieth century. On the one hand, communities scrutinized what teachers taught in the classroom and monitored their behavior outside of it. After all, they entrusted their children to these individuals; teachers served as role models, thus often causing community members to prescribe higher moral standards for classroom instructors than they placed on themselves. On the other hand, these people usually shunned personal associations with teachers because they seemed somewhat less than adult, represented effeminacy, and symbolized failure. These attitudes were reflected in modest salaries and low status for teachers, regardless of the community's size or economic standing. As Waller somberly noted in 1932 (p. 58): 'There is simply no place in this commercial culture for the teacher or the profession.'

Part II focuses on the relationship between teachers and their communities. Phyllis McGruder Chase, relying on diaries, letters, and oral interviews, traces the long, deep, and rich heritage of African-American instructors in Buffalo, New York, beginning in the early 1800s and moving well into the 1900s. Margaret Nelson, using oral histories, stresses the teacher's role in creating a sense of community in rural Vermont. Joseph Newman, tapping newspaper interviews and reports, examines religious prejudice and its impact on one public school instructor in early twentieth-century Atlanta. Alan Wieder, drawing from intense oral interviews, analyzes a more contemporary issue, teachers' perceptions of integration in New Orleans.

R.J.A.

Chapter 5

African-American Teachers in Buffalo: The First One Hundred Years

Phyllis McGruder Chase

We also wish to secure for our children, especially, the benefits of education which in several states is denied us and in others are enjoyed only in name.

Samuel Davis
Buffalo Teacher (1843)

Buffalo symbolized one step from freedom for many fugitive slaves; a short ferryboat ride across the Niagara River took them to Canada. 'Buffalo, New York, was an important step enroute to Canada for fugitive slaves. There was an active underground railroad supported by both Blacks and Whites, and a strong Anti-Slavery Society established in 1839 included some of the most prominent citizens of the day' (Graf, 1939, p. 1). Even Josiah Henson, the man after whom Harriet Beecher Stowe patterned her famous Uncle Tom character, passed through this city on route to Canada. Captain Burnham, a white Buffalonian, gave him the dollar he and his family needed to board the Waterloo Ferry to freedom (Henson, 1849). Approximately seventy African-American families lived among the 10,000 White people in Buffalo during the early 1800s. Whether freeborn or fugitive slaves, they had established themselves in the city: they owned property, maintained businesses, and built homes and churches. City directories listed them as barbers, ministers, doctors, teachers, and lawyers (Buffalo City Directories, 1828–1855).

African Americans and Whites appeared to live in harmony. African-American men, but not women or Native Americans, were allowed to vote if they owned property valued at a minimum of $250; this was not a requirement for White males (Brown and Watson, 1982, p. 52). Perhaps the mood or attitude towards Blacks can best be described by an article in a local paper:

Some little excitement was created in town yesterday afternoon by an attempt to secure and take away a young colored man named Christopher Webb, who was claimed as a fugitive slave by a person named Robert Perry, as the agent for the owner, and another person . . .

both of who are from Corington, Kentucky.... Perry and his associate recognized him and told him that he must go back to his master. Webb protested that he was free and should not go with them. One of the parties then seized him, at the same time drawing a six shooter and declaring that he would shoot the first person who interfered and dragged him by force down the stairs, when there was some interference to rescue him. He however was taken by the parties into a law office, where the crowd gathered in such numbers that Webb was permitted to leave. Some intimations were then made that Perry and his associate were to be arrested on a civil prosecution for assault and battery and false imprisonment.... The last that was heard of them they were proceeding at a rapid rate out of town with the Deputy Sheriff in pursuit, backed by several colored persons on horseback. (Quoted in Grendel, 1965)

In the years before emancipation, it appeared that Buffalo served as good a place as any for African Americans to live. Therefore, when the common school system opened, African-American parents petitioned City Council for their children to attend.

But, here the line was drawn. White Buffalonians shared the same general beliefs as the rest of the country, that is, African-American children were so inferior to White children that they should not be allowed to share the same classroom. Oliver Steele, Superintendent of the Buffalo school system, made this clear in his annual Report for 1838:

They require greater patience on the part of their teacher, longer training and severer discipline than are called into exercise in the district schools, and generations will pass before they possess the vigor of intellect, the power of memory and the judgement that are so early developed in the Anglo-Saxon race. Hence the importance of a distinct and separate organization of the African school. (Steele, 1839, p. 3)

In response to the demands of the African-American citizens, but in no way compromising their beliefs, in 1839, City Council established an African School. Many African-American families, viewing the segregated school as a symbol of their oppression, petitioned the White school system for admission and led boycotts against it for thirty-three years. However, the majority of parents welcomed any opportunity for their children to become educated; some wishing to improve their own educational level, perhaps even to become literate, attended school with their children.

The history of African-American teachers in the Buffalo Public School System begins with the opening of this African School, and with the first three teachers hired for the African School, who were males: J.C. Wilson, in 1839, Walter Fuller, in 1840, and Samuel Davis, in 1842. These African-American teachers represented a unique experience in the urban North. They were either fugitive slaves or freeborn, while most of the other members of their race in America were enslaved. These men were literate, while a majority of Americans were illiterate. These three teachers were given the opportunity to educate members of their race, while in other parts of the country people were beaten or jailed for attempting to do the same (Steele, 1839, p. 4; Kingsley, 1841, p. 5; Hawley, 1842, pp. 17–18).

This history of Buffalo's African-American teachers covers 150 years. This period is significant. Unlike Buffalo's other ethnic groups, African-American teachers taught during the enslavement of their race by their own countrymen; when their President issued an Emancipation Proclamation for the members of their race; throughout a civil war which divided their country — a war which most Americans were taught to believe was fought to free the slaves. In the twentieth century, they taught while witnessing the deliberate segregation of their race within the Buffalo Public School System; in 1954, the Supreme Court's Brown vs. Topeka decision gave Buffalo's African Americans a legal basis to fight the injustice of segregation. They waited and watched through twenty more years of legal maneuvering before a Federal Court ordered the Buffalo School System to desegregate in 1976 (Arthur v. Nyquist, 1976).

The three teachers, who will be described in some detail here, are included not only because they were African-American instructors in the Buffalo public school system, but because they represent the eras in which they lived and taught. The first two, Samuel Davis and Bishop James T. Holley, taught in the first half of the nineteenth century. Ida Fairbush, the third teacher, was hired in 1896 and made the transition from the nineteenth to the twentieth century. Certainly, just the fact that they were highly literate place Davis and Holley in the upper classes of their times. Those who knew Miss Fairbush likewise remember her as elegant. She was also closely associated with Mary Talbert, one of this nation's leading Negro Clubwomen. They have left us traces of their lives in their writings as well as official records.

Samuel Davis

Samuel Davis, the third teacher hired, may have been related to the Davis men who were listed in the 1828 City Directory in a section reserved for the 'colored' men of the community. He certainly represented one of the first African-American families in Buffalo. There is also no question that he belonged to that group of abolitionists and African-American activists (perhaps the terms are synonymous), both men and women, who dedicated their lives to the uplifting of their race and the oppressed of the world. They travelled extensively throughout the North and in Canada organizing and gathering support for their causes. Highly literate, they published their opinions and thinking in the journals of the day. They seemed to be talented enough to fit into any community. They served as clergymen, teachers, writers and laborers, doing whatever they must do for their cause and their survival.

In 1843, one year after being hired to teach at the African School, Davis was selected to serve as President *pro tempore* and keynote speaker of the Convention of Colored Citizens held in Buffalo. The leading African-American abolitionists attended, including young Federick Douglass. The convention centered on the 'moral and political condition of Blacks as American Citizens'. Davis (1843, pp. 3–18) gave an impassioned and eloquent plea for the 'colored citizens of America':

> I consider this a most happy period in our history when we, as a people are in some degree awake to a sense of our condition; and are determined no longer to submit tamely and silently to wear the galling yoke of oppression under which we have so long suffered.
>
> More particularly do I consider it ominous of good when I see here collected, so much wisdom and talent, from different parts of this great nation, collected here to deliberate upon the wisest and best methods which may seek redress of these grievances which sorely oppress us as a people.
>
> Among you are the men who are lately from that part of the country where they see our brethren bound and manacled, suffering and bleeding under the hand of the tyrant, who holds in one hand the Constitution of the United States, which guarantees freedom and equal rights to every citizen and in the other, the scourge dripping with human gore, drawn from the veins of his fellow man.... Our grievances are many and great; but it is not my intention to enumerate or enlarge upon them. I will simply say, however, that we wish to secure for ourselves in common with other citizens the privilege of seeking our own happiness in any part of the country we choose which right not unjustly and we believe unconstitutionally denied us in a part of this union ... We wish also to secure the elective franchise in those states which are denied us.
>
> We also wish to secure for our children, especially, the benefits of education which in several states is denied us and in others are enjoyed only in name.

A year later Davis established his own English-Colored School in Buffalo. Private schools were common at that time, with twenty-six private English schools including the Orphan Asylum and a German School. The tuition ranged from five cents per week to eleven dollars per quarter. Of the approximately 5500 children of school age in Buffalo, 1,200 attended private schools. Twenty-six of the one hundred school-aged children in the African-American community attended the English-Colored School, paying three dollars a quarter. Davis's private school had an impact on the African School, as noted in superintendent Elias Hawley's report:

> The Colored School has been taught this past year in the colored Methodist Episcopal Church on Vine Street which accommodates the school much better than the room occupied last year. A private school for colored children and youth has been in operation during the winter in the neighborhood taught by a colored gentleman who

formerly taught at the Colored public school. This has diminished the attendance the last two quarters. (Hawley, 1843, p. 17; 1844, p. 17)

There is no record of Samuel Davis being dismissed as a teacher from the African School. However, based on what we know about him, he probably resigned out of dissatisfaction with the lack of commitment by the city council to quality education for African-American children. Some parents apparently agreed with him, withdrew their children from the African School, and paid Davis to educate them.

The African School was expensive for the city. Davis thought that if one-fourth of the students left, the city's cost would be so great that the council would send African-American children to their neighborhood schools, there-by breaking down the barrier of segregation. School officials expressed some concern, but nothing changed. The disproportionate cost per pupil for the African School, compared to the other schools, did not deter a council willing to carry an extra financial burden just to guarantee that these children would not share educational facilities. The African School existed beyond the Civil War.

This represents the last mention of Davis in the Buffalo area, but true to the pattern of the activists of the period, he kept on the move between the United States and Canada. Leaving Buffalo, he moved to Detroit to minister to a Baptist congregation. By 1850, the American Free Missionary Society sent him to Canada to manage the Dawn Settlement in Dresden, Ontario. With the help of the British Institute, Josiah Henson had established what would now be considered a vocational college, including a schoolhouse, a church, houses, a sawmill, a black walnut forest, and his family home. The property and some of the original buildings exist today as the Uncle Tom Museum in Dresden. The Institute experienced some problems. John Scoble and others accused Henson of mismanagement. Although Davis saved the program, Scoble had taken over the Institute within two years, and Davis departed. He returned to minister to Detroit's United Baptist Church. Because of the Fugitive Slave Law, he had to return to Canada; there he worked with the Puce Indians near Dresden. In the mid-1860s, Davis returned to the United States and went South to assist the newly emancipated slaves. He acted as their minister and counsellor, helping them to adjust to their new lives, not unlike his earlier efforts at the Dawn Institute. Samuel Davis returned to Canada to spend his final years. For one whose life was dedicated to the uplifting of his race and all oppressed people of the world, he had lost hope for his native land: 'This is our own native land. I repeat it then, we love our country, we love our fellow citizens, but, we love liberty more.' (Quoted in Percy and Reed, 1986, p. 5).

James T. Holley

The city did not hire another African-American teacher for the African School until 1854, and this was due to the insistence of the African-American citizens of Buffalo: 'At several public meetings of the colored population an almost unanimous desire was manifested, that a principal teacher of their own color, might be employed. Accordingly at the commencement of the present school year, Mr. J.T. Holley, a colored gentleman of talent and education was appointed.' (Cook, 1854, p. 23).

Holley came from a privileged background. He was born free, in 1829, in Maryland. Two years later the family moved to Washington, DC, where his father established a successful shoemaking business; in 1809, he had made President James Madison's inauguration shoes. His father, a free man, knew how to prepare both of his sons to survive and develop as free men in a hostile society. They were taught the shoemaking trade, and received a formal education in a private school. In the 1830s aftermath of the Nat Turner rebellion, the racial climate in Washington, DC, was tense. The name calling and racist attacks suffered by the Holley brothers as they travelled several miles to and from school greatly influenced their attitude and thinking toward themselves and toward White people, and in reference to the survival of their race in America. Always striving for a better life for his family, his father moved the family to Brooklyn, New York. Here they lived near relatives and away from the brutal racism of Washington, DC; in Brooklyn, they found less segregation and more job opportunities (Dean, 1979).

These experiences had dramatically opposite effects on the brothers. At 19 years of age, James wrote the American Missionary Society requesting that 'they educate him in the medical profession' so that he might serve in Africa. His request was rejected. At the same time, Joseph was one of the first people in Brooklyn to subscribe to Frederick Douglass's paper, the *North Star*, which was dedicated to integrating African Americans into American society. James became a strong emigrationist while Joseph became a staunch integrationist.

After the death of his father, in the late 1840s, James moved with his brother, sister, and mother to Burlington, Vermont. Life in a small town was much different from city living; it is possible that the Holleys were the only African-American family in town. They opened a shoemaking business, but that did not deter the brothers from pursuing their beliefs. They communicated with the leading abolitionists of the day, and wrote letters to the various journals seeking support for their beliefs. The brothers even held public debates: James, the emigrationist, versus Joseph, the integrationist (Dean, 1979).

It was during this period, in Vermont, when James Holley's life took two important directions. A Roman Catholic, he became interested in the Episcopal church and he started corresponding with Henry Bibbs, who was a fugitive slave living in Canada. Bibbs was also the editor of an abolitionist journal, the *Voice of the Fugitive*, which served as a platform for his own emigrationist belief. In Bibbs, Holley found an ally; one of his earlier letters to the paper, 'From the Green Mountain' expressed his respect for Henry Bibbs and the philosophy they shared:

> I was agreeably surprised on the receipt of the late copies of your valuable journal, to learn that you had already projected, and was

agitating a plan for the systematic colonization of refugees in Canada West.... Your plan meets my hearty approbation, and I give my adhesion to it, as a humbler supporter of the same.... I think it now becomes the duty of the whole free colored population of the United States, to support your project as the most practical one ever presented for their consideration, and the most valuable for the emancipation of our enslaved brethren. (Ripley, 1986, p. 18)

Bibbs, likewise impressed with Holley, printed the following article in the *Voice of the Fugitive* on June 17, 1852:

PERSONAL MOVEMENTS

J.T. Holley, Esq. and Lady, of Burlington, Vt., arrived in Windsor on Thursday, the 3rd instant. This gentleman has recently been acting as travelling agent and corresponding editor of this paper, and has spent some six weeks travelling through Vermont, Massachusetts, New Hampshire, New York, and New Jersey on a mission for the 'Voice'. He is much gratified with the prospects of this place, intends settling down here, and will be associated with us hereafter.

This appointment afforded Holley the opportunity to express his beliefs and also to make himself known to the leading abolitionists of the day. He became co-editor and took charge of the paper. Bibbs lacked a formal education, making it an ideal situation for both men. At the same time, Holley pursued his studies in the Episcopal faith with a priest in nearby Detroit and converted in 1852 (Dean, 1979).

Life in Canada was not what he hoped it would be. He became embroiled in a controversy with some of the same people who had attacked Josiah Henson's settlement, that is, African Americans, both freeborn and fugitive slaves, who disagreed with the separatist philosophy and some of the programs endorsed and supported by Holley and Bibbs designed to help African-American refugees in Canada. They believed that integration in Canada was the key to survival and prosperity for African-American people in North America. But Holley remained firm in his belief that African Americans could not develop their full potential when living among White people. He was convinced that African Americans should take the best of White culture, leave the United States, and develop their own society. The *Voice of the Fugitive* went under. It was just too expensive to operate, and the same group who opposed it started a paper of their own, in direct competition. Bibbs was more interested in the lecture circuit.

Holley was disappointed with his Canadian experience. His first chance to emigrate had failed, and his enemy had been his own race. Holley, unemployed in Canada, with a wife, two children, his mother and a servant girl to support, welcomed the opportunity to teach in Buffalo, New York, for purely economic reasons (County Census, 1855). But he had to return to the country that held his race in bondage. Instead of addressing the world on the important issues of survival for his race, he found himself relegated to a segregated schoolhouse. The separation of the races did not offend him, but he abhorred the reason, perceived African-American inferiority, for the existence of the African School. It was impossible for Holley, under these circumstances, not to address the issues of emigration and colonization whenever he could. It seemed that Buffalo's African Americans reacted to Holley's philosophy as had their Canadian counterparts. His tenure as the Principal Teacher of the African School in Buffalo was considered unsuccessful by Superintendent Efram Cook (1854, p. 23): 'either from want of proper discipline in the school or on account of the dissension among its patrons the school is not in as good condition as under its former principal. There are in this school two organized departments in which have been registered within the year two hundred and sixteen.'

Despite all of the controversy in his public life, Holley was accepted for Holy Orders of the Episcopal Church in 1853, before leaving Canada. While in Buffalo he studied privately with Reverend William Shelton, rector of the most influential Episcopal church in that city. Holley became a priest in 1856. For the better part of five years, he served successfully as a parish priest and educator in New Haven, Connecticut. But his passion for emigration remained foremost in all that he did.

Holley refused any more appointments in the church, and in 1861 fulfilled his dream of recruiting a group of African Americans to form a colony in Haiti. The venture proved tragic. His wife, mother, and forty-three of the 101 colonists died the first year. Holley remained steadfast. He became a citizen of Haiti in 1862, but it was a constant struggle for the colony and his family just to survive. For the rest of his life, he never waivered from his commitment to his colony and to his faith. He was consecrated as Bishop of Haiti in 1874 and was the first African American to speak at Westminster Abbey:

> And now on the shores of Old England, the Cradle of that Anglo-Saxon Christianity by which I have been in part, at least illuminated ... here in the presence of God, of angels and of men ... I dedicated myself anew to the work of God, of the gospel of Christ and of the salvation of my fellow man in the far distant isle in the Caribbean that has become the chosen field of my special labors. (Quoted in Dean, 1979, pp. 71, 96)

Other African-American teachers taught in the African School after Holley. However, none ever again assumed the position of principal teacher, rather they were assigned as assistants to the White teachers. Not only was the African School key to the employment of African-American instructors in Buffalo, it was also the manifestation of the attitude of that city's White population toward the African-American population.

The African School closed twenty years after Holley departed. The City Council, pressured to close the school with the Emancipation Proclamation in 1863, found it necessary to restate school policy: 'Schools must be maintained in each of the districts now established by the Common Council to which shall be admitted all children between the ages of five and twenty-one years except colored children' (Sackett, 1863, p. 10).

Some African-American parents preferred that their children attend the African School. Others opposed the segregated school as an inconvenience, as indicated in the following petition from the grandparents of a child.

> We, the colored people, labor under great disadvantage in sending our children to the Vine Street School, out of their district. Some are so small that they cannot go without their parents taking them.... Some of us have been paying taxes more than thirty years. I took my grandchildren to No. 2 but they would not take them. The principal sent me to the Superintendent, saying if he had no objections, he had none. I saw the Superintendent and he said that he had no power, but that the Common Council could remove the disabilities so that the children could go to school. We thought it best to go before the Common Council and ask them to remove the disabilities, so that the children may go to school in their own district. We pray the Common Council will take it under consideration. (Quoted in Gredel, 1965, p. 3)

Superintendent Thomas Lathrop initiated the school's closing: 'There seems to be no good reason at this time why a school for colored children, exclusively should be maintained at the public expense, and it is recommended therefore that application be made to the legislature to repeal that clause of the City Charter which requires the City Council to maintain a school of that class' (Lathrop, 1870, p. 97; 1872, pp. 110–112). The Civil War and the Thirteenth, Fourteenth, and Fifteenth Amendments to the Constitution, which essentially gave African Americans full citizenship, could not be ignored. The City Council closed the school in 1872. African-American teachers lost their jobs when the African School closed. None of the names of the African-American instructors at the African School can be found in the yearly lists of teachers after 1872 (Buffalo Teachers Exams, 1892–1906). But twenty-three years after the closing of the African School, an African-American woman was hired to teach in the Buffalo public schools.

Ida Dora Fairbush

Ida Dora Fairbush was twenty-six years old when she passed the Buffalo Teachers' Exam in 1895. A graduate of Xenia Normal School in Ohio, she had taught almost two years at Wilberforce College in exchange for tuition. In 1896, the Board of Education appointed her to teach at the Annex of School Number 6 where she remained until her retirement forty-one years later (Fairbush, 1897). This represented a political appointment. In 1892, Richard Jolly and other men formed the 'Colored Democratic Club', breaking the political faith of the African American. 'This club had the Democratic candidate for Superintendent of Education promise if he were elected to appoint some well qualified person of the Negro race to be a teacher in the schools of the city. The Colored Republican League did the same thing. The Republican candidate Henry P. Emerson was elected and kept his word and appointed Miss Ida Fairbush' (Nash, 1940).

Ida Fairbush was everything she had to be: a member of a prominent Buffalo family, educated, respected by the African-American community, accepted by the White educational community, a leader in the African-American community, and a lovely lady of respectability. Not only was she the first African-American teacher trained specifically to become a teacher, but Miss Fairbush's career was unique, because she was the only African-American teacher in the system who never taught African-American children. Whether or not she was hired for that express purpose cannot be determined, but Miss Fairbush taught primarily the children of Italian immigrants (see Figure 5). Even when the East Side of Buffalo was evolving into an African-American community, she continued to teach immigrant children. A Buffalo principal recalled that his father, an Italian immigrant who attended school Number 6, would tell stories about his wonderful African-American instructor. His favorite memory was of Miss Fairbush playing the piano as they marched into their classroom each morning. Some former African-American students who attended the school recall that they never saw her or knew her. One prominent leader in the African-American community said that she can remember hearing rumors that there was an African-American teacher who was so talented that the White people kept her for their children.[1]

Many African-Americans living in Buffalo today remember Miss Fairbush. Their parents were her friends and their memories of her are both warm and pleasant. As a child, Ora Curry, who later became a prominent educator from Buffalo, remembered paying a visit with her mother to the home of Miss Fairbush; here was a memory of proper manners and elegance. Lanora Robinson, another prominent educator in Buffalo, recalled that Ida Fairbush wore herself out teaching immigrant children. She had a special talent; a good ear for the language.

One of the most delightful anecdotes comes from Mrs. Maria Harris, whose mother and Miss Fairbush belonged to the same card club. Mrs. Harris, then a child of 5 or 6 years, would attend the club meetings with her mother. She remembered that she would eat, listen to the conversations, and eventually fall asleep. Always fascinated by the stories Miss Fairbush told about her classroom, Mrs. Harris finally gathered enough courage to ask Miss Fairbush if she could go with her to see those children 'who sew their underwear on during the winter'. Miss Fairbush took her to school for a day which Mrs. Harris remembered as wonderful; Miss Fairbush loved her students.

Miss Fairbush worked closely with Mary Talbert. Among Mrs. Talbert's memorabilia at the Historical Society is a watercolor of her home painted by Miss Fairbush. Her close association with Talbert is significant, because even though she taught only White students, she was actively involved in the African-American community. Mary Talbert was known and honored worldwide as a civil rights activist. In Buffalo, Talbert organized a Christian Culture Congress which sponsored concerts by church choirs, and more importantly, brought in lecturers, including such notables as Booker T. Washington and Mary Mcleod Bethune. Nationally, Mary Talbert, raised money to support numerous causes, from the Dyer Anti-lynching Law 1921 to the restoration of the Frederick Douglass homestead (Logan and Winston, 1982).

Ida Dora Fairbush came from one of Buffalo's original African-American families and appeared to be comfortable living in several different sections of the city during her lifetime. She never lived in the neighborhood in which she taught nor in what was considered an African-American neighborhood. But she spoke affectionately of her students and worked hard as a teacher. She was concerned about her race and made an effort to change things. Serving as the only African-American teacher in the Buffalo school system during that period took courage. She taught the recently-arrived Americans, who had come in hopes of a new and prosperous life, while raising funds to support an anti-lynching law for her people. She never taught African-American children, but her work with Mrs. Talbert to raise money for the Federick Douglass Homestead helped to preserve a part of African-American history.

Ida Fairbush was in a highly visible position, but almost ignored by the school system. More than any African-American instructor who preceded or succeeded her, Miss Ida Fairbush was significant. She opened the door for African-American teachers in twentieth-century Buffalo. She was the 'only one' until the early years of this century. However, although White principals held her up as a role model to African-American teachers who came into the system during her tenure, the school system never acknowledged her forty-one years of service. Others, White teachers from the same school, were honored for what might be considered lesser contributions.

Ida Dora Fairbush remained a private person. She devoted a good part of her life to her crippled sister. All of her family predeceased her. In her final days, she seemed quite alone. The final memory of Miss Fairbush was that of a strong faced, stooped, elderly woman with shuffling steps. Miss Fairbush left no written words other than her will; she left all of her worldly possessions to her White physician and friend, Dr. Jennie Klein (Fairbush, 1939). Yet Ida Fairbush, a pioneer, made it possible for others to follow. The change was inevitable, but it would not have happened that early in Buffalo, nor would it have happened as gracefully if it had not been for her.

Few are aware that African-American teachers have taught for 150 years in the Buffalo schools. In spite of this, they are generally looked upon as newcomers, too impatient to await their turn to assimilate into the system. Since no written history of Buffalo Black teachers exists, it is important to begin with the urban pioneers of the nineteenth century. In this way, we are given an opportunity to begin to create an understanding of the African-American instructor from an informed perspective. African-American teachers in the urban North have always found themselves in unique positions, more obvious in the nineteenth century than in the twentieth century. An African-American instructor, teaching in the same city, in the same period

Figure 5

of time, and even in the same schoolhouse with a White teacher, viewed the situation from a much different perspective. To document these experiences and thoughts adds to our knowledge of African-American educators in Buffalo and to our general knowledge of the past; this can serve as a basis for a better understanding of the present and future (Button, 1979, pp. 3–9).

Note

1 I interviewed the following people to gather information about Ida Fairbush: Claude Clapp, October 1989, attended School No. 6; Ora Curry, September 1988, visited Miss Fairbush; Genevieve Harris, May 1988, attended a class; Mrs. Mack Lewis, October 1990, knew Miss Fairbush; Alice McAdin, October 1990, taught during the early 1900s; Russell Monteleone, March 1986, his father had Miss Fairbush as a teacher; Jessie Nash, October 1990, Miss Fairbush boarded in his home; Elma Plummer, September 1985, Miss Fairbush served as her role model; Mozella Richardson, December 1987, had heard of an 'excellent' African-American teacher; Lanora Robinson, May 1985, knew Miss Fairbush.

Chapter 6

Female Schoolteachers as Community Builders

Margaret K. Nelson

> Teachers were a thing apart ...
>
> Vermont Schoolteacher

Women who taught in the first half of the twentieth century in rural Vermont's one- and two-room schools gave frequent and rich descriptions of the central role they played in creating and recreating the communities in which they served.[1] Paradoxically, these same women often spoke about being forced into the position of peripheral or marginal community members, excluded from participation in the on-going life of the community. In this chapter, I analyze this contradictory finding. After a discussion of schooling and community in Vermont, I describe each of the components of the teacher's relation to the community in which she worked, that is, her central role as community builder and her more peripheral role as community servant. Finally, I offer complementary explanations about these two stances and I discuss the relationship between them.

Schooling and Community in Vermont

As in most states, public schooling in Vermont was initially organized locally: in the mid-nineteenth century, between two and three thousand locally controlled districts existed in the state, with an average enrollment of less than thirty students per school (Rosenfeld, 1977). Starting with a legislative option of creating a town system in 1870, the state initiated numerous efforts designed to eliminate the rural schools by combining them into larger units. Nevertheless, consolidation occurred only grudgingly.[2] In 1910, 2,249 schools served a student population of 18,331, but as late as 1933, 1391 schools remained, of which 82 per cent were one- or two-room buildings (Vermont State Board of Education, 1910; Rosenfeld, 1977, p. 46). The Proctor Report, the product of a Special Commission to study Vermont's system of education in 1934, gave enthusiastic support for the rural school system:

Most activities of life undergo more or less continual evolution. Some day we may awake to find the rural school has met a similar fate and outgrown its usefulness. But, we believe that such a day has not yet arrived. The direct and personal contact of the district school has perhaps greater possibilities for individual uplift and for fortifying our youth for the years ahead than any other form of educational preparation. The rural elements still constitute the heart of our renowned Commonwealth. . . . Who knows but what the great evolution we are now experiencing in industry, in government, and in other ways of life, may give new life in some form or other to our little hamlets and farms tucked away in these hills. They possess a charm and peace far too beautiful to ever lose. But they will pass with the passing of the district school. Until time shall have definitely indicated their fate may we cherish them as we would the life blood of this Commonwealth. (Proctor, 1934, pp. 23–4)

By 1950 Vermont had moved toward the 'passing of the district school', but the process appeared to be far from complete. There remained 486 one-room schools, and only 30 per cent of all towns operated a single elementary school (Vermont State Board of Education, 1950).

The school district referred to so elegantly in the Proctor Report represented a geographic area defined by distance from a central point and designed to insure that the children within a single neighborhood could walk to school. The district had no independent existence as an entity, that is, it had no political, religious, mercantile, or social meaning. (For these purposes, the relevant unit was the town — a combination of as many as ten separate districts — or, occasionally, the county).

These communities therefore maintained no cohesiveness; little if anything held the population together, or gave the inhabitants a common interest except the presence of a school. And the school which served a district stood in an uneasy relationship to the surrounding environment: the presence of a school building defined an area as a potential 'community', but without the unified action of the district residents, there would have been no school or, at best, there would have been only a poor one.

The standardization program, inaugurated in 1921 as part of a state-wide effort to improve the quality of Vermont's rural education, codified this circular relationship between community and school. Under this program, school conditions were rated on nine factors divided into two groups:

The first grouping [had] to do with the teacher, utilizing six measures: (1) training, (2) experience, (3) efficiency, (4) professional spirit, (5) results, (6) relation to the community. The second grouping [measured] the attitude of the community toward the school as shown by the character of the school building, adequacy of supplies and salary paid the teacher. Three measures [were] used: (1) building and grounds, (2) equipment and supplies, (3) community activities. (Proctor, 1934, p. 100)

Two ratings existed: standard, describing a school with at least 150 credits in the first year (and 160 thereafter), and superior, one with 180 credits out of a possible 200. These ratings assumed some significance for the teacher, because if a school received a 'standard' or 'superior' rating, the state gave a rebate to the town to be used toward the teacher's salary. Therefore, the pay received by a teacher depended on the quality of her school. The school's quality, in turn, depended on the voluntary actions of the district's members. For instance, painting the schoolhouse, planting shrubs around it, or purchasing a chemical toilet to replace an outhouse all represented actions which would result in an improved state evaluation and a larger state reimbursement for the teacher's salary. The voluntary actions of the district population depended on the presence of an enthusiastic teacher who could rouse her community. Moreover, in the absence of more formal system of supervision, the community's assessment of a teacher's enthusiasm became a basis for her evaluation and thus subsequent reappointment:

> With the time of the superintendent divided among numerous schools scattered over five or six towns frequent visits are impossible and a large measure of responsibility rests upon the teacher. Her importance to the community in rural districts can hardly be exaggerated. Upon her depends largely the attitude of the community to the school. She must create among parents an active interest in school affairs which will bring hearty co-operation and financial support. A comment upon a local teacher often heard in a rural neighborhood is, 'Oh yes, she is a good enough teacher, but she has no interest in community affairs.' There is probably no other field in the teaching profession which offers so wide an opportunity for social service as is found in the rural community. A well-equipped school, well-cared for grounds and an interested co-operative group of parents bespeaks a teacher who recognizes this larger ideal for the rural work. (Proctor, 1934, p. 99)

Center

As the evidence suggests, both Vermont's official rating system and the unofficial supervisory mechanism forced the teacher into playing a complex role in the community. The teacher, hired by a superintendent with the approval of a school district board, appeared to be a dependent actor. Yet she had the responsibility for developing among community members an 'active interest in school affairs'. In doing so, she brought into existence her own supervisory body: a more active community would be more aware of the teacher's effectiveness in the school. She could not do otherwise; her working conditions, her salary, and indeed the very existence of her position, demanded no less of her.

Mrs. O'Hara, born in 1903, graduated from a one-year teaching training program in 1922. She described the self interest as well as the broader concerns that motivated her to participate in this system in her first teaching job:[3]

> And I went around on snowshoes to some of the houses about this time of year. And I'm interested in them because there was a great drive on in the state to make our schoolhouses come up to standard.... The teacher received more pay and that wasn't only it, we really looked better from the state and the amount of money that the state gave to each school was more. So it was something to the parents, and people of the district, to have the school in better shape. Many times we raised money by various ways, having dances and having dinners and so on and then many times the fathers and interested people in the community would come on and do the carpenter work. So that, between the two helps, we really had some good standard schools and it was in that school that I started P.T.A. and that's how we standardized that school while I was there.

Other teachers spoke, as well, of this obligation to build the sense of community. One activity, to which the teachers referred most frequently as a regular feature of their job, was the provision of entertainments for the community on significant holidays. Through these entertainments, the teacher created an opportunity for the people in the district to assemble and to celebrate, at one and the same time, a specific calendar event, education and the school, and the community itself. Mrs. Foote described these festivities — and the very real sense of obligation surrounding them — as part of her reminiscences about the pros and cons of her twenty-five years of teaching following her graduation from a two-year teacher's training course in 1923:

> Every holiday — that is, Christmas, Thanksgiving and Memorial Day — we always had programs at the school and all the people of the district came. It was kind of an entertainment. Every teacher was expected to [participate] by the district people.... If you didn't do those thing you weren't a very good teacher — and it was really quite a problem that these teachers nowadays don't have at all.... I would never have tried getting out of it. If I had they wouldn't have thought I was a good teacher, I guess.

Another early twentieth-century schoolteacher, when asked whether she too became involved in such endeavors, responded with incredulity: 'Are you kidding? I was a teacher, wasn't I?' This obligation was so widespread that Vermont teachers were not even informed of it when hired: during a panel discussion of former one-room schoolteachers, held at a local historical society, a woman from Massachusetts described her first year in a Vermont school and explained that she had no idea that she was supposed to hold a Christmas program; she was about to leave to catch a train to visit her family when all of the parents showed up at the schoolhouse. The next year, she assured the audience, she started her preparations for the Christmas program in early October.[4] Another woman on the same panel received a hearty laugh from her co-panelists by mentioning that for two years in a row she went in as a substitute teacher right before Christmas. Clearly, they all knew that assuming a job at that time of year left her responsible, on very short notice, for one of the most significant teaching events.

Holiday entertainments constituted one set of community responsibilities; like Mrs. O'Hara, teachers mentioned many other responsibilities, including chaperoning dances, organizing spelling bees, and holding box socials to raise money for the hot lunch program, new seats for the school, or even a new school itself. Miss Waite described her role in a district where she taught for two years in the early 1940s: 'Cornwall was a very good community and I used to have a lot of entertainments at the school and I raised money for new seats ... and, well, we started just doing it, you know, for the community to get together. Card parties we had, and I always had entertainments at Halloween and Christmas.' Similarly, Mrs. Cady not only noted that she provided these entertainments in the community where she worked in the late 1930s, but fifty years later, she expressed considerable pride in how well she had done with them: 'We put on plays. You can't believe in these one-room schools the plays we put on ... and we had card parties all the time. That was the center of the whole community. There was nothing else. We had a supper one night ... it was in the fall ... and we put on the most fabulous supper you ever saw. Every person in that district came, every single person came.'

Thus, the pressure to engage in community-building activities within the school came as part of the 'normal' definition of the teacher's job. This obligation could extend beyond the school. Mrs. Manning remembered the demands placed on teachers during the late 1920s; she also remembered how she felt about these demands:

> A great deal was expected of you community-wise. They had a very beautiful library for a small town, and the librarian decided that the library should be a community center which was very commendable, but in making it a community center the teachers were expected, two times a month, perhaps, to go there and participate in games with children. Big deal. We hadn't seen enough of them for five days. And I don't think I was a gaming person. It was torture.

Others, in less exasperated tones, also noted that they had assumed responsibility for this kind of community-wide activity which expanded to suit particular needs at particular times. During the Second World War, for instance, schoolteachers assumed responsibility for distributing gas ration coupons. Miss Paul, who devoted her life to teaching and spent thirty-one years in the same classroom, perhaps summed up this set of expectations when she said, 'Teachers are always encouraged to be civic-minded.'

Periphery

While the teacher stood at the center of the community in both a literal sense — the school maintained a central location — and in a figurative sense — through her efforts the district's residents functioned as a community — she also stood at the periphery of the community, excluded from full participation in its significant events. As has been noted frequently in studies of schoolteachers in rural areas from the nineteenth century on, the community could restrain, limit, and control the behavior of its creator (Tyack and Hansot, 1982; Tyack and Strober, 1981; Waller, 1932). Not only did a different set of expectations apply to a teacher's behavior, but she also found herself excluded from certain activities. She was, in some essential sense, defined as 'other'. In reference to this unique set of expectations, Quantz (1983) has called teachers 'secular nuns'. The analogy is not entirely apt, if nuns are thought of as living a life separate from the world. Schoolteachers had behavioral prohibitions similar to those of nuns, but they were not encouraged or allowed to live a cloistered life. In fact, they had to assume an active role in the community. Like a minister or priest, they stood at the center of a 'parish' and created unique opportunities through which a 'flock' could come together as one.

All teachers had to conform to a unique standard of behavior. Mrs. Manning, when asked wether she had still other responsibilities toward the community beyond those of the holiday entertainments and the work in the local library, linked community building activities with behavioral restraints: 'I wasn't aware that I had any [other responsibilities] except that I walked a straight and narrow path character wise.... You just knew that that was expected of you.' When asked what it meant to 'walk a straight and narrow path', she responded that it meant 'to be a lady'. She then added with her usual touch of ironic honesty, 'I'm sure outwardly I was one; inwardly I rebelled.'[5]

Although they might have had different names for it, other teachers as well referred to something resembling a 'straight and narrow path'. One woman remembered that schoolteachers had to be 'up and becoming'; Miss Paul recalled that, in addition to being 'civic-minded', 'teachers were expected to set an example.... Questionable conduct would have been condemned.' Another lifelong teacher added:

> There were a lot of criticisms of teachers in your own private life. You had to be careful of the people you associated with. I think that was one of the things, just pick the people who had good reputations. You didn't want to be seen out with a group of people who weren't well thought of in the community. Especially the girls. You didn't want to be seen with boys that didn't have good reputations.

Some teachers mentioned specific precepts that fell within these broad definitions of propriety. One teacher recalled that she was asked about her views of drinking and smoking during a 1938 job interview, and was refused that position, because she admitted that she liked a cigarette every now and then. Another teacher told about receiving criticisms for square dancing with the children: *that* behavior was not sufficiently ladylike for community norms in the mid-1920s.

More important than these prescriptive innuendoes, however, were the ways in which the broad shape of a teacher's life could be controlled by the local community in which she worked. First, the school board could, and frequently did, build into contracts the clause, 'This contract shall terminate upon marriage.' Teachers hired on such a contract clearly had a major feature of their lives controlled by the community. By not being allowed to marry, or, thereafter, to give birth, the teacher was excluded from being a central actor in some of the community's most significant rituals. Although in chapter 3, I argue that in Vermont some of these restraints were more honored in the breach, their 'official' existence was significant. Whether or not a school board actually relieved a teacher of her responsibilities upon marriage or pregnancy, the fact that they could do so (and could even build that presumption into contracts) suggests a high degree of *potential* control.

Second, some communities imposed the requirement that the teacher actually live within the perimeter of the district in which she was teaching. Miss Paul noted that 'every teacher had to live in the district where she taught even though her own family might be within easy commuting distance.' This proviso ensured that the teacher's behavior could always be observed (during her work *and* her leisure time) and, perhaps, underlined her position as the servant of the community. She could not make her own home in the community: if she boarded with a family, she was always a 'guest'; even if she lived on her own or shared an apartment with other teachers, she remained cut off from her own roots.

Third, although the teachers acknowledged that they received community respect, to be discussed below, they also spoke of ways in which they were kept at a distance. Mrs. Cady thought the 'chilliness' she experienced stemmed from her being an outsider to Vermont. But Mrs. Manning, a lifelong resident of a neighboring community to Shoreham, where she began her teaching career, said she also seemed to be kept at arm's length: 'It was a cold community.... The parents were nice but they never became friends.'

In short, although the teacher created the rural community through her actions in and around the school, as a single woman the ongoing rituals of everyday life seemed to be denied her. Tyack and Hansot (1982, p. 174) describe such policies as having a bitter twist: 'The educator in a small community was expected to *conform* to the proper morals and mores of the town, but was often regarded as something of an *outsider*, not quite integrated into the social life of the community.' (emphasis added) Mrs. Boardman described the effects of these policies in a more personal, and particularly poignant, way: 'Teachers were a thing apart', she sighed, 'you couldn't do anything that other people did.'

Analysis

What is the link between two aspects of the teacher's relationship to the community in which she served — teacher at the center and teacher on the periphery? When she was 'required' to be a central actor in the district, why was she also forced to be a marginal member of that community? Some historians have suggested that the prescriptive control of a teacher's life represented a necessary component of the moral mission of the school. As Tyack and Hansot (1982, p. 175), argue, drawing extensively on Willard Waller (1932), the paradox of required conformity and maintenance of an outsider status,

> begins to dissolve when one realizes that often the public school served as a place where children learned that honesty is always the best policy, that the United States had statesmen of stainless steel, that proper diction and upright character go hand-in-hand. 'Among these ideals are those moral principles which the majority of adults more or less frankly disavow for themselves but want others to practice', wrote Waller; 'They are ideals for the helpless, ideals for the children, and for teachers.' As 'a paid agent of cultural diffusion' of these ideals the teacher must be shielded from the untoward realities of saloons and sigars, seduction and salacious talk. 'It is part of the American credo that school teachers reproduce by budding.'

This interpretation, while persuasive, cannot adequately explain why, when we still demand that our schools teach ideal rather than typical behavior, 'restrictive supervision' declined with the passing of the rural school (Tyack and Strober, 1982, p. 145). As complements, I suggest two interconnected interpretations. The first I call the 'literary' interpretation because it rests on notions about 'symbols' of authority; the other I call the 'socio-political' interpretation because it rests on notions about power.

According to the 'literary' interpretation, the effectiveness of school-teachers as community builders relied on their being the 'pure' embodiment of education in the community in which they lived. Nobody else so clearly stood for the ideals promulgated by the school. These ideals represented not only those signified by Waller's description of schools as 'museums of virtue', but also those of learning *per se*. As the pure symbol of education, teachers could build community around the school. But — and this is the catch — they had to remain 'pure'. Again, the analogy to a priest might help clarify the issue. The priest serves as the symbol of life of the spirit, the model of an ideal unattainable by most, but valued by all. As the symbolic representative of a specific standard, he can only build up the parish or church if he remains pure: no worldly allegiances or human ties are allowed. Similarly, then, the teacher served most effectively as the community educator or educational community builder if she was perceived as being attached only to the school.

This mantle of 'purity', or separateness, had particular significance when the teacher had few other resources to grant her authority.[6] As a young single woman she would have been a low-status member of any community; if she grew up in the same town, or a neighboring one, she could easily be subsumed by or incorporated into her familial role. And, in fact, the schoolteachers under investigation had few resources with which to combat either denigration or incorporation. Most of them were young: in 1924–1925 the median age for rural schoolteachers was 23.2 years (Steele, 1926, p. 18); in 1937–1938 the median age had risen only to 28.3 years (Bailey, 1939, p. 12). Many teachers claimed little education: in 1924–1925 the average rural teacher had only five years of schooling above the eighth grade (Steele, 1926, p. 21); in 1937–1938 a year or two of training beyond high school remained the norm (Bailey, 1939, p. 17); and in 1950 three-quarters of all Vermont teachers were still without college degrees (Vermont State Board of Education, 1950). Few of the teachers appeared to be highly experienced: in 1924–1925 the median length of experience among rural school teachers was approximately one year (Steele, 1926, p. 25); by 1937–1938 it had increased to only 6.14 years (Bailey, 1939, p. 14). The Proctor Report notwithstanding, the broader educational community frequently lambasted rural schoolteachers for their lack of expertise:[7]

> Only those conversant with the conditions know the worthless work performed in some rural schools under the guise of teaching, and were the patrons of such schools cognizant of the flagrant injustice committed against the children by the employment of young and untrained novices, they would vigorously demand a higher quality of instruction or the transportation of their children to better schools. (Vermont State Board of Education, 1938, pp. 7–8)

In such a context, a woman teacher would have found it difficult to assert her authority, and particularly the authority to command men (in the tasks surrounding school improvement), as well as older women and children, if she had not been accorded a special status that marked her off from the rest of the community. This status, in turn, served both to create and enhance her authority. And teachers remembered that they did receive the necessary respect: 'The teacher was quite somebody ... [she had] a great deal of respect ... I was always invited to everyone's house for a meal or a party.' Even Mrs. Cady, an 'outsider', remembered, 'You were God in your little community.'

The 'socio-political' interpretation of the center/periphery split in the teacher's relationship with her community has to do with restraints to her power, rather than the elaboration of her authority. The teacher represented a potentially powerful person within the community, with power derived from two sources. First, as the person with more knowledge than most others in the community (derived from her greater education), she had power of the sort that is meant when we say that 'knowledge is power', that is, she had been initiated into mysteries of the world unknown or unavailable to the mass of residents. The fact that the teacher did not have much education, judged by a wider standard, and that she needed enhancements to her authority does not undercut this assertion; rather, it demonstrates that those enhancements appeared effective. She often actually did have, and was perceived by the community members as having, knowledge that others did not share. Many teachers said with pride that they were the ones responsible for introducing children to such esoteric items as mirrors, toothbrushes, and pencil sharpeners. Teachers also recalled being enlisted by members of the community to help with a wide variety of problems: Mrs. O'Hara, for example, remembered being asked by a farmer to help him figure out the volume of a silo.

But the teacher possessed another kind of knowledge power as well: the knowledge of the intimate secrets gained through her close daily contact with the children and through living in and playing a central role in the community. One teacher said that she always got to school early, 'to make better contact with the children, and to hear the daily gossip'. Through such 'gossip', the teacher knew such details as whose father came home drunk last night, who did not have enough to eat, whose mother could not be bothered to sew a button back on. Another teacher remembered that when she did the 1960 Census in her community, 'she knew every single family'. Such knowledge made the teacher a potential threat, in a 'blackmail' sense. The means by which the community then chose to keep the teacher at the periphery — the behavioral restraints described above — can, in a way, be viewed as a form of containment. The teacher's power seemed curtailed because she was not 'real' and had no 'real' contacts.

Finally, I might add, the restraints might have made more acceptable the anomalous situation of men following the lead of women. The teacher needed enhancement of her authority in order to command men; but the community needed to restrain her as well, so that her leadership could not become a model to which other women in the community could aspire.

This theoretical apparatus makes an atypical assertion about rural schoolteachers — that they were potentially powerful. Many historical interpretations of women's lives stress their powerlessness, relative to men, women's status as victims (Cott, 1977, p. 197); this point of view has been applied to interpretations of the role of schoolteachers as well. Tyack and Strober's (1981, p. 145) argument that restrictive supervision rested on the helplessness of women is a case in point: 'Had mature men constituted a majority of the teaching profession, it is hard to imagine that school patrons would have insisted on such tight supervision of the morals and mores of teachers as they did in the case of young women. . . . It was the unmarried woman teacher, caught in a web of restrictive cultural expectations, who was most helpless to resist.' If schoolteachers seemed like 'victims', and in a sense I think they were, it was also true that they became so in part *because* people were afraid of them, because they had a power that had to be contained both in and of itself, and equally significantly, in order to prevent its becoming a model for other women to emulate. Women were kept in their place, not simply because it was easy to do so, but because they posed a threat to the social order.

Summary and Conclusion

I have argued that the rural area in which the school was located did not represent a community in a meaningful sense unless the teacher created it as such. Moreover, although the teacher created — indeed was required to create — community, she was also controlled and circumscribed by this same community.

In short, a set of contradictory demands were placed upon Vermont's rural schoolteachers. They were, at one and the same time, required to act as independent assertive community leaders and as dependent, self-effacing community servants. Effective enactment of the former role rested on an elaboration of the teacher's authority; this elaboration was necessary at a time when schoolteachers — because they were young, inexperienced, poorly trained, and female — had few genuine professional resources to call upon. The particular form of this elaboration, however, served also to contain the power that a schoolteacher acquired through her (albeit limited) training and through her community service. If she had a general knowledge that the community regarded with awe, she also had specific knowledge the community regarded with fear. A schoolteacher would be invited to a home as part of the respect due to her; she would rarely be made a friend. As a guest in the community she could rouse community spirits; as a single woman, she could not participate fully in community rituals. She might demonstrate female authority; the costs of doing so were high enough that she could not serve as a generalized model as such.

If the paradoxical situation of the early twentieth-century Vermont schoolteacher demanded 'restrictive supervision', exceptions to it are easily explained. As I have suggested in chapter 3, the exigencies of the period between 1910 and 1950 — both historical events and the shortage of teachers — were such as to call for extraordinary behavior on the part of men and women alike: the situation demanded a flexible response by some communities to individual deviations from the prescriptions. Not surprisingly, cultural norms were modified in the face of material constraints. The ultimate disappearance of restrictive supervision can also be accounted for. As the rural school gave way to the town school built (both literally and symbolically) on a stronger foundation, the teacher herself ceased to be responsible for maintaining the community. As a young, inexperienced teacher made room for her more professional peers, a teacher no longer had to rely on a 'mantle' of difference to mark her off from other community members. And finally, when she no longer played a central role in a small, ingrown community, the teacher no longer had to be contained. If the teacher lost a certain kind of 'respect' in the process, she also gained the freedom to be a normal member of the community and to lead a normal life — even as a single woman.

Notes

1 See chapter 3 for a complete description of the methodology on which this study is based.

2 For an analysis of the reasons for the slow pace of consolidation in Vermont, see Rosenfeld, 1977. Included among the reasons was the difficulty of transportation in Vermont's long winters and muddy summers, the slow population growth in Vermont, financial difficulties, and a fierce tradition of local control.

3 All names used are pseudonyms.

4 Although the teacher from Massachusetts represents an 'outsider's' perspective, the kinds of entertainments described are not unique to Vermont. In *America's Country Schools*, Andrew Guilliford (1984) describes similar ways in which rural schools throughout the country were used as community centers. The Massachusetts teacher had not had such an experience because she came from a more urban area, not because she came from outside Vermont.

5 For other evidence of this the teacher's 'dual self', see Quantz, chapter 12.

6 I have elsewhere argued at the 'restrictive supervision' served also to 'protect' the teacher against the threat of sexual harassment (Nelson, 1988). These two interpretations are complementary rather than mutually exclusive.

7 Interestingly, similar comments were made by superintendents about rural schoolteachers in Canada (Wilson and Stortz, 1988).

Chapter 7

Religious Discrimination, Political Revenge, and Teacher Tenure

Joseph W. Newman

> When one is discussing lack of freedom for teachers, [one] must remember that the majority of teachers do not need freedom, because they share the views of the community from which they sprang and in which they live.
>
> Howard K. Beale (1936, p. 636)

This chapter tells the story of a public school teacher/principal who stood out in her community because she was different. In an overwhelmingly Protestant city, she practiced Roman Catholicism. In an era when teachers were supposed to behave like grateful employees, she organized a teachers' union and publicized its fight for better salaries and working conditions. At a time when most women knew their place, she was assertive and, as she put it, unwilling to 'play safe'. After she worked for thirty years as a teacher and administrator, the School Board fired her.

What happened to Miss Julia T. Riordan in Atlanta in 1921 was dramatic, to be sure, but hardly exceptional. Across the nation, teachers who were at variance with the community risked losing their jobs, for teachers in most school systems did not have the protection of tenure. When the Atlanta Board of Education fired Julia Riordan, she received neither a statement of charges nor the opportunity to defend herself at a hearing. Throughout the United States, teachers who stood out as different often found themselves in the same position — out of work and out of luck. The rehearsal and restaging of this drama in one community after another led teacher organizations to press for tenure laws.

Julia Riordan's story, however, is much more than a study of how the teachers in one city won tenure. It is a study of the tension between an individual's desire for vindication and her community's reluctance to confront social and political controversy. Although the Atlanta teachers' union and the City Labor Council came to Riordan's defense, she was 'astounded' that their arguments rested entirely on due process and job security. What about religious discrimination? What about political revenge? Why did her colleagues refuse to tackle these issues, Riordan wanted to know. After all, two members of the Atlanta Board of Education had ties to the KKK, and two other Board members resented her political activities for the teachers' union. Why did no one but Riordan seem to be interested in telling the public why she had been fired?

Riordan discovered, much to her disappointment, what Howard K. Beale (1936) later confirmed: most teachers, like other workers, hold the dominant values of the community. Because most teachers find it hard to imagine having to defend their views or actions to the community, they will not stick their necks out to defend co-workers who come under attack because they are different.

Riordan's Early Career

Julia Riordan was the daughter of a rising middle-class family in post-Civil War Atlanta. Her Irish Catholic father, John W. Riordan, came to Atlanta in the early 1870s as a laborer but moved quickly up the economic ladder in the emerging capital of the New South. By 1877, Riordan worked as a buyer for a firm of cotton merchants, and by 1889 he had started a business in the cotton trade (*Atlanta City Directories*, 1874, 1877, 1889). Julia, his Atlanta-born daughter, graduated from Girls' High School, and like many women who continued their education through the secondary level, went to work as a grammar school teacher. Julia began her career in 1891 as a fourth grade teacher at Crew Street School, where she taught for eight years (Atlanta Public Schools, 1891, 1899). A photograph taken in 1895 shows Riordan as a tall, serious, attractive woman outfitted in proper attire for a weekend jaunt on a bicycle (Garrett, 1954, p. 331).

The career path for grammar school teachers in Atlanta, as in many other city systems, involved 'promotions' to higher grades every few years, sometimes accompanied by transfers from school to school. In Atlanta's completely feminized grammar school teaching force, experienced teachers who showed what superintendents called 'executive ability' could set their sights on administrative positions, for most grammar school administrators were also women. Julia Riordan's career followed just such a path. After sixteen years of classroom teaching, she became assistant principal of Fair Street School in 1907, moving two years later to the principalship of Davis Street School (Atlanta Public Schools, 1907, 1909). This Roman Catholic principal became a well-known figure in the Davis Street neighborhood, which was solidly working-class and Protestant.

As a charter member of the Atlanta Public School Teachers' Association (APSTA), Riordan helped steer the group through fourteen difficult years (1905–1919) as an independent organization. She served as APSTA director (representative to the policy-making council) from Boulevard School in 1906 and 1907, and the teachers at Fair Street elected their new assistant principal as director in 1908. After becoming principal of Davis Street School, Riordan served on APSTA's publicity committee from 1910 to 1912, with one year in the important post of publicity chair (APSTA, 1906; 1907; 7 November 1908; 1909; 5 November 1910; 2 December 1911).

Riordan's involvement in APSTA reflected the turbulence of that association's early years, when internal quarrels and external hostility from the School Board and the City Council made its very existence precarious. From 1914 to 1917, when authoritarian Board president 'Major' Robert J. Guinn had the teaching force so intimidated, many teachers were afraid to join APSTA; Riordan's Davis Street School was one of several schools unable to field a director (APSTA, 6 December 1913; 7 October 1916). During the 1917–1918 school year, however, teachers closed ranks against Major Guinn. Riordan returned to the Board of Directors and resumed her work as publicity chair (APSTA, 6 October 1917; 6 October 1918). A turning point for Atlanta's teachers came in June 1918 with a sensational City Council investigation of the school system. Riordan and other leaders of the teachers' association delivered damning testimony against Guinn's 'autocratic methods' and 'Prussianized administration' (Atlanta City Council, 1918). The Board president soon resigned in disgrace, APSTA's membership soared, and Atlanta's teachers faced the future with new confidence (Urban, 1977; Urban, 1982, ch. 2).

Regarded by her colleagues as courageous, outspoken, even verbally aggressive, Julia Riordan seemed the perfect choice to direct the Association's publicity campaign. Her forceful personality won her the respect of virtually all teachers, even if she was a close friend of very few (Barker, 1921a). As World War I and its aftermath filled the pages of the *Atlanta Constitution* and *Atlanta Journal* with military and diplomatic news, Riordan called the city's attention to the teachers' local battle for higher salaries. Never hesitating to state needs in terms of demands, Riordan argued in news columns and letters to the editor that, by local, regional, and national standards, Atlanta's teachers were grossly underpaid. Atlanta paid its teachers less than its firemen, policemen, and even some unskilled laborers, she pointed out, blaming City Council for shortchanging the school system ('Stanley will probe cost of living among teachers', 15 January 1919; 'School teachers issue statement', 16 January 1919). As a result, many teachers left their classrooms for better jobs in business and government. Early in 1919, as runaway inflation pushed teachers to desperation, the *Constitution* played up rumors of a teacher strike — rumors publicity manager Riordan neither confirmed nor denied ('Teachers of city to ask showdown . . .', 23 January 1919; 'Teachers ready to present plan', 25 January 1919). The outspoken Miss Riordan, one of APSTA's most visible leaders, was in the thick of every school controversy, or so it seemed.

As the Association considered affiliating with the American Federation of Teachers (AFT) and the Atlanta Federation of Trades, Riordan proved herself a strong union advocate. Teachers were city workers, the thirty-year veteran reminded her colleagues ('Stanley will probe cost of living. . .', 15 January 1919; 'School teachers issue statement', 16 January 1919). In several pivotal meetings she took the floor to explain the benefits of uniting with other workers (APSTA, February 1919; 14 April 1919). From a total APSTA membership of more than 500, she was one of nine members who signed the 1919 charter of the AFT's new Atlanta local. The following year she became one of the first teachers elected by her peers as a delegate to the Atlanta Federation of Trades (AFT, 1919; APSTA, 4 October 1920). In trying times, Riordan's words and deeds showed her commitment to organized labor. Her dismissal by the School Board soon tested organized labor's commitment to Julia Riordan.

Religious Discrimination

The Atlanta Board of Education struggled with the issue of religion in the schools from the system's inception in 1872. For more than forty years the board followed a policy of moderation, emphasizing its belief in the separation of church and state. Riordan became enmeshed in an earlier controversy that affirmed the Board's moderate stance. In the fall of 1916, the Davis Street principal asked the Board to investigate complaints that she and one of her teachers were teaching the superiority of the Roman Catholic faith. After concluding the two were innocent, the Board issued the following statement: 'We do not proscribe or discriminate against anyone on account of creed, or religious belief. This rule applies to patrons, teachers, and pupils — Protestant and Catholic, Jew and Gentile alike. On the other hand, questions of creed and particular religious belief have no place in the public schools, and we do not permit these questions to be injected into the schools by parents, teachers, school officials, or anyone else.' (Atlanta Board of Education, 26 October 1916).

Unfortunately the Board's handling of this case bore little resemblance to its actions over the next five years. The controversy at Davis Street School became a harbinger of growing religious intolerance in Atlanta, a city whose population of more than 200,000 was only 5 per cent Jewish and 2 per cent Catholic (Jackson, 1967, pp. 29, 260). From 1916 to 1921, the School Board changed its position on religion several times in response to public pressure and as new members influenced its mood. When representatives of Catholic and Jewish groups appeared at Board meetings to counter mounting demands from Protestants for required Bible reading, heated arguments broke out in the Board's chambers (Racine, 1973, pp. 64–66). Worn down by the protracted agitation, the Board finally submitted the matter to the voters of Atlanta, who in July 1920 endorsed, by a four-to-one margin, 'reading the [Protestant] bible [sic] in the public schools without comment' (Atlanta Board of Education, 9 August 1920). The Atlanta Board joined a national trend when it yielded to popular opinion and required teachers to begin the school day with Bible reading. The Board also accepted the offer of the Junior Order United American Mechanics (JOUAM), an anti-Catholic fraternal organization, to donate Bibles for use in the daily religious exercises (Atlanta Board of Education, 9 August 1920; Ecke, 1972, p. 134). The sole dissenter on the Board protested the policy as 'nothing more than a slap at the Jews and

Catholics of the city' ('10 Minutes will be devoted to daily Bible reading', 10 August 1920).

Agitation over required Bible reading set the stage for overt discrimination against Roman Catholic teachers. The School Board elections held in late 1920 brought a reign of religious intolerance to the Atlanta public schools as a Klansman, attorney Walter A. Sims, and a fellow traveler, attorney Carl F. Hutcheson, associate editor of the *Searchlight*, the newsletter of the JOUAM, took seats on the board (Moseley, 1973, p. 242). JOUAM membership served as 'an excellent recommendation for membership in the Klan', and many Atlantans saw the *Searchlight* as the Invisible Empire's official organ (Jackson, 1967, pp. 232–233, 261). Outspokenly anti-Catholic, Hutcheson never admitted membership in the Klan but supported the organization financially. Sims, who came to the Board as an ex-officio member representing City Council, exuded pride in his Klan knighthood. Continually attacking the Catholic church in School Board and City Council meetings, Sims would be elected Mayor of Atlanta in 1922 (House of Representatives, United States, Committee on Rules, 1921, pp. 11, 107; Moseley, 1973, p. 239).

While Hutcheson and Sims brought invisible government to the Atlanta public schools, the KKK spread its influence throughout the city and state. The modern Klan, reborn in Atlanta in 1915, received a corporate charter in July 1916. Within three months, Bible reading became a controversial issue for the Board of Education, and Julia Riordan ran into trouble at Davis Street School. By 1921, when the Board fired Riordan, the rejuvenated KKK had purchased a university, albeit a financially ailing one. Lanier University, a Baptist-related institution in the prestigious Druid Hills section of Atlanta, had been under Klan influence since its founding four years earlier, and now it promised to lead a collegiate drive for 'One hundred per cent Americanism'. Despite a warm reception from middle- and upper-class Atlantans, Lanier University declared bankruptcy and closed in August 1922 (Jackson, 1967, pp. 29–30; Dyer, 1978).

By then, however, the Klan appeared well entrenched in Georgia politics. In 1922, the year Walter Sims won the mayoral race in Atlanta, the KKK also helped elect Georgia's governor and one of its US senators. The Knights of the Invisible Empire included sheriffs, police chiefs, mayors, city council members, judges, and state legislators (Moseley, 1973, pp. 236–239). Thus the tentacles of the Klan extended throughout Georgia in the early 1920s. As Kenneth Jackson (1967) points out, the empire encompassed the South and much of the nation as well.

This was the context in which Hutcheson and Sims launched their anti-Catholic crusade on the Atlanta Board of Education. At their very first meeting, these two men engineered the election of another new member, the more moderate William W. Gaines, as president. Gaines, also an attorney but no Klansman, repaid the favor by appointing Hutcheson as chair and Sims as a member of the powerful Schools and Teachers Committee. These positions enabled Hutcheson and Sims to wield power over textbooks, curricula, and personnel. Hutcheson, Sims, Gaines, and ex-officio member James L. Key, Mayor of Atlanta, voted as a bloc on several critical issues that came before the Board in 1921 (Atlanta Board of Education, 10 and 12 January 1921). This majority of four stood against three members with prior service on the Board: Paul L. Fleming, a wholesale druggist; W.H. Terrell, a lawyer who led the fight for Bible reading in the schools; and William L. McCalley, an insurance agent (*Atlanta City Directory*, 1921).

The bloc of new and ex-officio members first flexed its muscle in May 1921 by ousting Superintendent W.F. Dykes, an up-from-the-ranks teacher and administrator who incurred Mayor Key's wrath during the 1918 school investigation (Urban, 1977, pp. 136–137). Key persuaded the new Board members that the system needed fresh leadership, and with no prior warning the majority bloc declined to re-elect Dykes, a twenty-seven-year veteran of the system who survived for only two years as Superintendent (Atlanta Board of Education, 9 and 14 May 1921).

Teachers felt vulnerable; they knew they could lose their jobs as easily as Dykes lost his, for the Board employed everyone on a yearly basis with no guarantee of re-election. APSTA responded quickly, passing a resolution that condemned Dykes' firing as an overtly political move. Upset over rumors that the Board planned to cut teachers' salaries to reduce debt, the association resolved to meet any such attempt with individual and collective resistance. It fell to the publicity chair, Julia Riordan, to forward both resolutions — worded strongly if cordially — to the School Board, City Council, and local press (APSTA, 16 May 1921; 'Teachers oppose salary reduction', 17 May 1921).

Teachers soon had evidence their fears were legitimate. Steering the Board into executive session at two meetings held in June 1921, Hutcheson tried to block the re-election of four principals and one teacher — all Roman Catholics. His crusade achieved limited success: the Board did not re-elect Julia Riordan. Factions shifted slightly as McCalley joined Hutcheson, Sims, and Mayor Key in voting to fire the principal. President Gaines abstained, leaving only Terrell and Fleming to defend Riordan. The Board voted to re-elect the other Catholics Hutcheson had attacked (Atlanta Board of Education, 8 and 10 June 1921).

Throughout the summer of 1921, the Riordan incident became one of Atlanta's top newspaper controversies — depending on the newspaper. The headlines of the 11 June *Constitution* trumpeted the story: 'Battle Over Teachers Fought Before Board: Miss Riordan Dropped.' The morning *Constitution*, which aligned itself with the 'traditional' wing of the Democratic party that opposed Mayor Key, reported the Board's actions in detail, branding Hutcheson's list of Catholic teachers a 'black list' ('Battle over teachers . . .', 11 June 1921). The afternoon *Journal*, a supporter of Mayor Key and and 'progressive' wing of the Democratic party, gave Atlantans a contrasting report that did not even mention Riordan's name ('Jobs for teachers contingent on tax increase', 11 June 1921). Throughout the summer the *Constitution's* coverage was extensive and highly critical of the Board. The *Journal* seemed almost embarrassed by the drama that unfolded, but even its restrained coverage revealed that feelings about the incident were running high throughout the city.

Defending Riordan

Members of APSTA scrambled to respond to Riordan's dismissal. Although the news broke just as many teachers were leaving the city for the summer, approximately 150 teachers gathered on 17 June for a called meeting. President C.E. Phillips, a Boys' High School teacher, appointed a special committee to investigate the incident. Mary Barker, an elementary teacher with seventeen years of experience in the system, served as the chair of the committee. Barker, APSTA's strongest advocate of religious and racial tolerance, had established herself as the resident liberal in a conservative teacher organization (APSTA, 17 June 1921; Newman, 1981a; Newman, 1983).

The association approved a letter Barker had drafted to send to each School Board member. While APSTA in no way condoned poor teaching, the letter began, a teacher should be dismissed 'only for cause' and only after an opportunity to face her accusers. Barker stressed due process and job security: 'Could we ask for less? ... The State demands a fair trial in the presence of the accused for even the lowest criminal.... We feel an injustice has been done in the schools in that [the Board's] action engenders a feeling of unrest and uncertainty among the teachers that is most detrimental to the morale of the teaching body.' Riordan was entitled to a statement of charges and a hearing, Barker concluded. A separate letter asked Board president William Gaines to schedule another Board meeting at his earliest convenience to consider APSTA's requests (Barker, 1921b; APSTA, 17 June 1921).

After receiving the letters, Gaines called APSTA president Phillips to his office. Anxious to preserve his moderate image and avoid further controversy, Gaines tried to smooth the matter over. The 'very nice and respectful' Gaines 'said so much (and yet so little) that I know not how to report the conversation', Phillips recalled. Choosing his words carefully, Gaines implied the Board *might* give Riordan a statement of charges and a hearing, *if* teachers avoided 'embarrassing' the board. Phillips tried to hold the line, insisting 'emphatically but politely that the only way out [of] the situation was the straight but narrow way'. Gaines replied that although the Board was opposed to calling a special meeting, it would act on APSTA's requests at the next regular meeting on 8 July — two weeks away (Phillips, 1921).

Phillips, Barker, and the special committee decided to 'take the publicity road' by pleading Riordan's case to civic and education groups. The teachers were disappointed at the reception they received. City PTA leaders said they felt 'hopeless' because they had tried — to no avail — to win reinstatement for former Superintendent Dykes after the Board fired him. An official of the Atlanta Woman's Club seemed unwilling to take any initiative. Julia Riordan appeared before the Atlanta League of Women Voters, an organization in which she was active. The League gave her only 'lukewarm support', along with the explanation that it could not allow controversy to taint its campaign to revise the city's charter (Barker, 1921a). Besides charter revision, the League and other citizens' groups had another reason to handle Riordan with care: Atlantans were preparing to vote at the end of August on a long overdue tax increase for the schools. Mayor Key and Board president Gaines had been working closely with civic and education groups to build public support for the taxes. Key and Gaines believed the less they said about the Riordan controversy, the better the odds the taxes would pass (Newman, 1978, pp. 80–82).

Against the prevailing political winds, the League of Women Voters finally agreed to send a representative to the next School Board meeting on Riordan's behalf, as did the Board of Lady Visitors, a group of civic-minded women concerned with the welfare of the public schools. A former president of the Davis Street School PTA circulated a petition in support of Riordan, which about two-thirds of the neighborhood's residents signed ('Education board refuses hearing to teacher', 9 July 1921).

Barker and Phillips asked Riordan to leave her defense in their hands. As Riordan later explained in an open letter to APSTA, 'It was, they assured me, the association's fight and not mine. . . . I obeyed that order implicitly, leaving my interests entirely in the hands of those in whose loyalty I believed as strongly as in my own, and uttering no word in self defense' (Riordan, 1922). Riordan sat on the sidelines, uncharacteristically quiet at her colleagues' request.

Holding her peace must have been difficult, for the School Board meeting of 8 July offered little hope that APSTA's 'publicity road' would lead to a resolution of the controversy. Representatives of APSTA and the other organizations failed to sway the Board. By a vote of four to two (the same sides as before, with Gaines again abstaining), the Board refused to reopen the Riordan case (Atlanta Board of Education, 8 July 1921). Nor were the members who voted against Riordan willing to give specific grounds for her dismissal. Hutcheson resented the very request for an explanation, sniffing 'It would be a pretty come-off if the board should go to the teachers and ask them what we should do.' Curiously, all members agreed that Riordan's firing 'was not based on a question of her character or ability' ('Education Board refuses hearing to teaching', 9 July 1921).

On what rationale had the Board based its action? Terrell, the advocate of Bible-reading who supported Riordan, said he had been asked to vote against her 'solely' because of her faith ('Teacher plans to make demands for affidavits', 10 July 1921). Given the open anti-Catholicism of Hutcheson and Sims, Terrell's admission hardly seemed surprising, but how did it square with the Board's unanimous statement on Riordan's 'character'? Did some members believe a teacher of unquestioned character deserved dismissal simply because she was a Catholic? McCalley raised further questions when he said he based *his* opposition to Riordan on the contents of certain affidavits: 'If those affidavits are true, I cannot vote to give Miss Riordan a hearing. If they are not true, somebody could be prosecuted' ('Education board refuses hearing to teacher', 9 July 1921). The front page of the *Constitution* reported that Riordan would go to court to obtain the mysterious affidavits, but McCalley destroyed them before she could act ('Teacher plans to make demands for affidavits', 10 July 1921; 'Mayor responsible for her discharge, . . .', 12 August 1921).

As Atlantans watched the plot thicken, the woman whose career and reputation were at stake made no public statement in her own defense. To be sure, Riordan apparently did tell the *Constitution's* reporter she might take legal action on the affidavits, but otherwise she maintained official silence — and with great difficulty. As Riordan explained in her open letter to the Association, she was 'astounded' to hear President C. E. Phillips tell the School Board on 8 July that 'we [APSTA] do not say that Miss Riordan is innocent; we do not say that she is guilty; we ask merely that you give her a hearing in order that her guilt or innocence may be proved to our satisfaction.' Riordan reminded teachers that, as Barker's letter had stated, 'the lowest criminal' is considered innocent until proven guilty. 'Surely, the least due me from my fellow members in the teachers' association was a belief in my innocence until the board proved me guilty of some dereliction of duty. Any other attitude on the part of the association would render its protest at my removal ridiculous' (Riordan, 1922).

But Barker and Phillips were convinced 'it would be useless to plead Miss Riordan to that board. We had talked with every member and we knew that the attitude of the majority was such that only an appeal on the merits of abstract justice could have any weight' (Barker, 1921a). Thus APSTA defended Riordan on strictly procedural grounds, while explosive social and personal issues smoldered just beneath the surface.

Labor's Cause?

Casting about for help, Mary Barker and her committee turned next to the Atlanta Federation of Trades. Barker assumed complete charge of Riordan's defense, for C.E. Phillips, battle-weary after three years of service as APSTA president, announced he was moving to North Carolina to take a less stressful job. Although a veteran teacher, Barker regarded herself as a 'novice' in the arena of city politics. The Riordan case, shimmering in the glare of publicity, had become a hot political issue, and Barker turned to a seasoned labor leader, Jerome Jones, the dominant figure on the Atlanta and Georgia labor scene — the 'Samuel Gompers of the South' — for help in handling it (Barker, 1921c).

Jones came to Atlanta in 1898 to edit the weekly *Journal of Labor* at the request of Gompers, American Federation of Labor president ('Jerome Jones', 27 September 1940; Evans, 1929, pp. 259–261). A strong supporter of public education and a longtime defender of Atlanta's teachers, Jones served as labor mentor to the idealistic Barker and a small group of like-minded teachers (Newman, 1978, pp. 99–100). Jones had already expressed qualified support for Riordan in the *Journal of Labor*. Promising to reserve final judgment 'until all the evidence is in', Jones editorialized, 'If the teachers hope to keep their professional standing they should make of this case one of self-interest and protection. The proceeding is out of harmony with trades union ethics' ('Did Miss Riordan get a square deal?', 17 June 1921).

An encouraged Barker sent a memorial to the executive council of the Atlanta Federation of Trades requesting a formal investigation. Barker, who had just been elected reading secretary of the Federation, warned that the rise of 'invisible government' in the school system would lead to 'interminable friction' between teachers and the School Board and 'neutralize largely the values of the schools' (Barker, 1921d). Barker's warning was the most direct public reference to the KKK that any of Riordan's defenders would make during the controversy, and Barker's brief mention of values was one of the few attempts to present the case as anything more than a labor rights dispute.

Jones led a labor delegation to the 8 August meeting of the School Board. Although well known for his religious tolerance, Jones stuck to labor principles before the Board. Like APSTA president Phillips at the July meeting, Jones argued neither innocence nor guilt but due process. The Board set a bad precedent for employees throughout the state, Jones maintained, 'working a hardship on a mass of people to whom, I am sure, you men would not do harm consciously' ('Organized labor sponsors Atlanta woman teacher's case', 12 August 1921). Jones' view of due process was even narrower than APSTA's: a statement of reasons for dismissal would suffice, he said. Gentlemanly and kind — sometimes to a fault — Jones was a highly regarded figure in Atlanta politics. Despite his fine reputation and polite demeanor, however, several Board members appeared rude and inattentive, prompting the labor leader to 'demand a respectful hearing' ('Reasons for discharge of Miss Riordan . . .', 9 August 1921).

Toward the end of the long, tense meeting, Jones pressed Riordan's antagonists hard enough to open a small hole in their wall of silence. Walter Sims quoted a statement from ex-Superintendent W.F. Dykes that 'Riordan gave him more trouble than all the other teachers'. Carl Hutcheson jumped to his feet, exclaiming, 'Since this thing's come out, I'm going to make this statement', only to reconsider when William McCalley, gesturing toward a reporter, cautioned, 'Remember the *Constitution*, remember the *Constitution*.' Sims suggested each member may have had a different motive for voting against Riordan. President Gaines, ever the conciliator, tried to quell the controversy by offering Jones a private explanation of the Board's actions ('Reasons for discharge of Miss Riordan . . .', 9 August 1921). Jones refused, but later asked his labor delegation to delay its report, for a 'reliable source' had told him the Board would soon go public on the case ('Organized labor sponsors Atlanta woman teacher's case', 12 August 1921). Even the *Atlanta Journal*, Mayor Key's ally, opined that Jones' 'fair request' deserved a 'fair response' ('A fair request: Why not a fair response?', 14 August 1921). Atlantans, watching the pages of their newspapers, awaited the promised revelations.

Political Revenge

Jones, trusting his 'reliable source', may have been willing to wait for a public explanation, but not Riordan. Just after the 8 August Board meeting she handed the *Constitution's* reporter a letter in which former Superintendent Dykes stated, 'I have made no charges whatsoever against you. I recommended you for re-election, and I consider that I am in no way to blame for the unfair treatment accorded you.' The *Constitution* ran the letter in its 9 August issue ('No formal trial ever given her ...', 9 August 1921), which also featured a full-page KKK ad. Writing from the Imperial Castle in Atlanta, the Imperial Wizard assured 'all lovers of law and order, peace and justice' that the Klan 'does not encourage or foster lawlessness, racial prejudice or religious intolerance' ('To all lovers of law and order, peace and justice, and to all the people of the United States', 9 August 1921).

On the front page of that same issue, Riordan proceeded to defend herself, explaining that in February 1921 she appeared before Hutcheson and Sims' committee on schools and teachers to respond to complaints about promotion policies at Davis Street School. Subsequently — and over her strongly voiced objections — Superintendent Dykes bowed to a parent's wishes and promoted a student who was 'unruly and deserving of no special privileges'. Hutcheson and Sims obviously ruled her insubordinate, Riordan maintained, yet the two Board members never leveled any such charges against another principal who appeared at the same committee meeting, embroiled in a similar dispute. 'She, however, is not a Catholic', Riordan observed. ('No formal trial ever given her ...', 9 August 1921).

Now the gloves were off. The headlines of the 12 August *Constitution* announced, 'Mayor Responsible For Her Discharge, Miss Riordan Holds'. Drawing on information provided by her two supporters on the Board, Riordan attacked not only Mayor Key but each Board member who had voted to fire her. Key had admitted he opposed her because she was 'trying to unionize the teachers', she said, but that rationale flew in the face of the Mayor's long record of support for organized labor. Indeed, Key won his office with the help of the Federation of Trades, and he wrote a letter specifically endorsing APSTA's affiliation with the AFT and AFL. Riordan stated that in her role as publicity manager of APSTA, 'it has been necessary for me ... to fight out in the open, often in opposition to Mr. Key's wishes.' Serving on the front lines of a running battle with city council had not endeared her to the mayor ('Mayor responsible for her discharge, ...', 12 August 1921).

Moreover, Riordan had tried to block the Mayor's efforts to make a political deal with the city's African Americans. As part of his efforts to win their support for bond issues and tax increases, Key agreed to let the Davis Street neighborhood, located in a racially transitional area, gradually become African American. This strategy ran into opposition from 900 White property owners, all under the capable leadership of principal Julia Riordan ('Mayor responsible for her discharge, ...', 12 August 1921). Riordan also orchestrated APSTA's response when the School Board reduced a pay raise for White teachers in order to supplement the raise for African-American teachers. This move, which infuriated White teachers, represented another part of Key's racial rapprochement plan (Newman, 1981b, pp. 132–135). Riordan concluded the mayor's 'personal grudge' against her for thwarting his 'political ends' accounted for his vote to fire her ('Mayor responsible for her discharge, ...', 12 August 1921).

Riordan then turned to her other opponents on the Board. Sims and

Hutcheson, as virtually everyone knew, opposed her because of her religious beliefs. Hutcheson had accused Riordan of conspiring with other Catholic principals to urge the adoption of *The History of the American People* by Charles Beard and William F. Bagley, a textbook both Hutcheson and Sims considered pro-Catholic. Hutcheson had boasted to a group of teachers from Davis Street School that he expected to see every Catholic in the system fired during his term on the Board. Focusing on McCalley, Riordan charged his opposition stemmed from her 'activities in the teachers association' and her 'political activities', including her work against Mayor Key's plans for the Davis Street neighborhood. Her political activities had included working in McCalley's campaign for the School Board, and now McCalley was showing his gratitude by spreading 'propaganda' based on secret affidavits ('Mayor responsible for her discharge,...', 12 August 1921).

If Riordan intended her no-holds-barred interviews to provoke her opponents into breaking their silence, she was highly successful. The headlines of the 14 August *Constitution* informed Atlantans, 'Contents of McCalley's Affidavits Are Bared: Claimed Teacher Sent Girls Home In Janitor's Care'. The janitor in question was African American. In an era when White newspapers regularly fanned the flames of negrophobia with lurid accounts of African-American violence, these were sensational charges. 'Absolute falsehoods', Riordan retorted, explaining how a White parent in the Davis Street neighborhood had been offered fifty dollars to say the African-American janitor had punished her child. The parent had refused the bribe, said Riordan, but McCalley circulated his propaganda anyway. Confronted with Riordan's explanation, McCalley quickly modified his story, now claiming he barely recalled the affidavits' contents — he had received them *after* he voted against Riordan ('Contents of McCalley's affidavits are bared', 14 August 1921).

Sims lashed out, insisting former Superintendent Dykes had called Riordan 'uncontrollable'. Sims opposed Riordan because of her 'attitude', he claimed, but since *she* had injected religion into the controversy, Sims felt moved to respond in kind ('Contents of McCalley's affidavits are bared', 14 August 1921). 'Watch out Mr. Weak-kneed Non-Catholic', the future Mayor warned. 'The more you investigate the more you will become convinced that the greatest menace to the public school system, not only in Atlanta, but in the United States, is the Roman Catholic Church.' ('Labor will pass today on answer ...', 18 August 1921). Sims wondered whether any teacher loyal to the Catholic church could also be loyal to the public schools. Adding gender insult to religious injury, he demurred, 'I do not wish to get in controversy with a woman.' Sims said he would be pleased, however, to discuss the matter further with the 'Catholic propagandists who are behind Miss Riordan' ('Contents of McCalley's affidavits are bared', 14 August 1921).

Sims' anti-Catholic diatribe, amplified by Hutcheson and other local politicians, grew so loud the Catholic Laymen's Association of Georgia issued a rebuttal to the press. Their statement, however, was a defense of the right to maintain parochial schools rather than a defense of Julia Riordan ('Catholics reply to Sims' charge' and 'Catholics and the public schools', 19 August

1921). Obviously pleased with himself, Sims taunted, 'Catholic propagandists, who are hiding and shielding themselves behind a petticoat, came out and attacked me personally' ('Sims continues Catholic attack', 28 August 1921).

The charges and countercharges continued throughout the month of August as the former principal and her antagonists did battle in the newspapers. Religion, politics, and now race and gender were in the fray. Julia Riordan still had not received an official statement of charges, much less a hearing, but now Atlantans knew why the Board fired her.

Labor Solidarity?

Meanwhile, Jerome Jones and the Atlanta Federation of Trades waited for the official explanation the 'reliable source' had promised. It never came. Instead, Board members sent the Federation a copy of their letter to APSTA. 'No question of her character or ability was involved,' the letter repeated ('Labor is refused reasons of board ...', 16 August 1921). The showdown for organized labor on the Riordan case came at the Federation meeting of 24 August. After Jones presented a mildly worded history of the case, the Labor Council adopted his report without debate and turned to other business. Musician Karl Karston, financial secretary of the Federation and a leader of its 'radical' wing, refused to let the matter rest, offering a resolution censuring the School Board. W.C. Pollard, president of the Electrical Workers' Union, immediately rose to brand Karston's resolution 'too broad'. Attacking the entire Board would put the Federation in a 'ridiculous position', Pollard argued; asking the members who had voted against Riordan for their individual reasons would be more appropriate. Pollard said he could see a difference between the Board's not rehiring Riordan and an employer's firing an employee. When asked whether he would feel the same if an electrical worker were involved, Pollard angrily replied he would ('Plan to condemn education board beaten by labor', 25 August 1921).

Jones took the floor: 'Anybody with intelligence knows that an individual answer is not acceptable.' Pointing to Riordan's long service in the school system, Jones argued, 'It's nearly a test case. If that occurred in one of the shops you know what would happen.' Once again, Jones tried to shift attention away from Riordan and toward labor principles. He reminded the Federation that APSTA — not Riordan — had asked for a labor investigation, 'fearful that some other member might get the same dose.' Karl Karston joined Jones in highlighting labor issues, arguing there was no difference between 'not re-elected' and 'fired'. 'When an old and tried employee is fired without an excuse this is sufficient cause in any organization for a strike', Karston said, but since the AFT prohibited teacher strikes, the Federation of Trades was obligated to help APSTA settle its grievance ('Plan to condemn education board beaten by labor', 25 August 1921).

Louie Marquardt, the Federation's corresponding secretary and a leader of the 'conservative' wing, stood up to observe dryly that Riordan's wounded pride rather than organized labor's principles seemed to be the real issue. 'I believe anybody who knows anything at all knows why she was dropped', Marquardt said ('Plan to condemn education board beaten by labor', 25 August 1921).

Riordan, who attended Federation meetings as APSTA's representative before her dismissal, sat stunned in the audience. The woman who tried to persuade teachers that workers should join hands and help one another was now 'forced, as the member whose rights were in question, to sit in silence and listen to remarks from the secretary which were not only insulting ... but which were utterly without excuse or reason'.

> I saw the spirit of religious intolerance lift its head, and clearly and unmistakably arrogate to itself the right to deny to a Catholic member the privilege which labor is pledged to secure for every toiler, irrespective of race or creed. At the conclusion of Mr. Marquardt's remarks, if there had ever been any doubts as to the reason why the Atlanta Federation of Trades would fail to fulfill its obligation to the teachers' association those doubts were forever removed (Riordan, 1922).

Riordan felt the KKK's power in the Labor Council, the power Marquardt slyly invoked with his 'anybody who knows anything' remark. The social conventions of the day forbade mentioning the Klan by name in public meetings — even known members claimed to 'know nothing' about the secret society — but everyone caught the subtlety of Marquardt's point. The KKK had wrapped its tentacles around the Atlanta Federation of Trades, for several labor leaders 'wished to gain the support of the klansmen for the labor movement'. The Federation opposed a gubernatorial candidate because of his anti-Klan platform, and Walter Sims seemed exceptionally friendly toward the Federation after he became Mayor (Evans, 1929, pp. 215, 289, 292, 295). Barker explained in her committee report on the Riordan incident that 'the sentiment ... in favor of Labor principles was outweighed, it appeared, by the sentiment of religious intolerance and fear of the political power of that intolerance' (Barker, 1921a).

The Atlanta Federation of Trades defeated Karston's resolution to censure the School Board by a vote of twenty-six to nineteen. As labor closed its books on the case, the last organized effort to defend Riordan had failed.

The Plot Untangled

To Julia Riordan, the summer of 1921 must have seemed a southern Gothic nightmare of religious discrimination and political revenge, with racism and sexism adding complexity to an already twisted plot. Riordan had to draw her antagonists out into the open to expose the interwoven strands of the plot — the reasons for her dismissal. Clearly, Carl Hutcheson and Walter Sims opposed Riordan primarily because of her religion. The two Board members launched their anti-Catholic crusade by firing the most visible, controversial, and therefore vulnerable Catholic in the school system. Hutcheson and Sims were also preparing to run for other political offices: Sims for Mayor and Hutcheson for a judgeship (Barker, 1921c; Jackson, 1967, pp. 38–39). Playing into their hands was Mayor James Key, whose motive for voting against Riordan stemmed not from political ambition but from political revenge. Key, not opposed to the teachers' union on principle, was determined to punish the outspoken teacher unionist who had interfered with his political plans. William McCalley's motives are more difficult to analyze. The racist allegations in his secret affidavits made sensational newspaper copy and left an indelible smear, but McCalley was probably being honest when he said he based his opposition to Riordan more on her political activities than on the trumped-up incident with the African-American janitor. William Gaines, the 'moderate' School Board president, stood by and let it all happen, withholding his vote and saying as little as possible. Religion and politics came together in a strange coalition to fire a thirty-year employee of the Atlanta Public Schools.

Key and McCalley broke up the coalition at the next teachers' election in June 1922. This time Klansmen appeared at Board meetings and loudly agitated against Catholic teachers and principals. Key and McCalley felt pressure to continue the purge, but the two stood firm against further dismissals — even after McCalley received a telephoned bomb threat. Mayor Key, never a Klan confrère, developed an anti-Klan reputation by banning masked parades in Atlanta and vetoing Councilman Sims' resolution to condemn the Knights of Columbus. These actions, along with his attempts to accommodate African Americans, hurt Key at the polls. Sims defeated him for Mayor in September 1922. Masked parades returned to the streets of the city (Atlanta Board of Education, 24 May and 7–8 June 1922; Racine, 1973, pp. 69–70; Jackson, 1967, pp. 33, 38). Hutcheson, however, lost his judgeship, blaming his defeat on the 'failure of his fellow board members to go along with him' (Barker, 1921c).

Even in this highly charged atmosphere, Hutcheson and Sims could claim only one victim, a principal who had too many strikes against her. She was a Catholic. She had made political enemies. She had been smeared with racist sensationalism. She was verbally aggressive or, worse, insubordinate. And she was a woman. 'It was never my policy to play safe', Riordan proudly stated, and she certainly held her own against the men who attacked her (Riordan, 1922). Sims' sexist taunts could not intimidate a woman who would not play safe. Matching Sims volley for volley, Riordan commented on his reluctance to debate a woman. Since he had taken a woman's job, told lies about her, and denied her a chance to reply at a hearing, she said, 'it is not surprising that Mr. Sims does not wish to enter into a controversy with that woman' ('Labor will pass today on answer of school board', 18 August 1921).

Riordan never worked again in the Atlanta Public Schools. Growing increasingly bitter toward the Teachers' Association and the Federation of Trades, Riordan cut her ties with her former colleagues. Approaching 50 years of age, Riordan took stock of the 'wreck of [her] professional career' and left Atlanta in 1922 (Riordan, 1921; *Atlanta City Directory*, 1921 and

1922). Believers in poetic justice can hope she left to find another teaching job.

As Riordan pointed out in her farewell letter to APSTA, however, her prospects appeared dim. The saturation of publicity brought her unwelcomed notoriety. At the congressional hearings on the Ku Klux Klan held in late 1921, Klan attorney Paul S. Etheridge of Atlanta told the House Committee on Rules that Riordan's firing was justified because she was an 'organizer and ... agitator' who caused 'friction between the board of education and the teaching force'. Speaking of the Board members, Etheridge said he knew them all personally, and 'there was not a Klansman among them' (House of Representatives, 1921, p. 61). After the Atlanta newspapers published Etheridge's testimony, newspapers across the nation reprinted the story. In her parting letter Riordan blistered APSTA for failing to issue a denial of Etheridge's statements. His 'uncorrected' testimony, she claimed, 'place[d] my name on the blacklist of every superintendent in the country, and render[ed] it practically impossible for me to pursue my work as a teacher in any up-to-date system of schools' (Riordan, 1922).

On the copy of the letter that Mary Barker received, Barker penciled, 'Where would we have been if we had undertaken to deny all the statements?' That question goes on to the heart of the bitterness between Riordan and her defenders. Two months elapsed while she sat quietly on the sidelines: 'two months when I might have done effective work in my own behalf.' (Riordan, 1922). Understandably, she wanted her job back. Failing that, she wanted to clear her reputation by responding to formal charges at a hearing. Failing that, she was determined to let the public know the reasons for her dismissal. Riordan wanted a vindication of who she was and what she stood for. Barker, however, believed from the outset that winning reinstatement for Riordan was a lost cause. A narrow defense based on due process and job security represented the only hope. Moreover, Jerome Jones convinced Barker that APSTA's decision to 'take the publicity road' was a fatal mistake. The Board *might* have given Riordan a statement of charges and a hearing, Jones believed, had APSTA not backed the Board into a corner. As Barker put it, the teachers 'had not realized that "saving face" was adult procedure, not just a juvenile practice' (Barker, 1921c).

Teacher Tenure and Social Vision

The Riordan incident left a permanent impression on Barker. Embarking on a new course at midlife, the 42-year-old teacher became radicalized — by southern standards, at least — as her experience in the labor movement gave her a new outlook on social and political issues. Although Barker and Riordan parted company with ill feelings, Barker became APSTA's labor conscience and, in some ways, Riordan's successor. Beginning in 1921, Barker moved into a grammar school principalship and assumed one leadership role after another: secretary of the Atlanta Federation of Trades, representative to the

Georgia Federation of Labor, president of APSTA, chair of the Southern Summer School for Women Workers in Industry, and most significantly, president of the AFT. She championed religious and racial tolerance, women's rights, union organizing rights, academic freedom, and teacher tenure, among other causes (Newman, 1983; Frederickson, 1980).

The Riordan case galvanized Barker into action on all these issues. Leading APSTA's successful campaign for a tenure policy was one of her first accomplishments. Barker enlisted the Atlanta Federation of Trades and the Georgia Education Association in the campaign, outmaneuvering Carl Hutcheson by going directly to the state legislature. Following the pattern established in other states (Scott, 1934, chs. 2 and 3), the Georgia legislature balked at passing a statewide tenure law. The overwhelmingly rural legislature, however, believed big-city (that is, Atlanta) teachers were especially vulnerable to political and social attacks. Overlooking similar injustices in small-town and rural Georgia school districts, the legislature amended Atlanta's charter in August 1922 to clear the way for a local tenure policy. In October, the Atlanta Board of Education adopted a policy that placed teachers on 'civil service' status after three years of satisfactory performance, with dismissal only after the presentation of charges and a formal hearing (Newman, 1978, pp. 89–91).

Barker celebrated the victory with other teachers, but in the remaining years of her career she grew increasingly disappointed with her co-workers. The more Barker advocated racial and religious tolerance, the more she alienated the members of APSTA. When she retired in 1944, she had become as much of an outsider as Riordan had been. Barker was indeed Riordan's successor (Newman, 1981a).

Howard K. Beale visited Atlanta in 1933 while researching his classic study, *Are American Teachers Free?*, and he found only sixteen Roman Catholic teachers in the Atlanta Public Schools — the same number as in 1921. Despite the KKK's decline as a major political power, Beale found such rampant anti-Catholic feelings in the schools and the city that Catholic teachers did not bother to apply to the Atlanta system. APSTA was an organization that cared about salaries and little else, he discovered. Atlanta's teachers had a strong bread-and-butter union, but they had no social vision (Beale, 1936, pp. 511–512, 614, 709). Julia Riordan would have immediately recognized the school system, teachers' association, and community she abandoned more than a decade before.

Chapter 8

One Who Left and One Who Stayed: Teacher Recollections and Reflections of School Desegregation in New Orleans

Alan Wieder

I never understood everyone's excitement about one little girl.

Margaret Conner
Frantz School Parent

On 14 November 1960, New Orleans began token school integration. Although the city viewed itself as cosmopolitan and tolerant (public transit and the library had been integrated without incident), struggle and conflict preceded complete school integration. On 6 November 1951, African-American community leaders called a meeting of the Ninth Ward Civic and Improvement League to solicit parent volunteers for a class action desegregation suit against the Orleans Parish School Board. Ninety-five parents volunteered, and on 5 September 1952, the local chapter of the National Association for the Advancement of Colored People (NAACP) filed Bush v. Orleans Parish School Board. Heard after the landmark Brown decision, Judge Skelly Wright on 15 February 1956 ordered the Orleans Parish School Board to submit a plan for school integration. The board replied two years later, after Judge Wright implied that he would facilitate a plan for comprehensive school integration if the board did not submit a plan. The Orleans Parish School Board submitted a plan that would begin 'token' integration in 1960. Although the planned integration appeared to be minimal, the state legislature fought integration, passing thirty bills on 13 November outlawing integrated schools. The New Orleans schools were the only ones open the following day when two previously all-White elementary schools, McDonogh 19 and Frantz, became integrated. United States marshals escorted three African-American children into McDonogh 19 and one African-American child into Frantz. By midday the majority of White children had been removed from both schools by their parents (Inger, 1969). The White boycott of the two schools lasted the entire school year. It appeared to be total at

McDonogh 19, while a small number of White children attended Frantz School throughout the year. Integration dramatically altered the ethnography of these schools. Prior to 14 November, each enrolled approximately 550 students, employed a principal, a secretary, a janitor, and eighteen teachers (Wieder, 1986, pp. 125–129). After 14 November, African Americans throughout the city experienced verbal and physical harassment as did the few White families who kept their children in Frantz School (Inger, 1969, ch. 1). The teachers at these two schools were greatly affected, and their stories provide valuable insights into school integration in that city.

Surprisingly, there have been few studies treating the recollections and reflections of teachers regarding school integration in the United States — and none gives teachers an active voice. Meyer Weinberg's (1981, pp. 659–680) massive bibliography contains 540 citations under the heading 'teacher'. Of these, only a few relate to teacher's reactions to integration and only one records the recollections and reflections of teachers — the others represent surveys and, although quite valuable, they do not provide individual recollections and reflections (Coles, 1964a, pp. 72–73, 90). This chapter provides that missing voice. The first section reviews the literature on teacher recollections and reflections of school integration. The second section presents two case studies on New Orleans teachers — one who left McDonogh 19 and one who stayed at Frantz. The third section draws some conclusions about teacher recollections and reflections on school integration in New Orleans.

Teacher Recollections and Reflections

The literature is sparse. Robert Coles' (1964a) article in the *Saturday Review* pieces together parts of his famous *Children of Crisis* (1964) series. Levinson and Wright (1976) recount the stories of five teachers from Chicago, Hattiesburg, San Francisco, and Detroit. However, only Coles' (1964a) essay offers similarities and differences in teacher reactions, pointing to uncertainty, racism, and the disparity between their beliefs and their roles. These concerns were mirrored by the New Orleans teachers. (Some of Coles' teachers are also New Orleanians.) A male teacher in Atlanta told Coles (1964a, p. 72) of his uncertainty:

> I almost had to pinch myself that first day when they came down the hall; and when the girl walked into my classroom I have to admit I was as confused as the boys and girls. You could hear a pin drop. In all my years of teaching I've never had a class so quiet. It was real strange the way she'd come in and a kind of stillness came over all of us. Talk about learning; we sure have been getting some.

None of Coles' teachers speaks in favor of integration. In spite of that, they grew less and less patient with the White mobs: 'Who can ever forget the looks on those faces? I always thought I was a segregationist, but I never heard such language, and they became so impossible after a while that they belonged in a zoo, not on the streets. That little nigra child had more dignity than all of them put together — it makes you stop and think.' (in Coles, 1964a, p. 73). New Orleans' teachers related similar experiences. Twenty-five years after the event in 1985, they felt on reflection that integration's time had certainly come in 1960. At that time, they might have sounded more like a number of Coles's teachers: 'I find myself torn. I never wanted this, but now we have to live with it, and whatever I say at home has nothing to do with what I have to do every day I come to work.' (in Coles, 1964a, p. 72). A second teacher stated it in even more precise terms: 'The crowds outside wanted me to boycott the schools, too; and I was with them, then, to be truthful. I mean I was opposed to desegregation. But I had my job as a teacher, and I just couldn't walk out of the building like that.' (in Coles, 1964a, p. 73). Similar words were spoken by the teachers in New Orleans (not by the two teachers interviewed below). In fact, a small number of teachers agree with the last of Coles's (1964a, p. 73) teachers: 'I just didn't believe it would work. I've known nigras all my life, and I didn't think they would adjust to our schools. I have nothing against them. I just thought their minds weren't like ours.'

Harry Edwards' (1980, p. 70) autobiography introduces a like-thinking teacher. Edwards, an African-American eighth grade student in 1954 when the Supreme Court ruled on the Brown case, recalled his response:

> I entered junior high school in 1954, the year of the Supreme Court's first major school desegregation decision. All my teachers seemed to be talking about it — to each other — but, with the exception of one old, Bible-thumping spinster about to retire with almost forty years of teaching behind her, none of them ever discussed the decision in any class that I attended. (And even this old woman's message to us was that 'you little darkies aren't ready for integration'.)

Florence Levinsohn and Benjamin Wright (1976) present a different set of teacher perceptions, based on the views of White as well as African-American instructors. Five teachers, Sylvia Fischer of Chicago, Helen Nicholson and Miriam Vance of Hattiesburg, Mississippi, Florence Lewis of San Francisco, and Nellie Brodis of Detroit, reflect on their experiences in desegregated schools. The editors' introduction to the teacher's stories is worth repeating. A similar statement accurately describes the frustrations of some of the teachers at McDonogh 19 and Frantz schools:

> It is not particularly astounding to discover, in reading their comments, that these teachers are angry. They are angry at the 'system' that has failed to provide them with an atmosphere in which they can use their skills most efficiently. They are, contrary to much received wisdom, deeply concerned about the children they teach. They are passionate in their concern for their schools. They see the center coming apart. (Levinsohn and Wright, 1976, p. 173)

Mr. Scharfenstein, the White teacher who left McDonogh 19, fits this characterization.

These teachers' views offer micro- and macro-levels of interpretation of the move to integrated schools. On the one hand, Sylvia Fischer, a veteran White teacher, provides a broad analysis of desegregation in Chicago. Although she was based at an integrated school in the mid-1960s, her reflections focus on school board decisions and the school board's 'will to fail' (Levinsohn and Wright, 1976, pp. 177–179). Ironically, the school Superintendent she speaks of in Chicago, James Redmond, served as the New Orleans Superintendent in 1960. The issue of the 'will to fail' is also often raised in analysis of school desegregation in New Orleans (Inger, 1969).

On the other hand, the Mississippi and San Francisco teachers offer more personal recollections. Helen Nicholson, a veteran African-American teacher at Hattiesburg High School, spoke of the pros and cons of integration: 'Yes, in my opinion, school desegregation is still a good idea for the purpose of providing adequate teaching materials and supplies and for dispelling of some of the fallacies usually associated with the races. No, desegregation is not still a good idea from a humanistic point of view.' (Levinsohn and Wright, 1976, p. 187). Nicholson's 'humanistic' point of view was portrayed in depth in Edwards' (1980) autobiography. What she is referring to is the all-African-American school as a community in itself. As in a family, everyone knows everyone else and everyone cares about everyone else. In spite of the above reality, Edwards opts for integrated schools. He, like Nicholson, does it with a critical eye. There is a price to pay, but it is worth paying he believes. 'Separate, but equal' schools were separate, but they were not equal. Nicholson discusses a second positive aspect of school integration: 'I also feel that school desegregation is still a good idea because it dispels some of the fallacies related to race, and everyone gets an opportunity to see for himself.... Blacks have learned that all whites are not smart, and whites have learned that all Blacks are not dumb; there are extremes in all racial groups.' (Levinsohn and Wright, 1976, p. 188). Helen Nicholson continues in this same vein. Although she does refer to problems, she spends a great deal more of her time supporting integrated schools. She believes that breaking down myths and stereotypes will facilitate a system that works for African Americans: 'It is hoped that Black students in the future will be given more positive recognition in areas other than sports, and that Blacks will not make up the greatest percentage of students in special-education and remedial-reading classes.' (Levinsohn and Wright, 1976, p. 189).

Florence Lewis, a White veteran English teacher at Lowell High School in San Francisco, reflects on her teaching experiences. She speaks with deep emotion of America's racism and the reaction to it by African-American students. She speaks with sensitivity as she recalls being hated because of her race.

> I know what it feels like to ask a human being a question and to have
> him turn away from me and walk down the hall as if I did not exist.
> The question is not am I big enough to take this acting out of what

others have done to him. The question is how long can I take it and
teach. The question is not whether I am elite enough to put a stop to
elitism but elite enough to say — Look, both of us are wrong if we
continue in this fashion. (in Levinsohn and Wright, 1976, p. 198)

'What others have done to him' is essential if we are to understand Miss
Lewis' reaction to school integration. She spends a large portion of her essay
discussing the education that Ellis, one of her students, has been cheated out
of because of racism: 'But what I am trying to make clear is the climate of the
sixties — how much injustice the Black kids had suffered, how much they had
been left out of a traditionally solid education and certainly the fun of going
to school ... how necessary desegregation was in order to give them a chance
because they were the dispossessed.' (in Levinsohn and Wright, 1976, p. 198).
Lewis's reflections offer a critical analysis of class, race, and the societal and
educational reality in the United States — she does it, however, from a
personal perspective. The issues she speaks of still have to be addressed.

One Who Left and One Who Stayed: Recollections and Reflections

The recollections and reflections of New Orleans teachers are similar to those
of the teachers introduced above. However, each teacher's social and cultural
situation, as well as different school realities, have had and continue to have
a direct effect on their memories and perceptions of school desegregation.
Family, religion, class, race, and geography have an effect on both how
teachers acted at the time their schools were integrated and how they perceive
that event today. The particular school situation is also important. New
Orleans public schools maintained an astounding student teacher ratio of 6:1
because of the White boycott. In addition to the White boycott, crowds
assembled daily at each school, violence permeated the city, teachers experienced harassment as they entered the schools, and the telephone rang nightly
with obscenities and threats at home. It is against this backdrop that we begin
to explore the recollections and reflections of two of the teachers — Mr. Les
Scharfenstein and Mrs. Josie Ritter.

Les Scharfenstein

I interviewed Mr. Scharfenstein in his office at the St. Bernard Parish school
board.[1] Mr. Scharfenstein had been director of food services in that district
for ten years but was a teacher at the time of the boycott. The district adjoins
Orleans Parish and served an important part in the White boycott at Mc-
Donogh 19 and Frantz when Leander Perez, Attorney General of Plaque-
mines Parish and a racist power broker in southern Louisiana, arranged
for the White children from Orleans parish to be accepted in St. Bernard
(Jeansonne, 1977, chs. 12, 13). In essence, the St. Bernard schools provided

one of two options for white children — another was a segregationist academy that was also supported by Perez.

Scharfenstein described initial confusion caused by the order to integrate the public schools, the day-to-day experience as a teacher in a boycotted school, the hope that White children would return, empathy for White parents, contempt for the integration process, and eventually his departure from McDonogh 19. Mr. Scharfenstein's confusion was unlike the confusion at Frantz School. Jack Stewart, McDonogh 19's principal, had notified the faculty about preparations for integrating the school for the morning of 14 November. Mr. Scharfenstein and the rest of the faculty had immediate duties (Wieder, 1986, p. 127).

> I was a sixth grade teacher at the time and we arrived at school to find people on the neutral ground and policemen on horseback. The principal called us together to get things organized. In fact he even stationed us at each of the entrances so only the children could enter. We would not allow the parents to enter the school but we assured them that their children would be alright.

The parents did not stay away for long though and by midday no White children had entered McDonogh 19 (Wieder, 1986, pp. 126, 127). The school had only three six-year-old African-American girls for the rest of the school year (Wieder, 1986, p. 126). The recollections of the school's Principal, Mr. Stewart, includes like praise for the faculty, who vainly tried to facilitate a traditional school day: 'The teachers went out of their way to see that they got good instruction. We still made the three of them file in a row to come down the steps. You see that's what school is about to a little child.' However, for Scharfenstein, this situation generated a great deal of frustration. His memories stress the lack of teaching: 'In the meantime we were left with no children to teach from early November. By Christmas time several of us were getting a little leery of doing busy-work. We became engaged in a curriculum study but it was really busy-work and we knew it and everyone else knew it.' Scharfenstein and the other teachers maintained the hope that the White children would return to McDonogh 19. By Christmas they realized differently; White parents had found alternatives for their children, enrolling them in either the Ninth Ward Cooperative School or in the St. Bernard Schools. Although Scharfenstein hoped the White children would return, he empathized with their choice:

> I spoke to a few people. I could understand their position. For a parent to have sent their children back to that school they might have been creating some problems for themselves in their own neighborhood. I can understand why they might not have done it, because of the pressure that was being brought to bear by their peers, by the people in their community. I certainly would not have advised them to do something that would have created a problem for them.

The local papers, the *Times Picayune* and the *States Item*, recorded the harassment of two families — the Foremans and the Gabrielles (Inger, 1969; Wieder, 1988). Each family encountered harassment on the way to school, in the work place, and at home; each was scared away from Frantz School.

Just as Scharfenstein viewed school integration as creating a dilemma for White parents, he felt that the White parents understood the dilemma of McDonogh 19's teachers: 'Those who knew us as faculty members knew that we were in the same position that they were in. We were having something forced on us that we really had no choice in. I don't think they held it against us personally. I think they understood our position as we understood theirs.' Jack Stewart's recollections concurred with Scharfenstein's:

> There was little harrassment of any of our faculty. Now I understand at the other school it was somewhat different. Our teachers never stopped parking their cars right out on the street. It was almost as if the community separated the faculty of the school from whatever else was going on. I think it was a credit to the teachers who were there. We could see them on the streets in the evening and they would talk about everything and anything. They did not come across to us with any animosity.

The word *force* appears often in the reflections of both men. Mr. Stewart is clear when he states that integration's time had come in 1960. Scharfenstein makes no definitive statement about the political issue itself, but he does say that he had nothing against teaching Black children. (That seems like an absurd statement to repeat, but it was not a given in 1960). Although Scharfenstein does not appear insightful in his critique of New Orleans school integration, he did not agree with the procedures: 'Force — this was the objection of most of the people. I think that integration might have been done differently. If they just had said we have the same assignments for all children, Black and White, as we had before. However, the doors of all schools are open to any student that wants to transfer to another school. I think this is really what Black people wanted at the time.'

Scharfenstein's analysis denies the tremendous amount of struggle by African Americans in New Orleans and throughout the nation for civil rights. Interestingly, the stressing of *force* changes the issue, that is, it implies that the imposition of the federal government represents a greater evil than the White racism endemic in American society. It also might be pointed out that the same people who resisted federal intervention in civil rights matters never resisted federal, state, or local White racism. This is not to say that school integration in New Orleans was conducted in the most humanistic or efficient manner. This is illustrated by the fact that two schools within affluent areas had volunteered to integrate. However, the School Board, which consistently made bad choices, selected two other schools — both in lower-middle/lower-class neighborhoods, which implied that the Board condoned integration only for poor Whites and poor Blacks. Thus, Scharfenstein's (and others') references to integration as *force* might help us understand the actions of the White community in opposition to integration, but they should not be used as justification — such actions were illegitimate.

Although Scharfenstein assures us that he did not mind teaching African-American children, his reasons for leaving McDonogh 19 differed from those of the boycotting White families. His departure requires further scrutiny. First, let us listen to his reflections on his move from McDonogh 19 to St. Bernard's Parish Arabi Elementary School.

> We had only those three children in the school. There really wasn't much for us. We reported to school every day. We met together. We didn't know what the future held. We didn't know what the response of parents would be. We did not know whether or not the children would return to school. I think we held out hope that they would. We expected that they would, but they didn't because other provisions were made. By Christmas of that year we began to wonder if there wasn't some possibility to be transferred to another school ... that is as teachers. Many of us felt we'd like to get back to teaching. I went to the personnel office — I spoke to the personnel director and explained how I felt. He responded that the Board's hands were tied. There was nothing they could do but keep us there. They had to maintain a faculty. My reply was that mine weren't. I came down to St. Bernard and spoke to the Superintendent, and sure enough there was an opening. In early January I began teaching in St. Bernard. I became a sixth grade teacher at Arabi Elementary School. As I said for me it turned out to be probably the best thing that ever happened.

According to Scharfenstein, the integration of McDonogh 19 'turned out to be probably the best thing that ever happened'. Although he is well aware that he was teaching many of the same children at Arabi as he had been before at McDonogh 19, he does not acknowledge the White boycott as a precondition of his being hired in St. Bernard. He does recollect being welcomed by the White children and their families: 'They were glad to see me come down there, although they might have misinterpreted my motives. When I came to Arabi I was kind of cheered. Anyone who asked me, I explained to that I was there because I wanted to teach. I felt good about being back in the classroom. I felt good about the move. It didn't take me long to like the idea of teaching down here.'

Scharfenstein does not appear to anguish over or analyze his decision. His words are important, because there is no discussion or analysis of the integrated schools. It seemed to be an individual choice, but he ignores the fact that the job at Arabi materialized because of the boycott of the newly integrated school. Although Scharfenstein had no qualms about teaching African-American children, his move to St. Bernard became possible only because the White people at McDonogh 19 refused to allow their children to attend an 'integrated' school and transferred them to a nearby parish. One cannot begrudge Mr. Scharfenstein his desire to teach, but the issue is more complex than his need for personal satisfaction. Teachers at both integrated schools were offered alternative positions at the Ninth Ward Cooperative School, yet only one teacher at each school failed to complete the school year. True, Les Scharfenstein and the other teachers at McDonogh 19 experienced pressure and stress. On the other hand, his departure, just like the White families' boycott, represented a political statement about the perceived importance of school integration in New Orleans in 1960 — whether he wanted it to be or not. Mr. Scharfenstein and the Whites who left might have been well instructed by Mr. Margaret Conner, the mother of one of the two White families who kept their children in Frantz. She spoke of the reaction to Ruby Bridges, the Black child who enrolled in Frantz: 'I never understood everyone's excitement about one little girl.'

Mrs. Josie Ritter

Josie Ritter's memories of school desegregation reveal a different tone. She seemed more descriptive, able, and displayed a strong sense of altruism. At the time of the school crisis, Mrs. Ritter had been a White teacher at Frantz School for seven years. Mrs. Ritter still retains pictures of the children playing in the schoolyard at Frantz School. Photos from 1960 show Ruby Bridges, the one Black child who integrated the school, playing with the few White children who still attended Frantz. Although Mrs. Ritter told me that she had not looked at the pictures in years, her face delighted in the smiles on the children's faces. At that time, smiles appeared to be rare at Frantz School. Like my meetings with Mr. Scharfenstein, the interview with Josie Ritter covered a number of themes — her initial reaction, that of the school's principal (a woman, Mrs. Barkemeyer, very different from Jack Stewart), the reactions of White parents, the daily reality at the school, the reactions of family, friends, and other teachers, and finally Mrs. Ritter's unhappiness with the school board.

Mrs. Ritter liked the Frantz School and the community. She spoke with me about the faculty being honored by the school's PTA just three days before the school was integrated: 'The parent's club had a celebration for us. They brought all different kinds of pies and cakes and they gave each of us a gift.' That same day, the principal was informed that Frantz would be integrated (Wieder, 1986). Unlike Mr. Stewart, Mrs. Barkemeyer kept the news to herself. Mrs. Ritter knew that school integration would begin on 14 November — she did not anticipate that Frantz would be one of the integrated schools. She drove to school with Earlene Schubert, a fellow teacher. She recalled their surprise that historic morning:

> When we turned the corner to the school we saw one of the TV stations shooting film. I'll never forget, she said, 'Son of a bitch, we're the ones that are integrating'. We were shocked. We could not park near the school so we went down the block. As we walked to the school the newscaster wanted a statement. We asked them what was going on and they told us that Frantz had been chosen to be

integrated. Well, we were absolutely shocked, we didn't know what to do.

Mrs. Ritter recollects confusion. The White children were already at the school; Ruby Bridges would not arrive until later in the morning. Rumors abounded and the school lacked a plan — there seemed to be no leadership. According to Mrs. Ritter, Mrs. Barkemeyer was nowhere to be found. One of the parents who kept her children in Frantz School throughout the school year, Mrs. Chandler, remembered Mrs. Barkemeyer speaking with White parents. She told the parents that the school was open under federal order and that they were welcome to take their children home. She then asked all the parents to leave. Mrs. Chandler never saw Mrs. Barkemeyer for the year (Wieder, 1988).

Mrs. Ritter also recalls an invisible Principal: 'Barkemeyer, we did not see her. She disappeared. She did not know her faculty and we did not know her, she was a stranger.' A second recollection is even more telling: 'Her brother and Mr. Moorehouse, a representative from the Board of Education, one on each arm would carry her into the school each morning. She wouldn't come in — I think she was scared, because when the police or anybody would come into the building she would say she was Miss Smith. She had her ranking teacher deal with them — she would hide.' Mrs. Ritter's memories might appear somewhat dramatic, but other teachers as well as the two White mothers whose children remained at Frantz viewed Mrs. Barkemeyer as a phantom. This is important because her absence promoted confusion and made the transition even more difficult. A good percentage of the faculty had been at the school for many years and feared the change. It is interesting that Mrs. Ritter firmly believed that the Principal who had retired the year before, a veteran both of the school and the community, would have provided leadership that would have supported the faculty and quashed the White boycott: 'She was a very straight-backed woman. She would have gone down those front steps and told those people to go home and leave her and the kids alone. There would not have been a boycott.' However, she had retired; teachers thus lacked support and White parents removed their children.

As at McDonogh 19, one of the teachers joined the boycott. Actually, she acted before Ruby Bridges even arrived at the school and before the parent student boycott began. As the first grade teacher, she was scheduled to teach Ruby. In some ways, her refusal to teach Ruby brought the other teachers together and gave them the strength to persevere. Mrs. Ritter remembers the teacher's discussion on the morning of 14 November: 'Everybody was talking about it. She lived in the neighborhood and she was at her house screaming and crying. She said that she couldn't do it, and she never did come. The other teachers who lived in the neighborhood came in and everyone signed in except her.' The teachers, although unsure of what they should be doing, seemed unsettled by the extreme actions of their colleague.

They also appeared shocked by the community's reaction — the same community that had honored them just a few days earlier removed its children before Ruby even entered the school, as Mrs. Ritter recalls: 'The parents all came and they were hauling their children out. They said they weren't going to let their children be at school with a Nigger. You know, that kind of talk.' Mrs. Ritter recalls the crowd growing outside the school and reacting vocally when the federal marshals escorted Ruby into the school. She offers an interesting insight into their reaction: 'The federal marshals brought her in the front door, and that is what really infuriated the white people.'

In retrospect, the initial actions of the crowds seemed mild considering what would happen in the days to come. The White families who kept their children in Frantz were unmercifully harassed. The teachers, Mrs. Ritter included, also felt antagonism; they were confronted directly by the Whites who left the school and victimized nightly by obscene telephone calls. Mrs. Ritter recalls some of her encounters with parents:

> There was one father whose child had lost a library book. They had paid for the book, but then the book was found at the school. The family made no attempt to get their money back. After the school was integrated the father came in and asked for his money back. What did he say to me? We were all 'Nigger lovers' and he didn't care if he had his money back before, but now he wanted his money back.

It would not be fair to portray the entire neighborhood as aligned against the faculty. Mrs. Ritter did receive supportive calls from the parents of some of her ex-students. Some said they wanted to keep their children in Frantz School, but the community pressure appeared too great — they were afraid. On the opposite extreme, the crowds that gathered outside of Frantz did not hesitate to spit at the teachers as well as at the White parents whose children remained in school: 'We no longer parked our cars on the street. We had to park in the school yard, or they would spit at us or damage our cars. The police had to escort us out of the neighborhood.' Josie Ritter also remembers the phone calls: 'We had to have our phone changed to a silent number. Oh, they would call, and what they wouldn't call me. It was horrible. There we were, the people they had honored just two days before, and they were saying that we should leave, but the words they used.' Mrs. Ritter and her family felt the stress. Her supportive husband encountered confrontation with acquaintances as well as workmates. Mrs. Ritter still expresses disappointment in the community's reaction to her and her fellow teachers. She sadly remembers the Whites who boycotted because of pressure and fear rather than intense racism. One parent told her, 'I can't send them back, Josie, I just can't do it. Your neighbors won't talk to you.' Another parent spoke similar words, 'I won't let my little girl go to Frantz and be subject to those people [crowds]. Not that I care if she goes to school with a Black child but I know what happens to the White kids on the way to school.' Ritter's reflections on the Frantz School parents are summed up in the following statement: 'The main thing that I would say was that the people that honored us turned on us so quickly. It is a shame that the people couldn't have accepted it. I never dreamed that these people would all pull their children out of school. Even after we knew we were integrated we still thought we were going to have a school.'

Because of the White boycott, Frantz did not function as a school in the traditional sense. Student demographics varied little from those at McDonogh 19; by the end of the year, the student body included Ruby, the four Conner children, and the two Chandler girls. A new first grade teacher, Barbara Henry, served as Ruby's teacher, but the teachers split their duties. In addition to the stress of the crowds and the community, teachers also suffered from the daily reality in the school. With no leadership, the faculty no longer worked at the same school they had known, and faced constant uncertainty. After all, were they really teaching?

Mrs. Ritter spoke of the frustration of being idle. With so few children, teachers had a great deal of free time. Mrs. Ritter became especially upset when teachers from other schools spoke cynically of teachers at Frantz and McDonogh 19 receiving their pay for nothing. Interestingly, the state of Louisiana cut funding for both schools in early December. A missed paycheck caused teacher morale to plummet. Although Mrs. Ritter did not elaborate on not being paid, Jack Stewart offered some interesting recollections:

> One day I was downtown, and I got back to the building and I knew something was wrong. Everybody was in their own room. You could just feel it. When you've got three kids, that's not typical. You know the faculty had had a blowup. I just got on the horn and said, 'I want to see you all when school lets out.'
>
> I just went around the table and apparently a few guys on the faculty were really hurting for money. I said, 'Allright, what do you want to do? Do you want to walk out?' After we chatted for awhile, we all decided we didn't know what to do, so we were going to do nothing. We just came back the next day.

In spite of these setbacks, the teachers tried to lift the spirit of each other and of the children. Mrs. Ritter spoke with fond memories of teachers, police, and US marshals dancing and singing at the school's Christmas party. When I mentioned that Mrs. Conner told me that one of her daughters learned to play the piano that year, she described the teaching:

> We did everything. We had crocheting. We had art work for them. Those children got the best education. There were two third grade teachers and one third grade child. She and I taught in the morning and she taught in the afternoon. We had all the regular subjects and so much more. We had programs and parties for Christmas and Easter. We made a lot of things go on for them — it was for us, too.

As much as they tried, it remained a long and frustrating year. The White children did not return and, although the faculty tried to make the best of it, they were happy to see the year come to a conclusion.

Josie Ritter's family and friends played important roles. Mr. Ritter worked as a foreman at an integrated utility company. He supported Mrs. Ritter and had no qualms about her teaching at Frantz. Most of the family's friends supported Mrs. Ritter, but a few disagreed. Some broke off their friendship and others got in their digs (and still do): 'Josie, you still a "Nigger lover"? — like that. And I say, "Yes!"'

Although Josie Ritter stresses that she thought it was time for the schools of New Orleans to integrate, she expressed concern about the way the change was accomplished. In that sense, she agrees with Les Scharfenstein. Mrs. Ritter thought that both schools appeared to be bad choices for integration. She does not speak about force or the federal government, like Mr. Scharfenstein. Instead, she names half a dozen schools that she thinks could have been integrated with less struggle and less resistance.

Mrs. Ritter's memories appear unique, because they are deeply personal. I am confident that her values and personality are reflected fairly in the above portrayal. We gain further insights into Josie Ritter as she reflects on how her daughter's school was later integrated:

> I was teaching and I was called to my daughter's school the day they integrated. The mothers were outside and they said that they didn't want their children going to school with Blacks. I told them that they were acting foolish. I said that I had been through this and that my daughter was staying right in that school where she belonged. One of the teachers was outside with the mothers, and she was asking what she should do. I told her that she should go back into the school and teach because that was what she was supposed to be doing whether the kids were Black or White.

Conclusion

Teacher reactions to school integration varied in New Orleans. Although neither Mr. Scharfenstein nor Mrs. Ritter offer extremes — he is not an the arch-segregationist and she is not a grassroots integrationist organizer — their stories do provide us with personal perspectives on school integration. Neither appears to carry the event with them twenty-seven years later. Mrs. Ritter told me that she seldom thinks of that time — only when people like me ask her about it. Mr. Scharfenstein still views it as a personal stroke of luck. He does not consider his move to St. Bernard in the same context as the White parents moving their children to St. Bernard. Although Josie Ritter comes out in favor of integration, she does not do so within the framework of resistance to the organizational and psychological White racism that still persists in American society. The point is that both teachers' stories are more recollection than reflection. How they each experienced the event — how it worked on them and how they reacted or worked on it — is more important than race and White racism as a social reality. Their stories may therefore help us to understand why *de facto* school segregation is still the reality in New Orleans.

There are very few teachers — or any of the rest of us, for that matter —

whose reactions to the beginnings of school integration are as sensitive as those of that San Francisco teacher, Florence Lewis. She has the wonderful ability to connect the societal/educational class disparity and white racism with what it does to real people. Les Scharfenstein and Josie Ritter do not speak about either White racism or their students. On the other hand, what Miss Lewis talks about is her relationship to her students — students who have been consistently ignored and disenfranchised. Although there are others like Miss Lewis, more of us are more concerned about how we are personally affected and are more than willing to confuse personal troubles with societal issues, thus paving the way to ignore class disparity and racism and to instead 'blame the victim'. This is not to say that if the teachers at McDonogh or Frantz schools would have been more like Miss Lewis, the school crisis might have been avoided. Rather, without more teachers like Miss Lewis, true school and social integration are an impossibility.

Note

1 I conducted interviews of Mr. Les Scharfenstein, Mr. Jack Stewart, and Mrs. Josie Ritter throughout 1982 and 1983.

Part III

Professionals or Workers?

The essential thing is that the public school teachers recognize
the fact that struggle to maintain the efficiency of the schools
thru [sic] better conditions for themselves is a part of the
same great struggle which the manual workers ... have been
making for humanity.

Margaret Haley (1904) quoted in Reid (1982)

Introduction

Historians have never clearly defined the concept of 'professional', except to describe its unfolding process and structural position, yet they have long characterized twentieth-century teachers as professionals. The underlying assumption prevailed that as professionals, teachers belonged to the middle class. To be separate and above the working class meant that they would never stoop to join unions or participate in strikes. The dominant paradigm of organized teacher behavior which emerged from these histories followed a 'gradual progression' towards high status (Ozga and Lawn, 1981, p. 10). The title of Willard Elsbree's (1939) classic work, *The American Teacher: Evolution of a Profession in a Democracy*, boldly testifies to this point. The evolutionary strategy for such development as an occupational group included expanded preparation, the acquisition of tenure and modest salary increases, and the formation and growth of professional societies, like the NEA. Teachers and their organizations seemingly functioned politically in a 'nonaligned' fashion, 'adopting professional models of "indirect" pressure' (Ozga and Lawn, 1981, p. 10).

Robert Reid's analysis of the professionalization of teaching represents a case in point. Teachers' 'self-conscious' desire to become professional grew out of the post-Civil War experiences of industrial consolidation and urban impersonality. This cultural formalization caused teachers to respond in kind. Their 'movement to elevate the standing of the occupation' originated in large cities, with female teachers seeking security and status through the formation of their own organizations (Reid, 1968, p. iii). The Chicago Teachers' Federation (CTF), formed in 1897, and Margaret Haley, its 'paid business representative', pioneered this effort, competing in a democratic fashion and as an interest group against the business sector (Reid, 1982, p. viii). The CTF led numerous 'crusades' over a twenty-year period, generating school revenue through litigation, which resulted in corporate property reassessment, fighting for improved salaries as well as pensions and tenure, and defeating a school centralization bill in the Illinois legislature. Reid sees the CTF as part of the 'organizational revolution', which served as a patterned response to industrial-urban America, and portrays Haley as a typical progressive reformer:

> As a former teacher and disenfranchised female, she performed as an educator, bringing the concerns of the teachers to civic organizations, church groups, labor unions, and women's clubs. In both word and deed, Haley conveyed the theme of citizen participation. Her identification with this egalitarian or 'democratic' side of the progressive movement stood in marked contrast to the centralist tendencies with reform in the first decades of the twentieth century (1982, pp. xi, xii).

Reid sees all of these efforts as purposefully intending 'to enhance professional attitudes of self-respect and autonomy' (1982, p. xxv).

These nonmanual, white-collar instructors never identified with manual, blue-collar workers, and never would. Reid thus downplays the CTF's 1902 affiliation with the Chicago Federation of Labor (CFL) as pragmatic and expedient, giving these female elementary teachers 'male allies who possessed the weapon of the ballot' (1982, p. xii). The CTF withdrew from the CFL in 1917 after the Illinois Supreme Court upheld the Loeb rule, which prohibited teachers from affiliating with trade unions. According to Reid (1968, p. vi), the CTF bequeathed its real legacy through its reform endeavors to address teacher issues within the NEA, culminating in the formation of the Department of Classroom Teachers: 'By 1920 the NEA had responded to the challenge. It assumed responsibility for promoting teacher welfare and, by reorganizing to ally state and local associations and vigorously recruiting new members, it furthered its claim to organizational leadership of the teaching profession.' Teachers' professionalization formalized their middle-class position with this organizational maturation.

Because of these developments, one might assume that classroom instructors reaped material benefits from their elevation of status, but this simply was not the case. The NEA, throughout the twentieth century, enrolled the largest number of teachers in the country, but its leadership, dominated by male school administrators given to strong rhetoric, took little concrete action, other than appointing investigative committees, to secure for teachers the amenities commensurate with professional status (Eaton, 1975, p. 173). For example, during the twentieth century, public school teachers' relative earnings, despite modest gains, have 'lagged far behind those of other professions' (Carter, 1989, p. 53). This organizational manifestation of the professional status of teachers seems abstract at best and nebulous at worst. The question remains: what is teacher professionalism?

Ozga and Lawn (1981), relying on the experiences of English and Welsh teachers, provide a provocative interpretation of professionalism, treating it as an ideology. This benefits the state since it denies class conflict, manipulates and coopts instructors, and relies on the ambiguous concepts of autonomy and service. The perspective of Ozga and Lawn assumes more significance when the social class position of teachers is considered, when teaching is juxtaposed against the ongoing process of proletarianization (Labaree, 1988):

> Through this process teachers are not merely made more like other workers in economic terms, i.e. less economically advantaged, more vulnerable to redundancy and pressure towards increased workload. The proletarianization process also involves a loss of control over the work process, a loss of definition by the worker of the essential elements of the task. Thus the teachers' broad self-image as an 'educator' is eroded and his/her function as a processor stressed. This in turn breaks down the teachers' individualistic professional self-image, and forces on them a revived recognition of a collective interest in organization against the employer (Ozga and Lawn, 1981, pp. 143–4).

This profoundly alters the notion of professionalism for public school teachers.

The campaign to define teachers as professionals may be viewed in this context as a defensive measure to fend off proletarianization (Apple, 1986). This is what Bergen (1982) found in his analysis of English elementary teachers during the late nineteenth and early twentieth centuries. These instructors, with working-class roots, perceived teaching as a mode of upward mobility, 'having risen above the working class, if not having reached the middle class' (p. 10). They based their being 'better' than workers on the rigorous selection process, their position of relative authority, superior education, and certification, among other factors. As Bergen observes, 'Clearly the varied attempts of elementary teachers to professionalize constitute an attempt to raise their class position from an interstitial one between the working class and middle class to the solidly middle class position of a profession' (p. 10). Thus, this occupational advancement to nonmanual tasks conferred respectability, with the illusion of status, and these insecure instructors strove to raise their job to a profession in the same sense as law and medicine. They failed.

Marjorie Murphy (1981; 1990) takes this analysis a step further with American teachers, that is, during the early decades of the twentieth century, some openly aligned themselves with the working class. She focuses on Chicago teachers to illustrate 'the shift in white-collar identity from an artisanal to a professional outlook', thus flatly refuting Reid's (1968; 1982) interpretation that Chicago teachers and the CTF pursued professionalization from the beginning. She argues instead that the CTF originated as a manifestation of working-class solidarity, not as an exercise to divorce white-collar workers from their blue-collar counterparts; both groups faced the proletarianization of their work. As skilled workers already realized, teachers too understood that 'the centralization of urban schools would undermine autonomy in the classroom' (Murphy, 1981, p. 197). Hiring standards also changed, and debate ensued over the need for a college education for teachers, as well as issues of transfer, promotion, and salary.

Teachers, led by Haley, appealed to an artisan tradition, asserting the idea of teaching as a craft to be mastered through classroom experience, like an apprenticeship. The CTF consciously identified with the labor movement, formalized by its CFL affiliation: 'Teachers negotiated salaries and working conditions, and inspired other women to organize. The teachers' craft ideal achieved its fullest form during the Progressive Era, and was essential to the strength of that movement' (Murphy, 1981, p. 3). However, the Loeb rule crushed this craft spirit and potential source of power for classroom instructors; that was precisely what school officials and city and state politicians wanted. This marked 'a turning point in labor history' (Murphy, 1981, p. 1). With the trade union movement among teachers effectively neutralized, the ill-defined notion of professionalization emerged, as embodied by the NEA. For Murphy, this administratively dominated organization functioned, by the 1930s, as nothing more than a 'company union' (1981, p. 368; 1990).

Although teacher militantism appeared — or reappeared, according to Murphy's perspective — during the 1960s, professionalism persisted as the goal. This elusive ideal is still sought amid the many recent school reform reports (Altenbaugh, 1989; Boyer, 1983; Goodlad, 1984; Holmes, 1986). However, both Susan Moore Johnson (1984) and Larry Cuban (1984) have demonstrated the enduring ability of teachers, as historical actors, to shape unions and school reforms, respectively, to suit their own needs and benefits.

The three articles that follow shed some light on the professional-worker nexus. Patricia Carter taps reports, autobiographies, and NEA surveys to analyze perceptions of teachers' status, reminding us of the gender basis of teaching and the gender biases of this country. Richard Quantz uses oral histories to arrive at a set of four metaphors which categorize the experiences and perceptions of small town (Hamilton, Ohio) female teachers, using them to explain their resistance to unionization during the 1930s. Professionalism appeared to be subsumed under more complex issues growing out of their individual experiences. Richard Altenbaugh's contribution focuses on the oral histories of Pittsburgh teachers to illustrate the varied and often contradictory responses by male and female teachers alike to the imposition of business efficiency methods in the schools. Pittsburgh teachers embraced science and expertise in their pursuit of professionalism, not realizing that this cost them what little autonomy they possessed. More significant, in all three cases, teachers never enunciated a clear, enduring sense of professionalism.

R.J.A.

Chapter 9

The Social Status of Women Teachers in the Early Twentieth Century

Patricia Carter

Ten years ago, after the final session of a spring term, I escaped from three years of bondage in the schoolroom. . . . My decision had been reached only after serious consideration and endless argument, my parents having shaken their heads dolefully and reminded me that I had spent four years at a state university in preparing to be a teacher. They reminded me also that as a teacher I had attained some success and that to abandon the one true and honorable vocation for a woman was little short of madness.

Donovan, *Schoolma'am* (1938)

The woman quoted above went on to become a business entrepreneur — one of the first of a group of women to do so in the 1920s. Her trepidation about leaving teaching, or at least that of her parents, underscored the dilemma faced by women of the early twentieth century when selecting a career — should that decision be based on social status or economic rewards? Throughout the latter nineteenth and early twentieth centuries, teaching represented, as noted above, the 'one true and honorable vocation' for women, serving as the one exception granted to the rather rigid social belief that paid labor degraded women and corrupted their moral character (Newman, 1985, p. 245). As a result women entered teaching in ever increasing numbers. By 1900, the ranks included women from all social classes and eventually from many races and ethnic groups. Women comprised over 82 per cent of all urban and 70.6 per cent of rural schoolteachers. Social injunctions against women's paid labor suppressed teachers' wages, as school boards reasoned that women worked out of community-spiritedness or religious self-denial, but not for monetary reward.

Yet, as the twentieth century progressed, increasingly larger percentages of women teachers left for opportunities in other fields, citing economics as a major factor in their decision. In opting for careers outside of teaching, women made conscious efforts to broaden their individual career possibilities, while expanding society's criteria for acceptable occupations for women, especially for educated women. Two major changes prompted this trend: a reconsideration of women's economic roles in society that resulted in the development of new career opportunities for women; and the decline of altruism among educated women as a primary motivation for entering the work force. I will focus on how these two factors increased the concern between 1900–1930 of women about the social status of teaching. Other forces further influenced these changes; most important among them being feminist ideology, the rise of the consumer society, and greater attention to economic factors, prompted by recessions and labor unrest.

The Origins of Altruism for Female Teachers

As early as the 1830s and 1840s teachers routinely earned less than their factory sisters (Kessler-Harris, 1982, p. 56). The rationale for the low wages accorded to women in the profession was based in the early nineteenth-century Protestant-republican ideology 'which freely mixed economic arguments with the religious and political for public education' (Tyack and Hansot, 1982, p. 21). Women were expected to become teachers, not for the monetary rewards, but out of duty to God and community. Reflective of this viewpoint was Horace Mann's 1860 article, 'The Female Teacher', in which he wrote, 'Christ's lessons never sounded so beautifully . . . as when spoken by the voice and ministered by the hand of a woman . . . if ever I envied a mortal being upon earth, it would not be the queen, . . . but . . . the devoted, modest, female teacher, conscious only of her duties, unconscious of ambition or earthly reward' (p. 1860, 157–8). Catharine Beecher echoed a similar sentiment when she identified those appropriate to the task of teaching as 'Christian females' who would work 'not for money, nor influence, nor for honour, not for ease, but with the simple, single purpose of doing good' (1846, p. 23). This belief, that women are naturally more altruistic than men, continued to suppress female wages in the twentieth century. But concurrently it allowed women to maintain a higher social status, since entering teaching could be judged an act of altruism rather than one of economic desperation. In fact, Beecher envisioned teaching as a 'casteless profession' which would 'eliminate the extremes of class identity'. She directed this message to factory workers as well as upper-class women (Sklar, 1987, p. 161).

As a community role model, the educator was expected to be intellectually competent and morally virtuous, cultivated in manner and behavior. Increasingly, the manner and behavior of women teachers came to be judged by external characteristics such as dress, place of residence, and forms of social entertainment rather than the Christian piety stressed by Beecher and Mann. Correct appearance guaranteed the community that one was a proper lady and thus an adequate role model for children. In the late 1880s this connection between teaching and social status led many advisers, including Ella Rodman Church, to declare: 'In spite of its care and anxiety and wearying tread-mill round of duties, teaching has always been a popular employment with the educated — principally because it is one of the few means of money-making in which a lady may openly engage without compromising her social status.' (Church, 1982, pp. 77–8).

However, support for teaching diminished in the second and third decades of the twentieth century, as women began to recognize other possibilities. Catherine Filene (1920) warned her readers that teaching afforded very little opportunity for advancement, financial remuneration was 'quite inadequate', and the stress of the work often resulted in 'nervous strain inimical to physical and mental health' (Filene, 1920, pp. 19–20). Caroline Dall (1914, p. 111) further cautioned that the poor salaries paid to women teachers jeopardized their standing in the community: 'Their meager salaries prevent them from dressing as ladies. . . . For the same reason, their boarding places are obscure and lonely. The upperclass look down upon them kindly, but they never think of inviting them to meet distinguished people.' This imbalance between wages and social requirements of a lady emerged as an even more significant source of dissatisfaction among teachers as twentieth-century modernism transformed the United States into a culture of consumption (Fox and Lear, 1983). As Lotus Coffman noted in 1911, 'The tastes of the teachers might be those of people of refined economic leisure, but the salaries, being those of mechanics and at-laborers or even less, prevent the enjoyment of these higher things' (p. 83).

By the turn of the century, inflation accounted partially for the greater attention to the economic condition of women. The US Bureau of Labor found that between 1897 and 1911 inflation increased by 44.1 per cent. Food prices had increased 61.7 per cent from 1896 to June 1912 (*Teacher's Salaries and the Cost of Living*, 1913, p. xi). Unfortunately communities often refused to recognize the effect that inflation had on teacher salaries. Cost-of-living raises appeared rare and as a New Haven teacher complained in a 1913 NEA survey, the public visibility of teachers' raises only incurred higher charges for community services:

> Since the last increase in salary, I have not been able to save any. Commodities have increased so, and as soon as the tailor knew I was a teacher, he charged me $2 more to make a suit. The dressmaker charges as much per day as I earn. The dentist charged me $3.50 to do the identical work for which I had formerly paid him $2 (about an hour's work). Upon hearing of our salary increase, our board in the country was put up $1 more per week and many extra charges made. I was formerly able to save about $140 over year, but now I occasionally have to draw on the interest of my savings. (*Teachers' Salaries and the Cost of Living*, 1913, p. 223)

A Denver instructor concurred: 'Teachers are required to pay a higher rate for board and lodging than are other workers because the public consider us better paid' (*Teachers' Salaries and the Cost of Living*, 1913, pp. 222–223). To compound matters, some women teachers perceived school and community expectations as sexist, as reflected in the following statement: 'More is expected of a woman teacher in the way of social life, accomplishments, culture, style of living. These things entail a large expenditure of money' (*Teachers' Salaries and the Cost of Living*, 1913, p. 221). Another teacher from Denver, in that same NEA report, noted the link between these expectations and the twentieth century cult of consumerism: 'In returning to school work after an absence of twenty-two years, I noticed a marked increase in the demands made upon a teacher's time, skill, and money. Teachers have to dress better and more is expected of them in every way. Special subjects like drawing and sewing take much time and make heavy demands upon the nerves. Salaries have not increased to these demands' (*Teachers' Salaries and the Cost of Living*, 1913, p. 221).

Though obviously connected with economic status, these complaints were usually framed in terms of 'keeping up the appropriate feminine appearance.' Few women wanted to approach their concern about unfair wages directly, for that might be considered 'unladylike' and too self-seeking. Instead they carefully explained that they were no longer able to meet the 'community's expectations' of the proper female teacher. In doing so they sustained the stereotype of the altruistic female teacher while generally attempting to enhance or at least maintain their own social status.

Taking the Direct Approach

Although social status may have been a primary determinant in attracting women to the teaching profession, economic factors increasingly became a source of dissatisfaction once they were there. As a result, some appeared willing to confront more directly the harsher realities of the poor wages paid to teachers, such as salary inequities between male and female teachers, or between teachers and other community services. Older women also voiced concern about their inability to save for their retirement. And stories about the heroic efforts of some women teachers to support siblings, elderly parents, and children appeared in the 1913 NEA survey:

> Outside work carried to an extreme is represented ... a woman grade teacher in one of the cities studied, who partially supports her mother. To her salary of $750 she added in 1911 the following items: $8 received for private lesson; $0.50 for proofreading; $30.75 for acting as a cashier in a dry-goods store for forty-one evenings; $8 profits on a personally conducted excursion tour; $32.73 for services as a waitress during the summer; $42 in tips from guests; $6.45 for clerical work in a store, and one or two smaller items making a total of $880. Her accounts show fair but not excessive expenditures for clothing and recreation but she states that her savings amounting to $50 for the summer use only. 'I feel absolutely obliged to do these extra things to earn money', she adds, 'every little bit helps.' (*Teachers' Salaries and the Cost of Living*, p. 233)

Others endured what appeared to be slow starvation in order to keep up the correct appearances. A widow supporting her two children on $1,235 noted:

> For twelve years [I] have practiced the most rigid economy where it could not be known. For instance, while I get dinner in the middle of the day I never allow myself — or rather seldom — anything more than bread and tea or coffee for breakfast or supper. Fear of being dependent in my old age had made me do this. I have many wealthy friends who have given me help — thrust it upon me. They have not the slightest idea of my economies for I keep a good outside appearance. (*Teachers' Salaries and the Cost of Living*, p. 228)

More public forums, such as the *Woman's Journal*, published pieces, such as the following poem written by a school superintendent in 1906 (Harris), which commented on the increasing dissatisfaction teachers felt about low wages and community expectations.

Everybody's Paid But Teacher

Everybody's paid but teacher,
Carpenter, mason, and clerk;
Everybody's paid but teacher,
She gets nothing but work.

Everybody's paid but teacher,
Toiling day and night,
Everybody's paid but teacher,
Drawing her slender mite.

Everybody's paid but teacher,
Butcher, baker, and cook,
Everybody's paid but teacher,
Grafter, fakir, and crook.

Everybody's paid but teacher,
Paid with a scowl or a smile;
Everybody's paid but teacher,
Whose work is not worth while.

Everybody's paid but teacher,
Seeking her pay above;
Everybody's paid but teacher,
Living on ethereal love.... (Harris, 1906, p. 20)

The denigrating reference to 'ethereal love' underscores the growing challenge to the prevailing notion that women teachers should be willing to work for altruistic reasons. While the poem compares the salaries of teachers with those of various other occupations, the author carefully avoids any reference to the salary distinctions within the teaching profession itself. Salaries differed dramatically from one part of the country to another and between women and men teachers. For example, cities such as New York, Chicago, Philadelphia, and Boston, which employed 27 per cent of all teachers in 1905, inflated the national median wage, since wages paid in those cities were comparatively high. Nationally, female elementary school teachers earned $650 annually, while male teachers with the same duties earned $1,161. At the high school level, men received an average yearly salary of $1,303 while women made $903 in a comparable situation. With the four cities excluded from the average, the median annual salary for female elementary school teachers is $556, and $653 for men. Of 1,500 men elementary school teachers nationwide, 900 were employed in schools in New York, Chicago, Philadelphia or Boston (*Survey on Salaries, Tenure of Office and Pension Provisions of Teachers*, 1905, p. 460).

Rural schools, especially those in New England, paid the poorest salaries. Due to the low number of students per school, a short school year, and a low tax base, rural schools found it impossible to compete with the city schools. One rural school in Connecticut reported that its teachers drew an annual income of $180 for thirty-six weeks of work. In Maine, the lowest salary reported was $206 for teachers who taught thirty-two weeks. As a result of the low wages, rural schools had trouble retaining a stable body of trained educators. With rural educators across the nation receiving a range of $6 to $12 a week and in larger cities like New York $42 to $55 a week, it was not unusual for teachers to gain their initial teaching experience in a rural or village school and then move to the city as soon as they were able to obtain a position.

Compared to other occupations in which women were beginning to participate, teaching demanded more training for less financial return. This was especially true when teaching is compared to clerical work, a field offering new opportunities for women. A New Haven woman grade school teacher with two years of normal school complained in the 1913 NEA survey: 'Have two sisters who went two years to high school. One receives $200 more a year than I do, the other about $500 a year more.' She explained further, 'One is a bookkeeper, the other a stenographer' (*Teachers' Salaries*) *and the Cost of Living*, 1913, p. 217). An Atlanta woman principal agreed: 'I consider the salaries paid to teachers in this section of the country very poor indeed, in view of the years of preparation for work. Much better salaries are paid here in other lines of work. I have a sister employed as a stenographer who receives several hundred dollars a year more than I do, and then too, without the years of preparation I have given for my work' (*Teachers' Salaries and the Cost of Living*, 1913, p. 217). A female grade school teacher in Cincinnati regretted her lack of forethought in selecting teaching as her profession: 'Had I given the thought, time, labor, and earnestness to any line of mercantile employment, I should today be earning a better salary, have more opportunity for investments, and not have had a nervous breakdown' (*Teachers' Salaries and the Cost of Living*, 1913, p. 219). A Denver schoolteacher compared her wages to others in the public service sector: 'In this city post-office clerks, policemen, firemen, and clerks in the Capitol and City Hall, and others serving the public are better paid than teachers, and organized workers in almost all lines receive a greater compensation' (*Teachers' Salaries and the Cost of Living*, 1913, p. 219).

The time and money spent in teacher education represented only one factor in the discontent voiced by women teachers about their salaries. The continuing need to upgrade one's training and skills was another. A Cincinnati grade school teacher explained:

> The demands on a teacher are very great in these progressive times. A teacher cannot confine herself to school work alone. She should hear the best in music, see the best works of art, be acquainted with all current events of interest, and all this with the salary of an average stenographer. The stenographer's education is completed in a year; the teacher's is never finished, or at least should not be. (*Teachers' Salaries and the Cost of Living*, 1913, p. 218)

Some women teachers expressed anger over unequal in salaries paid to male and female teachers. An Atlanta high school teacher complained: 'My work has been given unqualified indorsement [sic] of the Board of Education and the public and yet in our school system inexperienced men are given less advanced work than mine on a salary which exceeds mine by $263' (*Teachers' Salaries and the Cost of Living*, 1913, p. 243). A Cincinnati woman advocated the concept of equal pay as a remedy.

> In this city the men receive more salary than the women. In this school the men receive $500 more than women. Twenty-five per cent of the men have no one dependent upon them.... In every case the men's responsibilities consist of a wife and a family from a voluntary choice on their part. The women's responsibilities consist of mother and sisters. All the women, moreover, have a number of home duties in the way of housework and sewing which take time and energy from studies and professional activities. The additional $500 a year that men receive would, if also paid to women, enable them to pay to have such things done. To sum it all up: the women have the same amount of school duties as men, they have the same amount of family responsibilities, very much less time for intellectual pursuits, and less pay. Raising the salaries of the women to equal the salaries of the men would do the men no injustice, and would only be doing justice to the women. (*Teachers' Salaries and the Cost of Living*, p. 239)

School boards remained unconvinced of the legitimacy of the theory of equal pay for equal work. On the one hand, since women constituted a large majority of the teaching staff in most schools, raising their salaries commensurate with those of men would require a substantial increase in the school budget. Taxpayers, it was believed, were not anxious to support the burden of equal pay. On the other hand, the idea of downgrading men's salaries to the level of women's appealed to no one. Men would not work for such poor salaries when they could find better paying occupations. Since male teachers seemed essential in administration and as role models for boy students, school boards appeared willing to pay men a higher salary.

Race, Ethnicity, and Social Status

Inequalities based on race and ethnicity exacerbated gender issues within the teaching profession. School boards did not particularly encourage African-American women to pursue teaching careers, and in 1895 Susan Elizabeth Frazier had to institute legal proceedings in order to gain her position as the first African-American woman to teach in an integrated New York City school (Davis, 1982). Frazier represented a group of women who composed only 4 per cent of the nation's teaching profession. Between 1890 and 1900 African-American women teachers increased by 72.6 per cent and by another 30.2 per cent during the next decade (*Statistics of Women at Work*, 1907, p. 118). This rapid increase of African-American women as teachers has been attributed in part to the preference of white male supervisors of segregated schools for female over male teachers (Strober and Tyack, 1980). But others note that teaching became sex-segregated for African Americans for the same reasons that it did for whites: teaching represented a socially acceptable public extension of the female domestic role; it provided an opportunity for women to utilize an advanced education; it provided one of the best salaries available to women; and it offered social prestige and status within their communities (Harley, 1982, p. 256). In fact, the feminization of teaching occurred even more rapidly among African Americans than for whites. As of 1890 7,864 African-American women and 7,236 men held jobs as teachers, but in 1900 the number of men remained relatively stable while women nearly doubled to 13,524. By 1910, women had filled over two-thirds (or 29,772) of all the positions in the African-American teaching force. As was the case for Whites, African-American men left teaching when other professional opportunities with larger financial rewards or greater job mobility opened to them (Collier-Thomas, 1982, p. 180).

During this period, the charge to use one's education to 'uplift the race' was never understated (Davis, 1982, p. 276). The urgency and moral obligation of the teaching profession, when combined with racist conventions about segregated schools, suppressed African-American women's wages even more critically than White women's. While some northern, urban school districts paid a relatively good salary to women, most African-American teachers found employment in the southern states (Harley, 1982, p. 255). Because of their remote location, poor facilities, and inadequate budgets, southern rural schools hired inexperienced teachers, usually with less than a high school education, at a minimal salary.

In 1916, at the age of eighteen, Septima Clark joined the ranks of these teachers. Educated in a private school in Charleston, South Carolina, Clark had always wanted to be a teacher. In her last year of high school, she took the teacher's examination and received a first-grade certificate. Though she was encouraged by her teachers to attend Fisk University, her parents could not afford the tuition and she began to look for work. Her own hometown of Charleston would not hire African Americans to teach in the public schools. With the help of a local Methodist pastor, she was able to secure a position in a segregated school on nearby John's Island. In the intervening summer months, she took a job in a bakery to earn enough money to buy the 'appropriate clothes' for her new position. Her parents proudly supported her intention to become a teacher. Clark notes: 'Teaching was honorable work that ranked well above most other work available to Negro girls. And it would be a life of service.' (Clark, S.P. and Blyth, L., p. 28). Her father had feared the consequences should she fall into the wrong line of work, such as domestic service or hotel work. On the street where the Clarks lived four women had become the mistresses of White men, a condition her family felt shameful and linked to the degradation and underemployment of African-American women. They had warned Septima and her sisters about situations in which they might make a similar error.

Despite her lack of training Clark received the rating of 'principal', which gave her a salary of $30 a month; local White teachers of the same rank received $85. Clark taught 132 children, from preschool through eighth grade, though teachers in the nearby White school had as few as three students in their classrooms. She believed that African Americans were more committed teachers than Whites (p. 40), because they had to compensate for inferior school facilities, work for low pay, and tolerate hostility by some in the White community. Despite the difficult conditions, Clark enjoyed her work, but after her first year she gratefully left the island school for a better paying position at her alma mater in Charleston. During her first year there, she worked with the NAACP to collect 10,000 signatures in support of African-American employment in the Charleston public schools. This successful campaign opened positions for many women, including Clark (Clark, S.P. and Blyth, L., pp. 60–61).

At the turn of the century, the US Census combined Native-Americans and Asian-Americans under one category in descriptions of women's occupational status. Nevertheless, these groups comprised a tiny percentage of teachers, even when compared to African Americans. In 1890 the teachers' ranks included only ten women of either Native-American or Asian-American origin, but in 1900 this number climbed to 255 (*Census Statistics of Teachers*, 1905, p. 20). This increase is related to the addition to the Census of Native-American women working as teachers for the Bureau of Indian Affairs (*Census Statistics of Teachers*, p. 14). A majority of Native-American women teachers found employment with the BIA in the western and south-central regions of the United States (Rogers, 1915, p. 260). Although listed as teachers, most Native-American women held positions of lower status than those of White women or men, or even Native-American men. For instance, during the 1899–1900 school year, Native-American women accounted for only 2.75 per cent of all general subject teachers, but 14.89 per cent of all the assistant teachers. No Native-American women served as principal teachers or school supervisors (*Annual Report of the Commissioner of Indian Affairs* ..., 1900).

In 1891, Congress declared school attendance compulsory for Native-Americans and in 1893 authorized the BIA to 'withhold rations, clothing, and other annuities from those parents who resisted sending their children to school' (Adams, 1988, p. 3). By 1907, 173 boarding schools and 168 day schools registered 25,802 students, well over one-half of all Native-American children (*Annual Report of the Commissioner of Indian Afairs* ..., 1908). Since reservation schools did not offer teacher training, Native-American women who wished to enter the profession usually did so in eastern boarding schools. Some began the process as small children who left their reservation homes to attend BIA boarding schools.

One such student was Zitkala-Sa (1921), of the Sioux nation, who described her education as both isolating and demeaning. At the age of 5, she and the children of many different Native-American societies began their years of physical and emotional abuse in a curriculum that deprived them of their native customs, foods, and languages (1921). The schools discouraged home visits for fear that the students would not return or would come back with bad 'Indian habits'. Thus, when the children finished their schooling, they often returned to villages where their Anglo habits and values created problems for them and their families. Some, like Zitkala-Sa, did not return to their homes but became BIA teachers. Like most Native-American teachers, she did not receive an appointment to teach on her own reservation in Dakota, but was given a position in 1897 at the Carlisle Indian School. There she became increasingly and painfully aware of her part in the destruction of Native-American culture, and felt despair: 'In the process of my education I had lost all consciousness of the nature world about me. For the white man's papers I given up my faith in the Great Spirit.... On account of my mother's simple view of life, and my lack of any, I gave her up, also' (Zitkala-Sa, 1921, p. 96). She quit teaching, took up writing, and eventually became a well-known editor and advocate of Native-American rights.

Little has been published about the lives of foreign-born women teachers, or those born in the United States of foreign parents. Statistically this group represented a rapidly increasing population of early twentieth-century teachers. Between 1890 and 1900, the population of native-born White female teachers with foreign-born parents increased by 52.8 per cent and by 25.5 per cent for foreign-born White teachers, while the percentage for native White female teachers fell by 4 per cent (*Statistics of Women at Work*, p. 118, Table CLV). Thirty-three per cent of all women teachers had foreign-born parents, though less than 6 per cent (5.1) had themselves been born in countries other than the United States most notably in Ireland, Germany, England, and Wales (pp. 111, 115, Table CXLVIII).

In developing a portrait of the average woman teacher in these two categories, one would most likely envision a 24- to 35-year-old native-born woman with parents from Ireland, teaching in the North Atlantic region. One description of such a teacher is presented in *Little Citizens: The Humors of School Life*, first published in 1904 (Kelly, M., 1931). As an ex-schoolteacher of Irish descent, author Myra Kelly used her own experiences to detail everyday life in a typical big city school with its diversity of students and teacher backgrounds. The book follows a year in the life of a fictitious teacher, Constance Bailey, an ambitious first-year instructor of fifty-eight first graders from New York's east side. Her students, the majority of whom are the children of recent Jewish immigrants, provide the counterpoint to Bailey's own new and rather tenuous position within the professional class. On meeting her students she realizes how cloistered her Irish Catholic life has been. These are street children, whose illiterate parents are forced to work in dingy sweatshops fourteen or sixteen hours a day. The children fend for themselves as best they can, joining street gangs for the only protection on which they can count. Bailey does not want to respond emotionally to the plight of her students. She simply wants to be a good teacher and provide them with the fundamental skills to be successful students and become integrated into American life. Before she realizes it, she is drawn into their lives. She arbitrates family feuds, is asked to become a godmother to one of her Jewish students, and becomes an advisor to her student's lovelorn father and his new wife-to-be.

Implicit in this story is the checkered past of the schools' efforts to Americanize immigrants (Tyack, 1974; Berrol, 1981; Olneck and Lazerson, 1988). Although middle-class Protestant values dominated the concept of Americanization, teaching placements often reflected a higher priority, that is, insuring the 'best schools' received the 'best teachers'. Ironically, the better role models of White Protestant womanhood usually received assignments to exclusive middle-class public schools, such as Wadleigh in Manhattan or Erasmus Hall in Brooklyn, while the lower-status teachers, especially those of recent immigrant stock, were more likely to be placed in the schools within slum areas (Graham, 1974, p. 164). Without access to the cultural capital of their more well-to-do sisters, working-class Roman Catholic teachers, such as Kelly, found themselves in the odd predicament of trying to teach poor Jewish children the values of middle-class Protestant life in America.

However, *Little Citizens*, as the title suggests, is a collection of humorous but true-to-life vignettes of classroom life told from a teacher's perspective. Cultural dissonance is the prevailing theme but so is sensitivity and fair-mindedness. The reader understands that Bailey's own impoverished background increases her empathy for students, but her almost total *naïveté* about the colloquialisms, mannerisms, dialects, and religious customs of her Jewish students is humorous. Apparently, she has never before considered that such differences could exist. As an illustration of her cultural isolation, she forces the rabbi's grandson to wash out his mouth as a punishment for swearing. The soap, made of pork fat, compromises the child's religious principles. Though the boy protests that the soap is 'traef', Bailey does not understand the meaning of the word or its importance in Jewish culture, until the rabbi pays her a call. Though Bailey is humiliated by her lack of sophistication, the rabbi is tolerant and together they reach a solution — kosher soap.

In another episode, Bailey's romantic relationship is sabotaged by her students in an effort to protect her from a man that they are sure is a 'Krisht'. When Bailey assures the students that she knows all about 'Krishts' (Christians) and, indeed, is one herself, the children are flabbergasted. They promise not to tell anyone the truth of her horrible disgrace. For all their differences, the students and teacher are bound together in their mutual respect for each other and their shared distain for 'Gum Shoe Tim', the associate superintendent of schools. His nickname is derived from the soles of his shoes which allow him to sneak up on unsuspecting teachers in their classrooms. He is described as temperamental and ethnocentric, repeatedly demanding that Bailey 'stamp out the dialect' in her Eastern European students.

Altruism played an important role in motivating ethnic and racial minority women to become teachers. Going into education as a means of uplifting the people of one's own community assumed self-sacrifice on the part of minority teachers, like Septima Clark. It also granted a high status within that same community. However, as in the case of Zitkala-Sa, whose Anglo education left her isolated from her Native-American community, the price of this status came at too high a price.

Summary

Although the altruism associated with teaching allowed women to enter the profession without compromising their social status, their assumed altruistic motives also justified their low wages. The emergence of a culture of consumerism in early twentieth-century United States increased the standards for social respectability and ladylike appearance beyond the means of the average woman teacher. Teachers complained that fine clothing, suitable lodging, regular entertainment, and charitable contributions absorbed their entire salaries, leaving them nothing for savings or for retirement. To further complicate matters, many community merchants believed that teachers made a comfortable living and charged them accordingly, often raising their rates each time the teacher received an increase in pay.

Between 1900 and 1920, dissatisfaction increased as closer scrutiny of the woman teacher's situation, prompted by feminism, found that not only did men have a wider range of socially acceptable careers, but that even within teaching, they climbed career ladders not readily available to women. School boards based the salaries of male teachers on their potential advancement within the profession, while women's potential contribution to teaching remained identified with their domestic and maternal roles. They viewed a man's role as family breadwinner as an incentive for him to excel in his profession while a woman's roles as wife and mother seemed irreconcilable with her teaching duties. As a result, women's relationship to teaching came to be viewed as temporary, further justifying the inequities in male and female salaries. Thus, the changing image of the woman teacher, from that of altruistic social servant to the socially-conscious but fiscally-concerned worker, signaled the beginning of the professionalization of women teachers and their general acceptance within the permanent workforce.

Chapter 10

The Complex Visions of Female Teachers and the Failure of Unionization in the 1930s: An Oral History

Richard A. Quantz

I think they expected you to be an outstanding person. And I think we were selected because maybe we were.

Bertha C.

We were all a little knit family and we did everything together. We'd go to shows together, go out to eat together and when somebody had a birthday, we celebrated.

Linda A.

I thought that the most important thing in life was to be married and have a family. That was my goal.

Sallie D.

Until recently, historians have tended to treat teachers as nonpersons. Female teachers especially have been portrayed as objects rather than subjects, as either the unknowing tools of the social elite or as the exploited minority whose labor is bought cheaply. Rarely have they been treated as subjects in control of their own activities. Seldom has the world of schooling been presented through their eyes (For some interesting exceptions see Finkelstein, 1970 and 1979; Clifford, 1975 and 1978; Hoffman, 1981). This chapter attempts to reverse the traditional angle of vision and explore an educational event from the perspective of the teachers involved. Specifically, it explores the failure of unions to organize teachers during the Great Depression.

The failure of unionization among teachers in the first half of the twentieth century has not been ignored by historians. Joel Spring (1972) discusses the inability of organized labor to influence school boards or unionize teachers. David B. Tyack (1974) tells of administrative methods that wielded the hard club of threat and the false allures of professionalism. Both authors present these events as a conflict between unions and school elites for the allegiance of teachers. Both suggest that the elites won. For example, Spring (1972) blames the crushing power of corporate America and the conservatism of teachers for failure of unionization, whereas Tyack (1974) points to the veiled coercion of administrators and teachers' naive desires for professional status. Although these arguments are forceful, both authors constructed their arguments with little input from teachers.

Wayne Urban (1982) has provided one of the few analyses that include the voices of teachers, arguing that teachers formed unions and professional associations to gain material advances and to protect their seniority. His analysis portrays the teaching profession as an interest group which, like any other, acted to protect its own needs. This dispels any notion that teachers' organizations, union or professional, organized to improve conditions for the students or any other altruistic purpose. If teachers organized themselves to protect their power and material interests, then one would assume the National Education Association (NEA) became more popular with teachers than the American Federation of Teachers (AFT) because it was seen as better able to protect those interests. But Urban, like Tyack, shows very clearly that the NEA was primarily an organization of administrators, not teachers, and worked more against than for the interests of teachers.

Why, then, did teachers prefer to join the NEA? Urban (1982, p. 153) attributes the failure of unions in the 1920s to the 'lack of a real *raison d'etre*', but certainly the depression of the 1930s provided such a reason. The payment of teachers in scrip, the shortening of the school year, and the over-crowding of classrooms provided enough reasons to organize. Yet, even though some increase in union membership occurred during this period, the increase was not as dramatic as conditions might predict, and ultimately, the movement failed.

Spring (1972), Tyack (1974), and Urban (1982) fall short of fully explaining this failure, largely because they ignore teachers as self-directing people. More recent work by David Tyack, Robert Lowe, and Elisabeth Hansot (1984) provides detailed descriptions of the everyday lives of depression-era teachers, skillfully weaving anecdotal evidence with statistics and analysis and providing an enriched and powerful history for the reader. Unfortunately, the anecdotes are used as a way to round out, fill in, and add interest rather than as an analytic foundation for understanding the historical event. Even though their study concentrates on the Great Depression, tries to include teachers, and addresses the question of the influence of educators on public policy, it develops only slightly more than Tyack's earlier work the question of teacher unionization during this era. It leaves us with the impression that the organizing of teachers failed in most districts during the 1930s simply because they were conservative or because their communities were so conservative that professionalization was more likely to succeed than unionization. Too often it explains teachers' actions in terms of structural forces bigger than the teachers themselves.

Must we accept the idea that teachers were simply game pieces in the hands of administrators and other powerful men and that they were too timid or too powerless to act as subjects in their own world? Were teachers relegated to acting the pawns in reality conjured by others? To understand teachers, we need to do more than treat schools as little black boxes with interchangeable parts, which take inputs and create outputs, and which are manipulated by those outside them. If unionization failed, it is because real people made choices concerning their own very personal worlds. Attention to the larger forces of history provides a framework of understanding, but without knowing the finer detail of the participants' subjective realities, we fail fully to understand the dynamics of history. By following only macro-history we are in danger of 'failing to see the trees for the forest'. In our eagerness to map out the great movements of 'man', we sometimes forget that historical events often involved real women living in their own subjective, but equally real, worlds.

This study represents an oral history. Its goal is to describe the shared subjective reality of one group of women teachers during the 1930s and to compare that reality with some assumptions historians make about unionization. Based primarily on interviews and influenced by ethnohistory (See Quantz, chapter 12), this chapter presents a group definition of schools and life in a small midwestern city (Hamilton, Ohio) during the Great Depression. As such, it brings an anthropological perspective to historical study. By attempting to discover the cultural definitions of participants in an historical situation, it investigates the subjective side of history. This research is less interested in portraying the way things really were than in how participants perceived them. As a case study, it lays no claim to a generalizable truth. It should not be understood as presenting anything but a piece of the mosaic. Resulting from a study of Hamilton, Ohio, it should not be used to try to explain Enid, Oklahoma; Riverside, California; or any other small city. On the other hand, any historical analysis that purports to make a general explanation of the unionization movement of teachers during the 1930s and fails to consider the subjective reality of teachers, such as those found in Hamilton, makes a false claim.

The typical structural approach to history fails to explain fully why unions could not organize teachers during the 1930s. Citing structural causes, while important, tends to minimize the force of subjectivity in human life. In Hamilton, unions failed, at least partially, because of the cultural concepts women teachers constructed to organize their realities.[1] Second, the exercise of social and political power reflects the personal visions of ordinary people. As might be expected, school superintendents were likely to hire young women who presented an image corresponding to their concept of a teacher. In Hamilton, the appropriate candidate was likely to have been the daughter of a proper family and to have excelled in local schools, not through intellectual genius, but through competent conformity. By selecting 'safe' teachers, superintendents were able to guarantee a nonunion workforce. Power was exercised through normative controls (see Etzioni, 1961) without the need for clubs or delusion. As will be shown, the teachers of Hamilton, an over-whelmingly female group, having been raised in a world where success was achieved at the cost of control over their full social lives, contributed to their own lack of power.

Most of Hamilton's teachers in the 1920s and 1930s came from upper-working class or lower-middle class families. Most grew up in Hamilton, had excellent high school records, went to one of three nearby colleges, and returned after one to four years of higher education to live at home and teach in their old school system. They were obviously known quantities to the superintendents who hired them. Like teachers everywhere, they had to make sacrifices to get through the troubled economic times of the 1930s. They occasionally worked without pay, sometimes received scrip, and effectively subsidized the schools from their own bank accounts.

Complex Visions, Contradictory Metaphors

These facts only show the typicality of the city and teachers being studied. In this study, these facts are less important than the subjectively created world of the teachers themselves. Regardless of the historical 'facts', the definition of the situation accepted in common by the group can help us understand the relationship between teachers and unions. This definition, seen through the eyes of the women teachers, can be described using four metaphors: the subordinate authority figure, the school as family, the natural female avocation, and the dual-self. These four metaphors show clearly the world within which these women taught and lived and is best explained through the stories these women tell.[2]

Metaphor A: The Subordinate Authority Figure

The teachers of Hamilton provide us with a view of teachers built on conceptions in conflict. For example, the teacher is understood as someone worthy of receiving respect, while at the same time expected to follow orders. Forged in childhood, this view of the teacher seems to present the teacher as, at least in part, a powerful force; someone whose very presence may make us misspeak; whom, out of respect, we should avoid whenever possible. Linda A. shows us this idea clearly in the following anecdote.

As children, Linda and her friends used to walk to elementary school together. They would laugh and talk on their way to school staying on the west side of the street and keeping one eye out for Miss K., their second grade teacher. Miss K., who usually walked the mile from her home to Taylor School on the east side of Pleasant Avenue, occasionally would start out on the west side. When she did, Linda and her friends crossed the street to the other side. That way they would not have to speak to her. 'We just admired her so', Linda said, 'we were afraid we'd say something we shouldn't.'[3] Other teachers present the same image. As Barbara B. put it, 'I stood in awe of my teachers.' Bertha C. believed that teachers were very dedicated when she was a student. This attitude became embedded in their own concept of a teacher. 'You were the teacher', says Sallie D., 'and you demanded a certain respect and it was given you.'

But in a second anecdote Linda A. shows that she did not lose her respect for authority even when she became the teacher. Linda had been hired after talking to the principal, Miss J., on the phone. They had never met in person. On her first morning of school Linda arrived and immediately ran into her new principal.

Linda A.: 'Are you new?' And I said, 'Yes, ma'am. Fifth grade.' 'Oh', she said, 'You'll have a new teacher.' I started to say 'I' and she said 'hush!' to me, you know. She said, 'You go sit here', and she took me into that little office and she said, 'You sit here and I'll talk to you later.' She went back and forth to her room, back and forth, and she called the supervisor and said, 'The new teacher isn't here yet.' I even raised my hand. She just shook her head and walked out. 9:15 she called again and said, 'What am I gonna do? That new teacher isn't here yet. You said she was so reliable! You were so thrilled! She was gonna . . .' and all this rigamarole. Finally I said, 'I am Miss A.' She said, 'Why didn't you tell me in the first place?' I didn't have the heart to tell her, you know, that she wouldn't let me talk.

Fearful of authority, Linda A. could not tell the principal that she was the teacher, not a student. She even tried to raise her hand, an obvious gesture of subordination. Another teacher, Barbara B., was not only in awe of her teachers but 'always stood in awe of everybody who was in control.'

Teachers were expected to carry out orders, not initiate them. Susan E. puts it this way:

Susan E.: You were told what to do. You were told to get this, so much work done, and so much was laid — I mean — from the main office so much was laid out. . . . You carried out what you were supposed to do. You didn't know any different.

Interviewer: Did you ever think that they didn't know what they were talking about?

Susan E.: I did later. But then I wasn't — I guess, I don't know. I — you never — you didn't used to question authority.

Barbara B. is able to laugh now about the structured atmosphere and her fear of the supervisor.

Barbara B.: We did have very structured [pause] everything. The children had to be very quiet. You had to keep on your schedule. Outside of our door we had posted our schedule, and when the supervisor came, you had better be having what it said you were to have [laughs] even if you had to stop in the middle of a word, which is a little exaggeration, but he was very adamant about keeping on schedule.... I really was frightened of him. I was really fearful of him.... I guess I was afraid I would do something wrong, and that was just a no-no. Oh, one of the things that he was very strict about was shades. They must all be at the same level, which I thought was a little silly, but I was very careful to have them that way....

Interviewer: What if you disagreed with him about what was right?

Barbara: You didn't.

But teachers were not uncomfortable in this situation and can even talk about the freedom they had. Peggy F. explained, 'But there was a lot of freedom in music and plays and games within your own classroom. Then later on, teachers were assigned to go on the playground; and you could organize your games, you know, "Farmer in the Dell", and ...'

The first metaphor shows that teachers were people to be both respected and respectful, feared and fearful. Creativity and individual initiative were frowned upon except within strict boundaries, which perhaps explains one teacher's thankfulness for teachers' manuals. 'They assume you don't know anything and take it from there.' Teachers were seen as leaders of children and followers of men.

Metaphor B: The School as Family

In a different series of anecdotes Linda A. portrays the school with family-like metaphors.

Linda A.: Oh, I just loved teaching. Even when I was little in grade school, all I always said I was going to be was a teacher. I think that they could do anything to me, and I would have still loved it.... I was one of a large family and I was second in line and took care of them as though I was mothering them. I always wanted a large family. I didn't have it. I don't know, I just thought they were all my children, every year.... And we all felt like, I think the children thought you were their other mother too. I always stayed at school, usually, and talked and graded papers till about 5:30 or 6:00. The janitor would run us off. He was a doll. He always said 'darling' to us and he put a shower in the basement for these little ones that didn't come very clean if they were going on a trip, and

our mothers always wondered where the old towels and
washcloths and soap went, then after they used them the
lady across the street would wash them for us and bring
them back and once in a while a child would take a towel
home or a washcloth or a bar o'soap, but we didn't care.
They wanted something at home, too, you know, you
can understand it.... We were all a little knit family and
we did everything together. We'd go to shows together,
go out to eat together and when somebody had a birthday, we celebrated.

Sally D. had the same vision. 'Everybody was sort of a close family.' Beth M.
agreed, 'I prefer just to have my own class ... like a little family.'

Certainly, close, even sister-like relationships developed among many of
the teachers. Peggy F. states, 'I enjoyed the companionship of all the teachers
there because we stayed together so long. Nobody would ever be asked to
move.' Although all the teachers seemed to get along well, there did seem to
be a split between the older and younger teachers that mimicked the generation gap that often occurs between mothers and daughters. Susan E. remarked, 'I was eighteen, and I was thrown with women who were older and
had been teaching longer and I — well, whatever you did, you were younger
and you were "on the pan" quite often, in other words. And what you were
doing was nothing. I mean it wasn't ... there used to be a time when you, as
I say, you had to be so guarded in things that you did socially and all that sort
of thing.' Roseanne G. remembers the dress that her principal gave to her.
'She had a blue silk dress from the early 1900s that she probably had worn in
somebody's wedding — I don't know why she had it. And when she looked
at me she said, "I think you could wear my dress!" [laughs] I didn't know
what was coming next! So one day she brought it and had me try it on. It was
a beautiful dress with a wide skirt, you know, sort of bouffant, and little
tucks in the bodice part, which is what, I suppose, people wore then.... And
so I ... was able to wear it.' While hand-me-downs were certainly not the
rule, it is not difficult to imagine the relationship that developed among a
faculty that typically consisted of several very young women and a few much
older women.

If there is any doubt about the teachers' use of family metaphors to help
understand the sister-like and mother-daughter-like relationships among the
faculty, the mother-child metaphor used to describe the teacher-student relationship is clear. Linda A. makes it explicit. Susan E. also seems to have used
her colleagues and especially her students as a second family: 'I loved the
people. I love kids. I've never had any children, but I love kids, and I loved
the people I worked with.... And I had a room down there — I made
silhouettes of all the kids, and they went all the way around the room, pigtails
and all.' One teacher became so involved with one little girl that she adopted
the student when the girl's mother could no longer afford to care for her.

Although the images of family are not universal, many described the
close relationships that grew among the young women and the friendly but

reserved relationships they, as younger teachers, had with the older women. Certainly the same motherly, tender, and proud references to their 'kids' might be heard among teachers today.

In spite of, or perhaps partly because of, this 'family' image, women teachers were expected to be single — either young women not yet married or 'spinsters' or widows. In 1931, the Hamilton School Board adopted a policy of hiring only single women and firing all women who married. As in many other places, this policy was justified on financial grounds. 'Why should we allow two-income families', the argument demanded, 'when there are single women without jobs?' But, of course, there is no inherent logic in firing married women and maintaining single women who lived at home with their families, often wealthy ones. In fact, a well-established father probably required a supplementary income less than a young married husband. Lois Sharf (1980) suggests that such bans on marriage were the result of a trend that began long before the depression years. The financial problems merely accelerated a practice that had started in the 1920s when the teacher supply became large.

The no-marriage rule affected women in several ways. At least two women believed the ban interfered with their ability to find serious suitors. Alice H. explained, 'This discouraged the young men. Because, like I said, it was depression years and they couldn't swing a house on their salary. So they looked for girls who were secretaries or nurses or something like that who could marry and bring in another salary. So if you were a teacher, why the men — you were untouchable.' When asked to react to the idea that the no-marriage rule put a strain on their social relations with men, Susan E. wholeheartedly agreed, 'Oh, it did! It did!' Others do not completely agree, but the stories of delayed marriages are legion. Several of those women interviewed waited seven to eight years to get married, until they could wait no more; finally, the Second World War and threatened legal action lifted the ban in the 1940s.

The women I interviewed claim that they felt, even then, that the no-marriage rule was grossly unfair, but they believed that public sentiment during the depression was against giving a job to a married woman who had a husband to support her when many single women were without income. Although they complained to each other, they really did not think of trying to fight the rule. Roseanne G. explains, 'In those days teachers accepted, more than they would now, what was decided up at the Board and by the superintendent.' So the image of the single and subservient woman was strong enough to prevent any reversal of this rule. And in place of their own families these single women 'adopted' their students at school.

Metaphor C: The Natural Female Avocation

While still young girls, many women decided to teach. Linda A. had always dreamed of being a teacher. Sallie D. shared that dream. 'Well, I always, I always, from the time I was small, enjoyed being with children. And that was all I ever thought about — getting to be a teacher someday.' Peggy F. told her mother, '"Oh, I want to be a teacher"! I loved my teachers so much.' Many of those interviewed expressed similar sentiments — a deep-down belief, even as girls, that teaching would provide them with personal fulfillment.

Certainly this coincides with the public view of women teachers — hard-working, dedicated, willing to undergo any sacrifice for their students. Such teachers taught for personal fulfillment and would probably teach even if not paid. Such an image was certainly true for some of these women, but not all. In fact, many went into teaching because their parents wanted them to. 'I guess I never really decided to be a teacher', said Barbara B. 'My parents decided for me.' Bertha C. wanted to go into welfare work, but her family talked her out of it. Many of the women taught simply because they needed a job. For women, teaching was the best paying job around. Certainly the selection of occupations was limited. Gladys H. commented, 'Well, I wanted to be either a nurse or a teacher. Somehow, teaching was the choice.' Asked why she taught, one woman said simply, 'Because I went to college.'

Susan E., one of those who taught mainly because she needed a job, did not like the self-sacrificing image placed on teachers and the difficulty it created. 'You just didn't do it [demand a higher salary]. It wouldn't be professional. It wouldn't be — I hate the word — it wouldn't be dedicated. I just hate that word because I wasn't *dedicated* to teaching. I just liked it.' She taught because she needed a job, and this was as interesting and well-paying a job as was available.

Women were not supposed to be interested in careers. They had learned that true fulfillment came through marriage and having children. Even some of those who never married confided that their true goal in life had been to find a husband.

Sallie D.: My goal was always to have children of my own. Since I love children anyway, that was the most important thing in the world for me at that age. I was 17 when I started college so I was teaching at 19. I thought that the most important thing in life was to be married and have a family. That was my goal. I think that was instilled in you ... back in those days. [One] never thought about a career being the most important thing in the world to you.

This idea was not openly discussed, but it was implicitly understood. Sallie D. reflected others' thoughts when she said, 'I don't think — I never discussed — a lot of those things you just sort of keep inside you and you don't verbalize all your desires and hopes for the future. But I know that — my friends, that was one of their goals, to find a husband, get married, have a home.'

Teaching was one way for women to bide their time until marriage and to improve their skills as mothers. Perhaps the family and mother images placed on the schools made teaching a most inviting profession. Teachers were respected, in their way, even if also clearly subordinate. Women could learn how to order and organize their own world, while remaining, at the same time, dependent on others and ignorant of the world outside their own realm.

All but two of those women interviewed lived with their parents the first several years of teaching. The two exceptions lived at the Young Women's Christian Association (YMCA). Living at home allowed many the luxury of not worrying about money. Their salaries were more like a large allowance. They used it to buy fur coats and go on trips, or saved it for future use. These women were often quite oblivious to worldly affairs, even to the effects of the depression.

> Linda A.: We had a meeting and one man said, one man teacher said, 'See the handwriting on the wall,' and all of us dumb little single girls, we looked back where he was pointing and there was no [handwriting] [laughing], but one year we taught a month free. We did take a few cuts, but you know things were so cheap then I don't think we realized....

Although many of the women lived a life of dependence, many others learned that others depended on them. They were often the sole support of a widowed mother or sick father. Their income was needed to hold the family together. The majority may have lived with fathers until they could find husbands, but a large minority shouldered the financial burden of their families until they could find men willing to shoulder it for them. This latter group, to their surprise, often found few men who were willing until after the women had fulfilled their family obligations.

The only truly legitimate realm for most women was the family. The most appropriate way to fulfill their function was to marry and have children. This could not be done, however, until all obligations to their parents were completed and a man could be found to marry them. Until then one had to have a job, and teaching represented a good choice. Schools, as we have seen, were often pictured as extended families and teachers as mothers, sisters, and daughters. What a perfect way to earn money and satisfy one's perceived needs as a female.

Metaphor D: The Dual Self

In return for her cooperation, the teacher was given a special place in society. For many this was accepted in stride. Linda A. indicates easy acceptance of her status. She and her fellow teachers marched in the fire prevention parade every year and helped in the community drive to pass the school bond levy by making posters 'and all the rigamarole that goes on'.

Linda A.:   That was just part of the job. You know, it just went with it and, as I said, I think at the university they stressed that you get in the community and you should live in the community where you teach, to know the people, to get in on their things, and go to church with them. Of course, we all had to teach Sunday school. As soon as you started teaching you had a class....

Interviewer: Did any of you, or any of the teachers that you know, feel that you were inhibited, that you weren't able to do what you wanted to do?

Linda A.:   I don't think so. I just think we thought what was expected of us.

Interviewer: You were comfortable with that role?

Linda A.:   Oh, yeah.

Others agree.

Elsa K.:   I enjoyed my life in Hamilton. You were respected and part of the community.

Interviewer: Did they treat you differently than they might have other young women your age?

Elsa K.:   I don't know. I don't think they did treat me any differently. But, I think, I mean, well, yes! I think they had respect, you know.

And Bertha C., when asked to describe teachers' status, replied,

You were not just an ordinary person; people were interested in knowing you. People were interested in talking to you.... I think they expected you to be an outstanding person. And I think we were selected because maybe we were.

Many others, however, found this special status burdensome rather than welcomed. Roseanne G. explains, 'I mean, if I didn't know the [answer] right off, if I couldn't tell you the capital of Rhode Island or something, they'd say, "How do you teach your children if you don't know —?"' Peggy F. complains, 'Well, I think we were censored. Not knowingly, I mean things we did.... Well, it wasn't really censored, but maybe it was ridiculed.... I mean we had to be careful; what you did was everybody's business in other words.' Merle J. adds, 'Oh, you were expected to be above reproach in every way. *They* could do certain things that a teacher couldn't do. It was a terrible thing if you took a drink or smoked a cigarette in those days.' Sallie D. and Susan E. were afraid to wear colored nail polish. When sued for causing an automobile accident, Susan E. settled out of court. She and her boyfriend were afraid a public court appearance would cost her her job.

There was at least one major problem with the place of a teacher in society. Unlike the majority of young unmarried women, even proper ones, teachers were not supposed to present themselves as sexually attractive. The teacher's role, with its emphasis on nurturance and a teacher's special status in the community, could only satisfy a part of a woman's self-image. Therefore, most of these women engaged in an almost surreptitious private life. Susan E. said, 'If you went to a dance, if you went to a party, if you did all of the things that a lot of us did, you had to do it on the QT. You couldn't just do it openly'. Most of them did have an active social life. It was not really secret and was certainly circumspect. As Peggy F. pointed out, 'You never felt guilty about going out on dates or dancing. Everything was OK, you know. It was fun. We had a wonderful time.' This was so, even if, as others told me, you had to go to a roadhouse outside of town for a drink and to Cincinnati for a dance, because a dance at the local hotel could start the rumors flying!

The no-marriage rule created a whole new obstacle to many women's lives. More than one teacher dared take an out-of-town trip with her long-time fiancé, a deed that even today these women are afraid to make public. Several teachers were secretly married and living apart. A few continued to teach until they became pregnant. One teacher was able to hide her pregnancy until the newspaper published her name in the 'New Births' column. At that point the school authorities told her that if she did not announce her marriage, she would have to adopt her own child. She had to quit her job. She had been married for six years.

Secret marriages appeared quite common, but one wonders how secret they really were. Sally D. discussed her secret marriage.

Sallie D.:   Other people knew about it. . . . You just didn't . . . discuss it, broadcast it, but everybody would know about it, yes.

Interviewer: [Did] the principal know it?

Sallie D.:   No, I don't think the principal knew. Although I'm sure he might. He had to know it eventually because I became pregnant before the year was out, and he knew it, [but] he didn't say anything.

Teachers maintained a conspiracy of silence. They all seemed to understand the duality of their situation, even if many of them despised it. Most of them portrayed the appropriate public image and violated it only very carefully or in the secret company of their peers, like the woman who wore high heels to school every day even though she changed into flats while in the classroom, or the young woman who, on a summer vacation with her young friends, told the Canadian border guard that she was not a teacher but a stripper from the Gaiety Theatre.

These four metaphors provide a framework for the description of the commonly accepted reality used by many of the women teachers in Hamilton during the 1930s. It would be a mistake, however, to believe that all women shared these conceptions. A woman might share only one or two of these ideas, or change her mind about them at different times in her career. The degree to which a teacher shared these views depended on many work-related factors, such as the particular school in which she taught, the neighborhood in which the school was located, the character of the school's administration, and whether the school was elementary or secondary, and on many personal factors, such as religion, marital status, personality, desire to teach, and need for income.

To believe that a complete picture can be found in these four metaphors simplifies a complicated array of individual perceptions. It is possible that few teachers actually perceived their world of school as presented in these abstractions. People tend to approach their daily lives in the concrete. This study does not argue that this is the way the world really was. Instead, its thesis points to a publicly affirmed, cultural view — a culture of the schools within which proper women had to operate. Even if they did not personally share this view, they still had to accommodate to it. Few individuals may actually have accepted this world-view in its entirety, but they would all have recognized it, for they had to act within it or in opposition to it.

An Exception

One woman who did not use these metaphors is Patricia I. Partly because of her own confidence, courage, and independence, and partly due to her religion and divorce, Patricia operated within a different framework. Her story indicates a surprising number of concepts that do not parallel the others. As an exception, her story confirms the cultural creations of the others by its difference, and gives an indication of how individuality can be maintained in a seemingly homogeneous community. It also suggests that individual factors are an important determinant of one's willingness to accept and operate within the public culture.

Like many of the others, Patricia I. learned to respect teachers as a child, but she also learned that there were limits to that respect.

> Patricia I.: We had one [teacher] that every time you would stand up to answer a question and you didn't know it in Spanish or Latin, she would say, 'Jew, sit down. Zero for the day'.... I was a senior at that time; my father was very aggressive and he went to school; instead of going to the principal, he went to her directly. And he says, 'Listen here,' he says, 'I've been in this town since 1906. I've lived here all my life; I have paid all my taxes; I support everything that the city needs. And you're not going to treat my daughter that way.' He says, 'But you are going to stop picking on the Jewish children, and if you don't, I am going to talk to the principal and then I am going to the superintendent', — both friends of his.... No one except my father, that I know of, went to school and told the teacher off. It was not the thing one did.

After high school, Patricia I. went to the Ohio State University and majored in journalism.

> Patricia I.: I was just a playgirl.... I just went there to have a good time. In those days girls weren't expected to amount to anything; they were supposed to get married and have a family. So, I went a year and a quarter, found a guy, married him. Married six years and that was the end of that. And I thought I was getting nowhere in life so I decided to go back to college.... And I had a critic [teacher], you know, when you did your practice teaching, and she was the nosiest thing that ever lived. And somebody had told her that I was divorced, and she questioned me about it and I says, 'It is none of your business what I had happen to me in my private life. I am here for one purpose only. It is to prepare myself to make a living.'

Like the other teachers, she lived with her parents, but unlike the others, Patricia found living at home a disadvantage.

> Patricia I.: I should never have been in a school where I was known because they [the students] were all in my neighborhood.
> Interviewer: You think that causes problems?
> Patricia I.: It's better to be a stranger — then they don't, then they don't know what you are or what you can do.... After all, out of school I was Patricia and in school I was Miss I.

In trying to learn how to teach, Patricia asked other teachers for help. 'And those that were my friends', she says, 'would tell me, and those who weren't my friends would tell *on* me.'

> Interviewer: You mean teachers didn't just sit down and talk?
> Patricia I.: No, no, God forbid. You couldn't complain about anything.... You'd get fired.... I had a hard [time] breaking down the people to accept me, the teachers. Which they finally did.
> Interviewer: Because of the divorce?
> Patricia I.: I think that and my religion.

After suspecting one student of stealing money from the school, Patricia 'went to the principal and I asked him what to do about it and he says, "I don't know what you can do." He wouldn't give me any assistance or anything. So I went to the boy's home and told his mother.... They found the money under the bed.'

Patricia tried to sue the school system so that she could get married, but her lawyer pointed out that she would have to marry first and get fired before she could sue. As a result, she and a small group of friends talked one of the former teachers into bringing suit and helped her by paying for the legal fees. This action helped force the school system to eliminate the no-marriage rule.

Compared with the others, Patricia I. based her world on different conceptions of teachers and women. Teachers were to be respected, but not blindly. Authority was to be accepted, but not absolutely. At no time in her narrative do we find any allusion to a mother-like role; nor do we find a warm, comrade-like atmosphere in the school. There is nothing that suggests family images. Patricia clearly saw teaching as a job, and familiarity actually inhibited her. As a divorced woman, Patricia was able to establish her independence. She also showed that her subordinate position did not require submissiveness. Finally, when faced with the obvious violation of her rights, she felt no qualms about bringing in the law.

That Patricia I. provides a very different picture of teachers and women does not invalidate the images portrayed in this study. We must assume that other individuals for their own unique reasons challenged the accepted world presented by the four metaphors. Patricia I. is but one possible other view. These differing views in different communities at different times might form the basis for actions in these societies. And these differing views vying for acceptance in Hamilton might help explain the change in Hamilton schools that most of the retired teachers reported. Patricia I. was an outsider and as such her difference was the exception that proved the rule. She showed that the view shared by the others was not the only one possible, only the one publicly accepted.

The four metaphors described above appear to represent conceptual views of schools, teaching, and self shared by many of the female teachers of Hamilton during the 1930s. Certainly not all of the women teaching then shared all of the metaphorical assumptions, but conversations with these women indicate that those who were part of the mainstream group had to operate against the backdrop of these conceptions. Even so, these metaphors should be considered ideal types that make possible our analyses, rather than concrete entities that existed ontologically. To the extent that these ideal metaphorical types were shared by the teachers, a culture of female teachers existed.

Complex Visions and Unionization

Their conceptions offer complex views that were often in conflict. The contradictions can be found between metaphors, but more importantly contradictions exist within each one also. The subordinate-authority-figure metaphor hints at both a need to carve out a personal realm where power could be exhibited and a recognition that one's power rarely crossed the boundary. The school-as-a-family metaphor suggests that since family was the most legitimate female institution, the school had to resemble a family to make it a legitimate area for women to work. Of course, one's true duty was to one's real family; hence single women rarely gave up the hope of marriage, and married women were not permitted to teach. These first two metaphors support the third — teaching as a natural female avocation. Teaching was loosely called a profession, of course, but it was really not considered much more than a practice for marriage. The women seem to have accepted this image, even though for many it was not practice at all, but a job and important in itself. Finally, the respected status teachers received could only be maintained by having two selves — a public self, who tried to live up to the community expectations, and a private self, who needed to allow her own humanness to develop.

Against these contradictory visions, we can place the dilemmas of unions and professional organizations. One question revolves around whether teachers should organize at all, whereas a second is concerned with what form that organization should take. In the Hamilton of the 1930s, both questions seemed to be easily resolved. The women teachers organized professional organizations that served more as social and mutual support groups than as professional organizations or unions. Among the groups most frequently mentioned were the Classroom Teachers Association, the Federated Women's Clubs, and the American Association of University Women. When asked to describe these organizations, most remembered gathering for luncheons and a speaker. Luncheons, and other such activities, are hardly the kinds of activities that one would expect to find if the teachers were organizing for the protection of salaries and seniority. Why did they not join a union? Why did the professional organizations take the shape that they did?

Consider the first metaphor — the subordinate authority figure. To a person who divided the world into order-givers and order-takers, one's place in the hierarchy is important. Although it is certainly true that these women were at the bottom of the job hierarchy, they were also at the top of the classroom hierarchy. When the male supervisors gave orders, the teacher followed; but in the daily, moment-to-moment activities of the classroom, she remained in control. The teacher just did not feel the power of the administration often enough to create the feeling that she occupied the bottom rung. Instead, she felt in control. Randall Collins (1975), argues that the more one gives orders in the name of an organization, the more one believes in what it stands for. Teachers strongly identified with the organization, since they spent every minute of the working day giving orders in the name of the school. Their middle place in the order-giving hierarchy contradicts the image of a union laborer.

When we consider that the socially expected role of women closely paralleled their professional position, we realize that another of the metaphors, teaching as a natural female avocation, adds more to our understanding. It was almost universally understood that women should follow the orders of men: at home with father; on the job; and in marriage. However, she would have limited authority over the children. Forbidden to think of careers, women saw teaching as an avocation, as a service to the community until it was time to raise her own family. To join a union, or even a professional organization, designed to fight for material and job benefits was to acknowledge the primacy of a career over family obligations. Such action not only admitted personal failure and invited social disapproval, but also was 'unnatural'.

The conception of school as family also worked against unionization among women teachers. During the 1930s, in Hamilton, the elementary school principals were still principal teachers. They were still seen as peers by the other teachers. In fact, the teachers taught in a situation that closely resembled a smoothly running family. Just as the father/husband would leave the family at home in order to take care of 'more important' business, the male supervisory principal and superintendent spent most of their time over-seeing the district office. In both situations, the adult women were left to take care of the children. Accustomed to thinking of the school as their family and those in the schools as their fathers, mothers, sisters, and children, women found it difficult to join a union. How does one strike against one's father or mother and hurt one's children?

Finally, teachers were expected to uphold a moral ideal in their behavior, an ideal defined by the middle class. The relatively high status of teachers conflicted with the low-class status of unions. To join a union would be to forfeit their middle-class status. The material benefits to be gained through a union must be greater than the social status lost. On the other hand, to join a professional organization did not interfere with one's position, unless it started to use the tactics of labor.

What emerges from the conceptualizations of the teachers in this study is a definition of reality that competes with the easy acceptance of organizations that work for the kind of benefits that, as Urban (1982) argues, define the purpose of teachers' unions. In order for organizing to be successful in Hamilton, either external forces would have had to overcome the internal world of teachers, or the metaphors would have had to be altered in such a way as to be more compatible with unions. When Spring (1972) refers to the conservatism of teachers, he may be referring to the hegemonically con-structed subjective reality of teachers described in this chapter. When Tyack (1971) and Urban (1982) argue that teachers were misled or coerced into professional organizations that represented administrative interests, they do teachers a disservice by portraying teachers as incapable of deciding what was in their own best interest given their understanding of the present realities. On the other hand, when historians point out the rise of bureaucratic struc-tures that increased the number of full-time male administrators and widened the distance between the principal and the teachers, they point out conditions that could lead to the dissolution of the school-as-family metaphor. Since the Second World War created a change in the social universe of women, Urban (1982) may be on track when he points to that war as a major influence in the rise of teachers' organizations. Changing social and economic conditions, including population growth and new roles for women, forced the schools to adopt different policies. These included the impersonality of bureaucracy and the hiring of women from other geographic locales. This new generation of teachers developed their own visions of reality under different structural conditions and made possible the unionization that eventually occurred in Hamilton. The interaction of structural changes and teachers' subjective redefinitions made it possible for teachers to think of themselves in ways other than the four metaphors described in this chapter, or at least, in a way that deemphasized them.

In the broad sweep of events, Spring (1972), Tyack (1974), and Urban (1982) may all be accurate in their description of the 1930s. Tyack, Lowe, and Hansot (1984) certainly have moved in the right direction; educational historians must begin to include the visions of ordinary participants. But to understand more fully the human behavior that created the ultimate results, we must unveil the personal worlds of individuals *along with* the explicated forces of social structures as the basis for analysis. Perhaps the stories of the women teachers of Hamilton can help clarify how history is created by the ordinary participant acting within structural constraints. By using the metaphors described in this chapter as guidelines for their lives and their jobs, teachers may have participated in their own powerlessness and been part of broader social movements, while merely acting within their own subjective worlds.

Notes

1 Interestingly Cuban (1984) refers to the 'culture of teachers' as an important, even if partial, explanation of the situationally chosen classroom practices. Of course, Cuban uses culture in the sense of a macrophenomenon structuring the whole teaching community, rather than as a local microphenomenon constructed by the teachers themselves.

2 Cuban (1984) acknowledges the importance of metaphor in influencing the form of classroom practices. He writes, 'There is also another less direct, more subtle use that I see for this study of classroom instruction. Powerful metaphors dominate the thinking of practitioners, policy makers, and scholars on schooling.' (Cuban, 1984, p. 7). Cuban is referring specifically to the metaphor of 'school-as-factory' which dominated the writing of educational policymakers and scholars. As will be seen, the teachers of Hamilton did not seem to use this metaphor.

Since the original publication of this article some people have pointed out that 'the subordinate authority figure', 'the natural female avocation', and the 'dual-self' do not fit the form of a classic metaphor, since these three appear to represent essential rather than figurative comparisons. But one of the basic theses of this article is that the language of the participants indicates articulated meanings, rather than accurate representations of the world, and therefore, can claim to be no more than tropes. I recognize that this extends the ordinary usage of the term 'metaphor', but I believe it captures an important meaning. If you wish you might say that I use the term 'metaphor' metaphorically.

3 All interviews were conducted by the author.

Chapter 11

Teachers and the Workplace

Richard J. Altenbaugh

> I've walked my picket line ...
>
> Mary Helen B.

The adoption of the business efficiency model by school administrators during the early decades of the twentieth century and its ramifications for teachers' work has been well chronicled by educational historians. Yet they have failed to address teachers' responses in any detail. Because of this oversight, it has often been assumed that teachers quietly and passively submitted to their plight. But did they? When faced with similar circumstances during the early part of the century, skilled industrial workers acted in a number of ways: few sabotaged the new management techniques, some simply acquiesced, while still other workers collectively organized to resist the 'degradation' of their work (Braverman, 1974; Montgomery, 1979; Taylor, 1911).

This chapter, relying heavily on oral testimony, attempts to shed some light on the responses by twentieth-century urban, public schoolteachers to the imposition of a corporate structure on the schools, first, by briefly reviewing the general impact of scientific management on teachers' work. Second, it focuses on specific types of teacher responses to the growth of the school bureaucracy through a case-study analysis of Pittsburgh metropolitan schools between 1911 and 1968. Perhaps the generalizations drawn from this local, historical study may be extrapolated and applied to other similar experiences involving teachers' work, past and present.

Scientific Management

The school bureaucracy was well entrenched in urban districts by the latter half of the nineteenth century. Scientific management, however, did not fully manifest itself in the schools until the early twentieth century, the heydey of the efficiency movement. As part of broader Progressive reforms, 'business ideology' became a pervasive element in American culture (Berman, 1983; Hays, 1964; Kaestle, 1974; Katz, 1975; Tyack, 1967a; Tyack and Hansot,

1982). In the flush of enthusiasm over efficiency methods, attempts were made to relate the principles of scientific management to many aspects of American life, Raymond Callahan argues in *Education and the Cult of Efficiency*, including the armed services, the legal profession, the household, and the church. 'It was, therefore, quite natural for Americans, when they thought of reforming the schools, to apply business methods to achieve their ends' (Callahan, 1962, p. 5).

Scientific management basically had a twofold impact on the schools and, ultimately, on the teaching force. First, business-minded school administrators substantially reduced the decision-making role of teachers. Leading proponents of scientific management argued that efficiency would only prevail with the centralization of authority, and the direct supervision of the schooling process by administrators. This segmentation of teachers' work — the separation of conceptualization from execution — resulted in the proletarianization of teaching (Apple and Weiss, 1983; Ozga and Lawn, 1981). When describing the emergence of the field of school administration in 1908, William Estabrook Chancellor (1908, p. v), District of Columbia superintendent of schools, delineated a class clearly apart from teachers:

> . . . a class of school directors, administrators, and supervisors, whose function is management rather than instruction. These school managers see the schools from a point of view different from that of the instructors. The subject is defined not as the instruction and control of individual pupils, but as the organization, maintenance, administration, direction, and supervision of schools.

Chancellor described a division of labor in the schools, as school administrators made the decisions and teachers implemented them.

Second, school administrators relegated all educational considerations to questions of cost. Since teachers' salaries (i.e., labor costs) represented the largest single budget item, school managers sought to make this factor the most efficient. In their efforts to ensure cost-effectiveness, administrators transplanted yet another industrial innovation, the speed-up. 'Clearly, the way to economize was to get more work out of teachers, either by increasing the size of their classes or by increasing the number of classes they taught or both' (Callahan, 1962, p. 233).

Administrators also derived 'objective' methods to measure the efficiency of teacher performance; after all, it was reasoned, 'the measurement of teaching efficiency is related to the efficiency of the school'. The zeal of school superintendents and principals 'to determine the relative value of their teachers' resulted in the use of 'score cards' to 'measure' teacher efficiency. Intellectual capacity, industry, grasp of subject matter, and skill in questioning appeared on the rating scales, of course. But concerns over teacher efficiency occasionally transcended 'academic equipment' (Boyce, 1915, pp. 9–10). School officials also evaluated teachers on personal and moral criteria, such as appearance, integrity, cooperation, and habits. For William C. Bagley, author of *Classroom Management*, 'unquestioned obedience' served as the hallmark of the efficient teacher (1910, pp. 262, 265–66).

Intrusion into the personal lives of teachers, that is, 'personal equipment', encompassed their loyalty and patriotism as well. For example, during the First World War, school administrators, such as Frank Spaulding, then superintendent of the Cleveland schools, developed and implemented loyalty oaths. Spaulding (1955), a leading proponent in the quest to 'promote the efficiency of teachers', likewise conducted loyalty investigations of over fifty cases of alleged 'pro-Germanism' by teachers. As he recalled, 'none were summarily dismissed, but a few were not reappointed' (1955, p. 616). Thus, academic freedom was sometimes sacrificed for purposes of efficiency. As Howard K. Beale wrote in *Are American Teachers Free?* (1936, p. 744), 'Another reason for suppressing freedom is the belief of superintendents, principals, and school boards that it interferes with the efficient conduct of schools. It is the old problem of obtaining efficiency and unity without autocracy.'

School administrators even adopted business nomenclature. Schools became *plants* while school boards assumed the label of the *directorate* and teachers served as the *working force*. Urban districts not only adopted business methods and jargon, but businessmen often came to dominate school board membership as well (Callahan, 1962; Counts, 1927; Curti, 1935; Hays, 1964; Issel, 1970; Nearing, 1917; Plank and Peterson, 1983; Tyack and Hansot, 1982). Hence, the corporate mentality permeated the urban school setting.

What was the result for teachers? No golden age of decision making ever existed for teachers, but, because of the imposition of business methods, they slowly realized that they were blatantly treated as objects. As Jennifer Ozga and Martin Lawn point out, 'This situation is common to all kinds of work but occurred later in the white collar field. Depersonalization of work, where the job not the job holder is important, also meant that control over work tended to be, not personal, but by the application of formal, bureaucratic procedures and rules' (1981, p. 101).

Teachers' Responses

Initially teachers responded, as Callahan (1962, pp. 110, 120–21) generalizes, by 'meekly but resentfully' accepting business measures, such as rating scales, that evaluated their productivity. Some early dissent did exist, however. In large cities, New York and Chicago in particular, strong teacher unions were evident (Tyack and Hansot, 1982, p. 114).

At the 1904 meeting of the National Education Association (NEA), the 'insurgent' Margaret Haley, a former Chicago elementary teacher, representative of the Chicago Teachers' Federation, and later co-founder of the American Federation of Teachers (AFT) railed against '"factorizing education", making the teacher an automation, a mere factory hand, whose duty is to carry out mechanically and unquestionably the ideas and orders of those clothed with the authority of position, and who may or may not know the needs of the children or how to minister to them'. In a speech entitled 'Why Teachers Should Organize', she appealed to teachers to join with labor to fight 'commercialism, which subordinates the worker to the product and the machine'. She continued,

> The essential thing is that the public school teachers recognize the fact that struggle to maintain the efficiency of the schools thru [sic] better conditions for themselves is a part of the same great struggle which the manual workers ... have been making for humanity thru [sic] their efforts to secure living conditions for themselves and their children; and that back of the unfavorable conditions of both is a common cause. (Hoffman, 1981; Reid, 1982, pp. 279–87)

Aaron Gove, who represented the 'old guard', followed Haley to the podium and spoke on the topic 'Limitations of the Superintendent's Authority and of the Teacher's Independence'. [References to Gove's speech can be found in NEA, 1904, pp. 145–57; Reid, 1982, p. 137 n.; Tyack, 1967b, pp. 334–39.] Gove, long-time Superintendent of the Denver Public Schools, alluded to the industrial model of organization as he outlined what he envisioned as the ideal decision-making structure of the 'school corporation'. The ultimate power for policy decisions rested with the board of education while the superintendent possessed the authority 'to execute' these directives. Gove completely objectified the teachers in this process. 'The instruments used for that execution, namely the teachers, are furnished to this executive officer, who is instructed to use them in the performance of his duties, he having the knowledge and skill and ability to select given instruments for given purposes in order to obtain the results.' He not only likened the school hierarchy to the business model, but also paralleled it with the highly stratified military command structure. Giving teachers a share in decision making was anathema to Gove: 'An apparently growing feeling seems to exist — in truth it does exist, especially in one of the large cities of the country [referring, of course, to Haley's union activities in Chicago] — that the public school system be a democratic government. This is a false conception.' Gove reviewed this tendency with alarm, belittled the contributions of unions in general, and condemned teacher unions in particular. 'Concerning neither administration nor educational policies can the teaching body be entrusted with the final decision.'

Gove then shifted from an autocratic tone to a paternalistic mood, invoking the school-as-family image. He perceived teacher unionism as cultivating a confrontational relationship between administrators and teachers — which opposed the imposition of scientific management — and preferred to avoid unionism, because 'contest, conflict, and suspicion, and strife are fatal'. Rather, Gove proffered a decision-making atmosphere that fostered less formalized exchanges: 'as the good daughter talks with the father and mother; as the kindly son participates in the counsels of the home'. Thus, teachers were to be childlike and deferential to their superiors. After all, Gove sardonically concluded, teachers still maintained some autonomy:

The teacher has independence and can have independence like that of the man in the shoe factory who is told tomorrow morning to make a pair of No. 6 boots. The independence of the workman consists in the fact that he can sew four stitches in a minute or forty, can work rapidly or slowly, as he chooses or as he is able, but his dependence is that the boots must be made and made exactly, according to the order both in size and quality and execution.

But, as the record reveals, skilled workers seldom retained even this bit of independence due to the segmentation of their labor. Teachers similarly lacked any fundamental role in the policy-making process. Ironically, Gove's address lent little credence to its title, that is, school administrators appeared to wield 'unlimited authority' while teachers possessed 'no independence'.

Teacher protests were suppressed in more blatant ways as well. In *School and Society*, Felix Arnold (1915, p. 157) concluded an article about the cost and efficiency in school management by ominously proposing that 'those who oppose the [business] scheme most loudly should be selected for closest investigation'. Principals, clerical help, and teachers were all to be under close scrutiny. The protestor was either rated as inefficient and fired, or intimidated into acquiescence and silence. Protests were thus effectively suppressed. Many school districts fired teachers for their union allegiances. The Chicago Board of Education barred teachers from affiliating with national labor. In 1916, the Cleveland School Board released seven female teachers for their association with the AFT. The St. Louis School Board instituted a yellow-dog contract in 1919 that remained in use through 1937. San Francisco and Lancaster, Pennsylvania, fired teachers in 1920 (Eaton, 1975, p. 20; Urban, 1982, p. 157).

Pittsburgh Teachers

Still, the worst fears of school managers were realized; a dialectic was indeed at work. Like their industrial counterparts, teachers responded to changes in the structure of their work in a complexity of ways: Some resisted, through largely individual acts; others passively accepted their lot; and many teachers continued their efforts to organize collectively in order to assert their role in decision making (Gitlin, 1983; Urban, 1982). For those teachers who mounted active opposition, either singly or collectively, their actions were at first covert and, later, overt. These actions centered on the role of the administration, personal matters, political issues, and eventually control of the workplace, that is, the classroom.

What follows is a case-study based on interviews of the experiences and perceptions of Pittsburgh schoolteachers between the 1930s and 1970s. The oral history technique proved valuable because it enabled me to view the school setting from a hitherto little explored perspective: that of the teacher (Clifford, 1975; Montgomery, 1981; Sutherland, 1983; Gitlin, 1983). Between 1981 and 1985, I interviewed thirty-six retired Pittsburgh career teachers, 'systematically' probing common experiences through cues from a semistructured interview guide that was developed, then further refined during the interview process (Bodnar, 1982, p. 3; Grele, 1975; Thompson, 1978).

The mean age of the narrators was 74 and their careers spanned an average of thirty-three years. Of the teachers interviewed, twenty-four were female, and most had taught in the elementary grades. Male teachers, by contrast, taught almost exclusively at the junior or senior high levels. Only 20 per cent of the female teachers eventually became administrators, while a much higher percentage of the male teachers rose to some level of administrative work. A teaching career, according to the narrators, was a mode of social mobility. Most of their parents were working-class, such as miners, foundry workers, and electricians.

Because of increasingly hierarchical relationships between administrators and teachers in Pittsburgh, these teachers expressed feelings of alienation. Teachers often perceived school administrators, at all levels, as remote and detached. Margaret E., a teacher for thirty-eight years, said, 'You hardly had supervisors, but instead of supervisors we had started to call them 'snoopervisors'. I don't know where they hid themselves. The big administrators, you never saw them, you never heard from them. All you read in the newspaper was about how their salaries were going up and up and up and they would appear on TV or something.'[1] One male teacher, who taught for thirty-five years, recalls 'I was lucky if I saw the principal three or four times a year. He just waved passing the door and that was all I'd see of him.' For Helen S., with forty years of experience, there was 'a big gap between the principal and the teachers'.

These experiences and perceptions did not appear surprising since the administrative structure of the Pittsburgh Public Schools followed the same development as other urban school districts. A decentralized ward system originating in 1834 with the passage of the Pennsylvania Common School Law governed the city's schools until 1855. At that point, the ward school boards, while still retaining a modicum of their autonomy, sent representatives, numbering as many as thirty-eight in 1900, to a central board that attempted to bring unity to the Pittsburgh schools. A formal school bureaucracy began to emerge as early as 1867 when George J. Luckey, the principal of a ward school, was appointed as the first school superintendent (McCoy, 1951).

In the spate of reform that permeated the Progressive Era, and typical of reform in other cities, a group of 'concerned citizens', led by the Voters' League and city newspapers, successfully marshalled public support for the School Code of 1911, which profoundly restructured the central board. During its campaign, the Voters' League published a pamphlet complaining bitterly that the existing ward system was corrupt, incompetent, and wasteful. The fact that certain classes of people and occupations maintained membership on the ward boards was particularly galling. The presence of saloonkeepers, bartenders, gamblers, 'thirty-six laborers, including the lowest grade of unskilled millworkers, drivers, watchmen, and waiters' appalled the League. The only remedy was to create 'good boards' that consisted of businessmen and professionals, that is, physicians, dentists, and attorneys (*Bulletin of the Voter's League*, 1911). The Russell Sage Foundation, Chamber of Commerce, and Pittsburgh Teachers Association likewise lent their support. The new administrative structure replaced the ward system with a court-appointed board of public education consisting of fifteen members, instead of the elected board. All power for educational and fiscal policy now emanated from the newly refurbished, centralized board of public education. The *Pittsburgh School Bulletin* (1911, November, pp. 2–7), the official organ of the Pittsburgh Teachers Association, lauded the new centralized board:

> Pittsburg [sic] is assured of the re-organization of its school system, along conservative, upright, and efficient lines. But most important of all, the really essential consideration is well supported in the appointments, the board is composed of representatives of large business and great educational interests, insuring the direction of our schools by men and women of 'intelligence, experience, integrity, and independence'.

Business people and professionals dominated the new board and, given their backgrounds, it was no surprise that they hired a superintendent devoted to the principles of scientific management (Board of Education Handbook, 1916; Issel, 1967; Black, 1972).

Sylvanus L. Heeter, appointed in 1912 as the first Superintendent of the reorganized Pittsburgh School District, had previously served six years as the Superintendent of the St. Paul Public Schools. His tenure in St. Paul, marked by 'efficiency and integrity', left little doubt that he intended to be even more businesslike with the Pittsburgh schools through an emphasis on centralized authority and teacher efficiency. His opening statement in the *First Annual Report* of the Superintendent of the Schools included a complaint about how the prior 'division of responsible authority resulted naturally and inevitably in great diversity of standards, both in school accommodations and teaching efficiency'. The goals of his newly unveiled administrative structure were '1) The organization of the department of instruction and supervision, looking towards a complete and ideal city school system. 2) The purchase of all school supplies systematized and placed under the management of a distinct and fully organized department. 3) The reappointment of a corps of department directors and supervisors.' Heeter further declared that the 'new school system' was 'the concrete expression of the Board of Public Education. Its ideas and ideals in fundamental aims and purposes ... and the development of that system must be wrought out by constructive leadership under the Board's control. Workers may change, but the work continues.' (Pittsburgh Board of Education, *Annual Report*, 1912, pp. 20, 22, 25–26; McCoy, 1951; *Pittsburgh School Bulletin*, 1912, March, p. 14).

Pittsburgh teachers at first demonstrated enthusiastic but naive support for Heeter's plans. Members of the Pittsburgh Teachers Association wrote and performed the following song for him at a welcoming reception, attended by 1,800 guests, at Carnegie Music Hall, on 19 March 1912.

> If we should cause him tribulation
> He will meet our approbation

> If he sings! If he sings! If he sings a melody
> And when he works for standardization
> By enforcing rule and regulation
> We'll sing! We'll sing! We'll sing! the Lorelei

They adapted the lyrics, sung to the tune of 'Dixie', from his inaugural address presented ten days earlier. An article also appeared in the *Pittsburgh School Bulletin*[3] clearly delineating 'The Place of the Teacher in a Rational City School System'.

> Specialization and differentiation of work lies at the base of the extraordinary developments in the manufacturing and commercial world during the past generation. In the place of the old shoemaker has been developed a process of shoe-making in which the shoe passes, through forty different processes before it is ready to wear, each process requiring a kind of work different from every other process. So in the work of the teacher. Formerly the teacher could be, and often was a perfect autocrat in her school.

She no longer was an autocrat, but now 'in our cities the teacher has come to be but one element in the system of schools'. This system, of course, required supervision and coordination of 'the work of all teachers' (*Pittsburgh School Bulletin*, 1912 April).

Heeter's successors followed suit. Summarizing the first year under the new School Code, Superintendent William M. Davidson waxed eloquent about the newly 'unified and centralized school system' that had introduced 'standardization': 'At the close of the first year the school organization was practically complete, the business administration was well established and recognized as efficient. There was, moreover, a large body of trained and earnest school workers.... Standards of teaching efficiency have been adopted.' Subsequent superintendents merely perfected the administrative structure. By 1916, the office configuration of the Superintendent of Schools included an executive secretary, a clerk, and two stenographers. Eight associate superintendents worked at the next lowest level of the hierarchy, with ten directors of special instruction managing such curriculum areas as industrial training, kindergarten, hygiene, music, and art, directly below them. Five departments and their staffs followed, overseeing such areas as buildings, supplies, legal matters, and the collection and disbursement of revenue. By 1925, the basic structure and number of departments had remained the same under Superintendent Davidson, but the number of people employed in these departments had grown dramatically. In 1928, a special, nonpartisan commission applauded the management of the Pittsburgh school system for its leadership, quality, and efficiency (Pittsburgh Board of Education, *Annual Report*, 1913, pp. 20–21, 1916, 1925; Black, 1972).

The administrative structure continued to grow, both vertically and horizontally, in the decades that followed, and subsequent commissions continued to heap praise on the management of the Pittsburgh schools. The number of departments as well as the number of supervisors, directors, and staff had ballooned by 1935, under the superintendency of Ben G. Graham, to include five departments and sixteen areas of supervision. In 1945, Superintendent Earl A. Dimmick headed an administrative system that consisted of an expanded department of secretary of the board, namely the accounting department, division of plant operation and maintenance, department of supplies, the legal department, the department of school controller, and the department of school treasurer, as well as an enlarged department of education that housed (fifteen) separate subdepartments. This administrative organization continued to grow, under Dimmick's direction, until 1955, when it encompassed a department of business, with (seven) subdepartments; a department of education, with (twelve) 'sections'; and six other major divisions overseeing such areas as curriculum development and research, extension education, guidance, personnel, public relations, and health services. By 1967, Superintendent Sydney P. Marland supervised a highly stratified authority structure: seventeen different departments or offices existed, many with several subdivisions, that controlled all of the district's major functions. The department of curriculum and instruction housed eight separate divisions alone, while the office of school services had five subdivisions that were further fragmented (Pittsburgh Board of Education, *Annual Report*, 1935–1936, 1945–1946, 1954–1955, 1966–1967).

However, many teachers gradually began to resent the usurpation of their decision-making role, particularly the standardization of curricula and texts. This phenomenon reflected an attempt in the industrial sector, *vis-à-vis* scientific management, to direct and standardize all segments of the production process (Gordon, Edwards, and Reich, 1982; Schatz, 1984). When asked who was responsible for the introduction of a new, and extremely difficult, math curriculum into her school, a female teacher responded, 'Not the teachers. I don't know. I just imagined it was the administration and the building principals. We [the teachers] were just told what to do.' Or, Helen S. recollects that 'I didn't like the English book that I had, but there was nothing I could do about it. The reading book was selected by a committee. We [the teachers] really didn't have much to say about it.'

School administrators prescribed class size as well. Margaret E.'s first elementary-level classroom in 1934 contained fifty-four students; her class appeared to be 'typical.' Another teacher, Helen S., describes her successful protest over large high school classes in the 1930s: 'I remember one time I had an English class that had sixty-five (students) and the principal walked in. He said, "Do you have room for six more?" I said, "Mr. _____, I don't have room for the principal." You know, he never came to supervise me after that.'

The Pittsburgh school bureaucracy not only dominated the policy-making process, but also attempted to regulate the personal conduct and political perspectives of its employees. Many teachers resisted these intrusions into their private lives. Until 1937, with the passage of the state tenure law, the Pittsburgh School Board fired female teachers who married. Yet, through collective collusion, numerous female teachers had already subverted this rule for many years. According to Margaret E.,

Once you married you had to leave teaching, but there were some married undercover. A girlfriend of mine, she went on teaching two years without them [the administrators] knowing. She lived quite close to where she lived before. You know, rooms at home. They never knew whether she was going home or ... and there were one or two others that I suspect that ... they were pretty shrewd about covering it up.

Madeline S. also remembers a married teacher at her school. 'We all knew [she laughs] that she was living with this man and we hoped she was married. Luckily, she didn't get pregnant.' More important, Madeline S. provides valuable insight into teacher attitudes toward this rule as well as the means by which they circumvented it. 'There weren't too many of them, but the ones that wanted to marry that was their business and not the school board's. Certainly, I wasn't the one who was going to "snitch" and neither did anybody else.'

In response to McCarthyism and the Red scare, the Pennsylvania legislature in 1952 passed a law mandating that all public employees swear allegiance to the constitutions of the United States and Pennsylvania and affirm that they were not a member of any organization advocating the overthrow of either government (Black, 1972, pp. 201–2). Academic freedom as well as the individual rights of teachers, which had always been the sacrificial lamb of efficiency-minded school administrators, again became expendable. (Beale, 1936, p. 714; Violas, 1971). Although they sometimes felt indignant, teachers were required to take loyalty oaths. All of the teachers I interviewed complied, but some, like Helen D., lodged protests:

We were all required a loath of loyalty [she laughs] ... an oath of loyalty. I loathed it. I took it under duress and I resented it for this reason. I had just spent three years in the Navy and I felt that it was self-evident that I was a loyal American citizen. I had taken an oath when I joined the armed services. I thought it was an insult.... It was a fear. Oh yes, it was a great fear, and so people did not talk much about it. I based my opposition to that not so much against McCarthyism, but I felt it was an insult.

When Helen D. consulted with her building principal, the only solace she received was that everyone had to obey. Another female teacher, like Helen D., 'was very much against Mr. McCarthy' and detested politics in the schools. However, they too submitted to taking the oath. A male teacher summarizes the tense emotions experienced by teachers at that time: 'There was a little concern about the loyalty oaths, but everybody signed it whether they wanted to or not. Just to avoid making waves, you signed it. Everybody went along very quietly. They didn't want to get blacklisted'.

Such conformity appeared to be prevalent, as witnessed by another male teacher:

The way it was ... you went in and things were always set up. There was sort of a pattern that you followed. The principal ran the school. Looking back on it, I can honestly say, like a rooster in an hen house; he called the shots. He was like a little god. Not that he was domineering, or very authoritative, but that was the policy. That was the thing that every school went through; the principal called the shots. Of course, at the time you were expected to conform. They would say, the Board of Education, this is, what we're going to do, and this is the policy, and we can make a few changes, but that was it [emphasis]. Gradually, you get into this system, and you sort of followed it. You hate to make a change because it just isn't done. If the principal wanted to do something a little bit different, then he could do it. The teachers, by and large, didn't make any waves.

Nonetheless, changes did begin to occur, especially 'when the teacher organization came.'

Collective teacher protest was manifested through teacher unionism during the 1960s. Although Pittsburgh teachers created Local 400 of the AFT as early as 1935, the Pittsburgh Federation of Teachers (PFT) failed to experience any sustained growth until New York City's United Federation of Teachers won national recognition for its successful 1960 strike. Narrators also point to other factors that stimulated unionism among their peers. Madeline S., although antiunion, notes that a combination of variables, namely, the gradual influx of male teachers, since World War II, teachers' working-class backgrounds, and poor working conditions, prompted interest in teacher unionism:

The men that entered the profession after the war were union-minded. Women in the profession came from a higher social structure usually than the men who entered the profession. I think that had something to do with it. There were a lot of people [teachers] whose fathers, husbands, and so forth were union people. They grew up with it. I can understand how people were driven to unionism. When people forget that they are dealing with human beings, they get into all kinds of problems.

Helen S., active in union recruitment, supported unionization because her father 'always fought for unionization'. Furthermore, teaching was no longer regarded as a profession.

Years ago to be professional you were supposed to serve society and that's it. But now the definition is that you get paid for your work. Now, I have a brother-in-law who is a lawyer, and I have a brother-in-law who is a physician and they say you teachers are not professionals, because they are not self-employed and because they submit to supervision. That's what makes a professional in the eyes of a pure professional. You know, that is really a come down!

As one male teacher active in union activities recalls, many teachers were at first reluctant about organizing a union. 'The thing is, some of the teachers, particularly in our school, this was a radical thing for them [emphasis]. They were conservatives. They didn't want to make any waves, they weren't gonna change.' With him it was different. His working-class background had profoundly shaped his attitude toward his life work, that is, teaching:

> I lived in a neighborhood where people worked in the mills. I always felt that the most dignified person is a guy that carries a lunch bucket and is willing to go on strike. He is willing to withhold his services if he feels that he is being dealt with unfairly. That's really what it's all about. Now, teachers were the same way. I felt that teachers that were being dealt with unfairly ... look [emphasis] withhold your services. One teacher can't do it because they'll replace him, but when you get a group that feels the same way they can't [emphasis] replace the whole group. I'm not really a radical. To make anything effective you got to stop the gears. You really [emphasis] got to shut it down. Tell them you mean business! And that's what happened! We got our [teacher union] organization in.

The allusion to mill machinery, that is 'gears', is a clear working-class reference, and the solution for teachers — the union and the ultimate threat of a strike — parallels mill workers' response to problems in the workplace.

After the run-off election and Board tactics to stall the process, Pittsburgh teachers walked out. For Helen S.,

> It was the winter of 1967–68, something like that. Well, the actual election was this one spring, but we had organized in the union for a long time, even before I joined it, I worked for it. I collected dues. I hounded people [she laughs]. We managed. It was tough; they were hard to crack, but, of course when they found out that this was it, they joined. Of course, some never joined.

Teachers encountered severe picketing conditions, but they received some unexpected support. Again, Helen S. recollects that

> Well, it was cold [she laughs]. It was terribly cold, but, of course, I thought it was easier than the classroom [she laughs]. We would circle the board administration [building] down there and got to look at the scenery that I hadn't seen before [laughing]. I liked that. We remained united. I remember one time we were circling the Board and there came along a retired teacher that had taught music. She had been out [of the schools] for a long time. She was there when I had been a student. And she stood there, and another woman stood there, and watched. And she said, 'Come on. Let's get in this!' And they

came and joined us in the marching! So, you see she showed she was sympathetic.

The police arrested Helen S. and some of her fellow strikers for their strike activities. 'I [laughing] was hauled into jail, but I really wasn't in jail. I was brought before a judge. I forget why. Anyway, we [laughing] were taken before a judge. He was very wise.' He released them.

Not all teachers embraced teacher unionism, of course. Numerous teachers, in fact, abhorred the union, because they perceived it as the source of conflict between school administrators and teachers. They either spoke fondly of the former Pittsburgh Teachers Association, or reminisced, in almost romantic terms, about a less-formalized administrative structure. In either case, even these preferences reflected a desire for a less-centralized authority structure and a share in the decision-making process.

The Pittsburgh Teachers Association originated in April 1904 when 900 teachers assembled to protest their low salaries. Its primary objective, according to its constitution, was 'to promote the welfare of the public schools, and to improve the character of the work therein'. Through petitions, legal suits, and, eventually, lobbying efforts with the state legislature, the Association won salary increases and retirement benefits for teachers. In addition to addressing the economic conditions of teachers, the Association typified progressive education reforms by working to improve instruction in the Pittsburgh schools through the implementation of truancy measures, 'high school entrance examinations', and 'industrial education', and generally 'to increase the role of professional educators in the operation of the school system' by spearheading the restructuring of the school board, which culminated in the Pennsylvania School Code of 1911 (Issel, 1967, pp. 221, 227, 231). Thus, the association played a large part in destroying the former decentralized school system. Association members hoped that the concept of a centralized board would further the role of the educator as an expert.

Ironically, the centralized, hierarchical school structure, so desired by teachers during the Progressive Era, proved to be a nemesis for their successors decades later. The Association continued to negotiate periodic salary increases for teachers, but it also endorsed the Pittsburgh School Board's efforts to cut teachers' salaries during the Great Depression. The Association, in fact, remained a staunch ally of the Board of Public Education (*Pittsburgh School Bulletin*, 1911, November, pp. 3–5; November, 1912, May, 1932, pp. 25–27; December, 1932, p. 99; May–June, 1932, p. 279; September, 1932, p. 323; Issel, 1967). Helen D., who was active in the association, recalls how it functioned:

We got the consensus of opinions of teachers and then presented them through the Teachers Association to the Board of Education for salary increases, for hours, or any matter that might come up. And I think it was quite an effective organization; it was so purely [emphasis] connected with the teachers. There were no administrators that belonged — it was just teachers.

The Association eventually merged with the Pittsburgh Teachers Education Association during the run-off elections against the PFT in 1968. The PFT won and the Pittsburgh Teachers Association passed into oblivion.

Other teachers simply favored a return to a less-centralized administrative structure. The Head Teacher scheme, which predated the building principal concept, was often mentioned in preference, particularly by the older teachers, to existing administrative mechanism. Each building, at one time, had a Head Teacher who worked in the classroom as a regular teacher for a portion of the day, and fulfilled administrative duties for the remainder of it. Since all were perceived as colleagues, the workplace seemed to be devoid of hierarchical relationships; thus, decision making involved more of a shared process. Put another way, these teachers opined that the union not only bred conflict, but it also failed to come to grips with more fundamental problems. More must be done according to Margaret E.: 'They end up giving the teachers more money and sending them back to the schoolroom, but that's not the answer. There's a lot more questions in there that they don't put in the papers that are bothering the teachers.'

Conclusions

Social relations between school administrators and teachers appeared to follow the same pattern as that between industrial management and labor. First, control of the decision-making process was steadily removed from the workplace, that is, the classroom. Administrators became increasingly, and, at times were, invisible, according to the teachers. Second, administrators emphasized teachers' production and efficiency over their human and intellectual interaction with students. Third, the work process became fragmented and standardized with the separation of conception from execution. Many teachers observed that curricula, texts, and class size were all increasingly determined by administrators rather than by teachers.

My interviews show that teachers, working in the schools between the 1930s and 1970s, responded to their dilemma in many of the same ways that skilled industrial workers had acted earlier. To repeat, a few resisted, many acquiesced, and others collectively asserted themselves. The predominantly working-class backgrounds of Pittsburgh teachers certainly influenced their actions. Individual resistance and compliance were conservative responses, to be sure, and reflected the generally conservative nature of teachers (Urban, 1982, p. 22). Covert responses assumed individual as well as collective attempts to subvert external controls over the teachers and the workplace. However, in spite of overt collective actions by teachers, vis-à-vis teacher unions, fundamental hierarchical relationships still persist today. Although teachers now assert more control — through their union — over much of the economic decision making, educational policymaking remains largely in the hands of school administrators.

Notes

I want to thank Michael Apple, Larry Cuban, Maurine Greenwald, Martin Lawn, Don Martin, David Plank, William Thomas, and David Tyack for reading earlier drafts of this manuscript. Their suggestions were most helpful to me, but they are in no way held responsible for the interpretation and conclusions stated in this study. Also, research grants for this study were supplied by the Office of Research and the School of Education (No. 01-031272), University of Pittsburgh.

1 The tapes and transcripts of the interviews eventually will be housed at the Archives of Industrial Society, Hillman Library, University of Pittsburgh. The identities of the narrators are protected in this essay and, in a few cases, total anonymity has been requested by the subjects. The interview procedures were approved by the Human Subjects Committee, School of Education, University of Pittsburgh.
2 The *Pittsburgh School Bulletin* later assumed the title of the *Pittsburgh Teachers Bulletin*.

Part IV

Conclusions

Men make their own history, but they do not
make it just as they please; they do not make
it under circumstances chosen by themselves,
but under circumstances directly encountered, given,
and transmitted from the past.

Karl Marx
The Eighteenth Brumaire of Louis Bonaparte

Chapter 12

Interpretive Method in Historical Research: Ethnohistory Reconsidered

Richard A. Quantz

> It will become evident that my effort is not directed toward furnishing as complete and well documented a picture of the past as is possible. Nor is it oriented toward the refinement or redefinition of period concepts in historical and literary research. Rather, I try to stimulate a more engaging dialogue or critical exchange between past and present in which the interpreter is implicated as historian and as critic.
>
> Dominick LaCapra (1987, p. 2)

Postmodern/poststructural thought permeates every field and has turned social research upside down. This is especially true for historiography, and those of us interested in keeping history engaged in contemporary themes must begin to consider some of the challenges of postmodernism and poststructuralism. We must consider how history can be written given the rejection of transcendental reason and foundational thinking, the decentering of subjectivity and culture, the declaration of the 'end of history', and the textualization of the social. This essay will address some of these themes by telling a story of one person's reflections on his own work and thinking as a result of reading postmodern and poststructural writing. This intellectual journey will attempt to reveal, not only in its content, but also in its form, some of the influences of these new themes. However, this essay does not presume to be another treatise on postmodernism and poststructuralism; rather, it traces the impact of such writing on one person's construction of history and, in so doing, provides new insights into the researching and writing of interpretive history. (For excellent discussions of postmodernism and poststructuralism, see Foster, 1983; Harland, 1987; LaCapra, 1987; Nicholson, 1990; Ross, 1988; for an excellent example of postmodernism in education see Boston University, 1988.)

In 1985 I published an oral history titled, 'The Complex Visions of Female Teachers and the Failure of Unionization in the 1930s: An Oral

History' (see chapter 10). I attempted, among other things, to portray a culture of women teachers who had taught in Hamilton, a small city in Ohio, during the Great Depression. My research identified four metaphors which I claimed represented this culture. The four metaphors contradicted each other and, in fact, suffered from internal contradictions. For example, two of the metaphors, 'the subordinate authority figure' and 'the school as a family' suggest contradictions between the need for women teachers to be both subordinate to the authority of male administrators while authorities over children, and to be both a 'mother' to children in school while being prevented from being a real mother outside the school. In exploring this culture I became convinced that it revealed no unitary themes, no central patterns; that culture appeared complex and contradictory. While my empirical findings led me in this direction, I had no theoretical basis for dealing with my findings. I was convinced of my research, but I had difficulty linking it with a clear theoretical statement.

That my theory and my research were not reinforcing each other became clear to me when I was first asked to write this chapter. In July 1987 I finished the first draft of this chapter which I titled, 'Interpretive History and Ethnohistory in Educational Research' (referred to as '1987 Draft' throughout the rest of this text). At the same time, I was also completing work on an article (Quantz and O'Connor, 1988) based on the work of the Bakhtin Circle.[1] What I learned through reading these Russian theorists placed my first draft of this chapter in doubt. But because this piece was supposed to be a reflection on the process I used to research and write an ethnohistory of teachers in Hamilton, Ohio, I convinced myself that I ought to remain true to my thinking at that time and write the essay as if I had never read the Bakhtin Circle, or Foucault, or Derrida. Today I can no longer pretend such ignorance, and I have rewritten this chapter, to incorporate both my thinking in 1987 as to how I carried out my research, and my understanding now of how such research should be considered. In developing both my thinking in 1987 and my thinking now, I hope to reveal not just the intellectual shifts that postmodern/poststructural thinking permits, but to model the reflexivity that such thinking requires. My orientation will draw heavily from the work of the Russian 'Bakhtin Circle', particularly the work of V.N. Volosinov, as well as the work of poststructuralists/postmodernists such as Foucault and Derrida. (See Bakhtin, 1981, 1984a, 1984b; Bakhtin and Medvedev, 1985; Derrida, 1973, 1985; Harland, 1987; also see Derrida, 1973 and 1974; Foucault, 1980; Volosinov, 1973 and 1976).

Poststructuralism/postmodernism might be understood as a continuing dialogue which challenges some of the fundamental assumptions of modern Western thought. Among the challenges to Western tradition important to the writing of this essay is the rejection of foundational thinking and transcendental reason, what Nicholson (1990) has called the 'Gods eye view'. Our academic traditions of scholarship build on the assumption that some standard exists against which all arguments (empirical or analytic) can be measured: that a logic exists that rises above political and moral positioning and that can be used to judge the adequacy of an argument. Poststructural/postmodern writing often argues that such assumptions can no longer be accepted: that all reason is imbued with political and moral positioning and that our scholarship must recognize this.

Besides the rejection of foundational thinking, the rejection of the centered Subject (or unified Self) and, by extension, the centered culture influences this essay. Western tradition builds upon the idea of a unified Self. Whether that unified Self takes the form of the liberal autonomous individual or the Marxist socialist worker, the assumption that an individual has an authentic center which orients the individual's place in the world remains unquestioned. The numerous variations of Freudian psychology, for example, assume that the modern traumatized, alienated person is estranged from the true Self and that psychotherapy can lead to the reintegration of the disintegrated Self. Poststructuralism/postmodernism, however, suggests that the fractured Self is not abnormal and is, in fact, all there can be. Building on an understanding of a decentered Subject leads to reconceptualizing many of the basic assumptions of Western human sciences. For example, the decentered Self, or (in Bakhtin's discourse) the multivoiced Self, forces us to reconsider the idea of a cohesive, coherent, unified culture. With a decentered, multivoiced individual, culture must also be considered decentered and multivoiced. Any attempt to portray it as otherwise imposes a center on a decentered entity and represents the imposition of a political and moral position.

One often finds a third theme in postmodern/poststructural thought which might be called the 'end of history'. As I am using it here, this is a phrase rejecting the idea that history is teleological.[2] That history might be understood as the evolution of culture toward more advanced and better forms of civilization has formed the foundation of both liberal and Marxist thought. While different historians may argue about the directness of the progression and point out regressive moments in our history, they more or less agree that civilization generally advances — the present being a more progressive moment than the past. This sense that history progresses in a linear fashion must be rejected and replaced by a sense that history has 'ended'.

While our present moment cannot be understood as a place on some timeline of history leading toward some end, history can be understood as embedded in the present moment. Through the work of the Bakhtin Circle, we come to understand that while history cannot be portrayed through the eyes of a removed and distant observer, it can be located in the particular and concrete dialogues of participants. Since societies are multivoiced, history can be revealed in the tensions and silences of these dialogues. This sense that history can be found in dialogues highlights a fourth important postmodern/poststructural theme — that social events can be understood as text. Social text, like literary text, is a cultural activity in which human agents construct cultural products that must be read by others. Understanding history as social text allows us to utilize many of the insights of literary theory in our analysis of not only the writing of history but also the historical event itself; or, perhaps more accurately, literary theory blurs the separation between the writing of history and the meaning of historical events. (For a particularly good development of this see LaCapra, 1983, 1985, 1987; White, 1973). These four themes — the rejection of transcendent reason, of the centered Subject, of teleological history, and of the representation of history as text — as well as numerous other insights from the contemporary debates in the human sciences — forces us to reconsider our approaches to historiography. This realization became startlingly clear to me in the process of reflecting and writing on my ethnohistory project. I hope that some of these insights might become clear to others as they follow my struggle to write 'Complex Visions' and this chapter.

R.A.Q.

While editing the final draft of 'Complex Visions', one of the journal editors suggested that I drop any reference to 'complex visions' in the title. Despite the request, 'complex visions' remained, although I must admit that I relied more on intuition than reason to fix on 'complex visions' as the fundamental metaphor for representing the culture of a particular group of women teachers. Certainly the editors had every reason for questioning my use of it, since I did very little to develop it theoretically in my essay. I had not developed it more clearly, because I remained unclear how to do so. While it was evident to me that the culture which I was representing appeared self-contradictory, standard culture theory had not prepared me for the representation of self-contradictory culture. My knowledge in 1984 of cultural theory had taught me to seek unity, and the appearance of contradiction made standard approaches seem inappropriate. I therefore settled on using shared, but contradictory, metaphors as unifying themes, providing cultural unity while allowing for the contradictions which I had read in the transcripts of the interviews. While I lacked a theoretical rationale for what I did, I am still satisfied with the results. By focusing my analysis on metaphors which were intrinsically contradictory, I presented a culture which explained the teachers' near universal opposition to active unions in the 1930s and yet, also illustrated the potential for the reversal of that position, which occurred some years later. Furthermore, by emphasizing the complexity of the teachers' culture through inherently conflicting metaphors, I unwittingly demonstrated two of the important points of poststructural thought: that knowledge is intertwined with discourse, and that cultural and subjective unity are a myth. I must point out, however, in 1984, when I was writing 'Complex Visions' and in 1987, when I was writing the '1987 Draft', I had still not fully grasped these points.

In the '1987 Draft', I was still working with a rather simplistic, even if well accepted, understanding of interpretive research. Here is a quotation from the '1987 Draft' which illustrates this:

> Research which acts on the belief that historical events must be understood as socially constructed by both the historian *and* the

historical actors, we can call 'interpretive history.' Interpretive history attempts to discover the social and personal constructions of the historical participants. It is less interested in objective facts and truth than in participants' definitions of the situation. Interpretive history attempts to determine 'perceived facts' which may or may not be at variance with 'known facts.' Using techniques of psychology, anthropology, ethnography, and history, the interpretive historian attempts to detail the cultural scene from the actors' perspectives. Before such questions as 'Why did an event occur?' or 'How did it occur?' the historian must ask 'How did participants organize their world in common?' or 'What were the cultural assumptions of the group?' Such prior questions must be answered before one can understand the full dynamics of the broader historical questions. This approach rejects the practice of ignoring the teachers' and students' worlds when discussing the history of education. It disclaims the normative assumption that scholars' structures are more valid than those of ordinary people. Rather it argues that the social constructions of historical participants must be described and then laid against a backdrop of structural constraints.

This description of interpretive method borrows language from several epistemological traditions: 'definition of the situation' from symbolic interactionist sociology, 'social construction' from the phenomenological sociology of Peter Berger (Berger and Luckmann, 1967), and 'cultural scenes' from the ethnographic semantics of anthropologist James Spradley (1970) (Spradley and McCreedy, 1972). By ignoring some of the crucial epistemological differences among these traditions and concentrating on some of their commonalities, I was able to claim justification for an alternative research method. Ignoring the epistemological differences may be disconcerting to the philosopher and the philosophically-minded social scientist, but for the active social scientist and historian, their apparent similarities for research methodology usually outweigh any philosophical questions that may arise. While it may be that symbolic interactionism has its roots in American pragmatism, and that phenomenological sociology has its roots in German idealism, and that ethnographic semantics has its roots in the German semantics of Von Humbolt, all of these research traditions reject the positivistic epistemology of Anglo-American empiricism. And while the response may be different for each, all three reject the idea that knowledge corresponds to the empirical referent, that is, they reject the idea that knowledge represents exactly the way the world exists outside of human experience and thought. Given this shared opposition, many researchers are willing to include in their rubric 'interpretive' any method which shows skepticism of history without human agency, of history which acts as if the forces of human action are natural and inevitable. As 'interpretive' historians, these researchers are interested in clarifying the part that human consciousness plays in the active formation of historical events. In other words, as I might have written in 1987, interpretive research seeks the subjective forces in historical action. In order to elaborate further what I was thinking in 1987, I am going to present another quotation from the '1987 Draft'. This section attempts to clarify the concept of subjectivity in interpretive research. Following this lengthy discussion I will attempt to reformulate a concept of subjectivity which is more sensitive to themes of postmodernism and poststructuralism:

Subjectivity and Objectivity in Historical Research
(1987 Draft)

In discussions of research, one often hears reference to 'subjectivity' and 'objectivity.' These two often muddled concepts tend to confuse rather than enlighten. This occurs because the concepts usually refer to the position of the researchers in relation to the reality they attempt to describe. In such usage, 'objectivity' is equated with a correspondence theory of truth: the described reality of 'objective' research purports to correspond exactly to the real world. On the other hand, 'subjective' research interdicts the personal vision of the researcher between the description and the reality. As such, 'subjective' research is believed to be contaminated by researcher and informant bias. When understood in this manner, 'objective' research is clearly better, because it is 'truth' while 'subjective' research is less desirable because it is biased and untrustworthy. But ever since the work of Einstein, Heisenberg, and Planck in the early part of the century and certainly since the work of Kuhn (1970) and Polanyi (1958), many intellectuals realize that a correspondence theory of truth is not possible. In other words, when 'objectivity' and 'subjectivity' are defined as above, 'objectivity' is a myth. When those terms refer to the position of the researcher, no research is objective and all research is subjective.

In order for 'objectivity' and 'subjectivity' to have any useful meaning in social research, they must not refer to the researcher but to those being researched. 'Subjectivity' and 'objectivity' should refer to whether the people being studied are perceived as subjects who are able to influence and partially create their own world or as objects who are primarily at the mercy of the power of the elites or the forces of society or history. Interpretive history acts on the assumption that the people who form the center of attention in the research are *subjects in their world* rather than *objects of the world*, that they act on and *partially create* the reality within which they exist, rather than simply being acted upon by reality beyond their control. Interpretive history attempts to leave behind, temporarily, the organizing principles of the researcher and take on the organizing principles of those being studied. The goal of interpretive historians is to accurately describe the world as their subjects interpreted it before any further analysis can be made. Interpretive history eschews the organizing structures of traditional academic thought when presenting its subjects' worlds. It does not attempt to apply a Marxist, or an anarchist, or a human capitalist, or a functionalist view to the evidence until after the participants' voices have been accurately recorded (unless, of course, one of those conceptual views is the construct used by the subjects themselves). When investigators substitute their own scholarly constructs for the constructs of the historical participants, they assume that historical figures act primarily from external design and that the internal constructs of the participants are less relevant to the understanding of history. Such an assumption must be rejected: historical participants must be treated as subjects who, while living within structural constraints, create social meaning and act on those constructions.

The search for scholarly rigor has often been equated with the reduction of subjectivity, but we must understand that the emphasis on structures and quantifiable variables, while possibly making such research more reliable, does not necessarily make it more valid. The search for objectivity is a misguided ideal because both researchers and historical actors view an historical event from a particular perspective. As Joan Burstyn stated in her History of Education Society Presidential Address, 'History is constructed reality; yet, as historians we often select material and shape our interpretations without self-analysis. We assume that because we were educated to be objective, we undertake our research, analysis, and interpretation in an objective manner.' (Burstyn, 1987 p. 167). But, of course, that assumption is not true. Rather, as Burstyn suggests, history is a story constructed by researchers of a 'play' authored and acted out by the participants. As researchers we must be aware of both the historian's story and the historical participant's 'play.'

Since reality depends on both external and internal contingencies for truth (Hanson, 1979), history should be both subjective and objective; it should portray both the structural constraints and the social constructions. Early educational historians like Cubberley were properly criticized for allowing their own subjective visions to interfere with the interpretation of historical events, but, of course, interpretation has always been, and always will be, an integral part of historiography. What differentiates interpretive history from traditional history is not simply recognizing the need for interpretation on the part of the historian, but recognizing that interpretation is an integral part of all human action. For this reason interpretive historians believe that any historical event is incompletely characterized if it fails to describe the subjective or intersubjective social constructions of historical participants. The potential contribution of modern interpretive history, then, is not interpretation itself, but the careful and detailed description of the interpretive construction of the historical actors. Since description of participants' interpretive constructions is its most unique contribution, historians who pursue interpretive history must be extremely careful to use methods for collection, selection, interpretation, and presentation of evidence as stringent, even if different, as those in traditional history.

Subjectivity and Objectivity Reconsidered

I have repeated this lengthy '1987 Draft' discussion of subjectivity and objectivity in this chapter, because I believe it not only accurately presents my understanding at the time I was developing my own approach to interpretive research, but also because it reveals both the strength and weakness of that earlier formulation. Its strength lies in its deliberate rejection of positivistic and empiricist notions of truth, while its weakness lies in its rather naive and simplistic reconceptualization of objectivity and subjectivity.

A notion of the subject as presented in the last section makes the assumption that a subject capable of some unified understanding exists in the historical event. If we are seeking the 'subjective' view as outlined above, then we must assume that there is a conscious or cultural unity from which actors interpret their world. I now reject this assumption. Certainly the phenomenological assumption that there is an experiential presence, which can serve as a unified referent, cannot be accepted any longer, nor can the Humboltian notion that the human psyche is the source of language. Even when these basic principles are understood to be tempered and filtered through cultural transmission, they depend on a unified consciousness in order to make sense. And while the pragmatism of William Peirce has a particular place in the development of symbolic interactionism, it is German idealism filtered through a W.I. Thomas (Thomas and Thomas, 1928) version of G.H. Mead's behaviorism that has had the strongest influence on Blumer (1969) and subsequent symbolic interactionists. If symbolic interactionism had built more on Peirce's 'semiotics' (see Hartshone, Weiss and Burks, 1933–58), it might have developed discourse capable of handling poststructural critiques, but by isolating and emphasizing Thomas' sense of the definition of the situation, symbolic interactionism has been overly dependent on a unified subject capable of constructing a definition. This is so, even if that unification is achieved through social mechanisms as in a Median sense of the social self. (After all, Mead's sense of the generalized other requires there to be a noncontradictory set of relationships for the individual to master.) This dependence on a unified subject and culture has led to a belief that while there may not be an 'objective' historical event, there are unified 'subjective' or 'intersubjective' historical actions. This assumption I can no longer accept. While I may still talk about 'consciousness', I now understand this term to refer to, what Volosinov (1973, p. 91; 1976, p. 88) calls, 'behavioral ideology' and that the most appropriate focus for interpretive research is, therefore, not consciousness *per se*, but the utterance in dialogue.

'Any human verbal utterance is an ideological construct in the small', wrote Volosinov (1976, p. 88). Since any utterance is ideological and because inward and outward speech permeates behavior, Volosinov argues, we should think of such speech as 'behavioral ideology'. Volosinov (1973, p. 91) replaces our sense of consciousness (whether Freudian or phenomenological) with a very social notion of speech.

> We shall use the term *behavioral ideology* for the whole aggregate of life experiences and the outward expressions directly connected with it. Behavioral ideology is that atmosphere of unsystematized and unfixed inner and outer speech which endows our every instance of behavior and action and our every 'conscious' state with meaning.... In the present context, we should prefer to avoid the word 'psychology', since we are concerned exclusively with the content of the psyche and the consciousness. That content is ideological through and through, determined not by individual, organismic (biological or physiological) factors, but by factors of a purely sociological character. The individual, organismic factor is completely irrelevant to an understanding of the basic creative and living lineaments of the content of consciousness.

When speaking of subjectivity, then, we must realize that we are addressing a particular form of ideology. With this understanding we must realize that while historical participants may, in fact, 'construct' unique 'definitions of the situation', such 'constructions' and 'definitions' are intimately tied to political positioning; while there may be a 'social consciousness' or 'intersubjective reality', we must understand such things in terms of peoples' positions in what Cleo Cherryholmes (1988) calls 'power arrangements'. 'Subjectivity' in research must be understood to be a very special version of ideological critique which retells, elaborates, and positions inward and outward speech in particular historical dialogues.

When researchers re-present the cultural consciousness of a particular historical event, such representations ought to be critiques which place the utterances in dialogue and the dialogues in social, economic, and political context. Certainly this is what I was trying to do in 'Complex Visions'. By concentrating more on the rhetoric of my informants' narratives and less on the content of those stories, I fixed the particular utterances in the larger dialogues of the period, and by discussing these metaphors in terms of unionization, I placed the particular dialogues into the discursive practices of educational politics. In retrospect, the elaboration of the hidden power arrangements imbedded in these discursive practices would have vastly improved the text. When 'subjectivity' is understood in this manner, then it becomes both more complex and intellectually defensible. No longer is it based on the apparent commonalities of three divergent epistemologies.

While Volosinov (1973, 1976) helps me understand subjectivity to be a form of textual analysis, he is much less helpful in clarifying objectivity. For Volosinov (writing in Stalinist Russia), political structures simply meant class conflict. Today such monocausal assumptions of power structures must be replaced with a model of power which is fractured and particular. But even with a new sense of multiple power structures, I am forced to recognize that the scholars' text (in which we posit structure) is another form of utterance.

As a researcher I narrate my own story of structured ideology. In other words, 'objectivity' can mean no more than research guided and molded by an abstract model of the scholars' own discourses. While I do not want to privilege discourse over political positioning in the lives of historical participants, one should never confuse a historian's renditions of people's lives with the social encounters themselves. As historians and social researchers our published research must always be understood as text. As such, any claim to 'objectivity' must be understood as a rhetorical claim rather than an epistemological claim, and as a rhetorical claim, 'objectivity' can best be read as a form of ideological critique in which the original utterance (almost all historical evidence is in fact also an utterance) is abstracted out of context and reconstituted as part of the academic dialogue.

When stated this way, both 'objectivity'and 'subjectivity' can be understood to be 'reported speech' within an academic utterance. As such they can be analyzed rhetorically to gain greater understanding of their narrative power. If 'subjectivity' is reported speech placed into a particular, concrete context, and 'objectivity' is reported speech placed into an abstract context, then 'subjectivity' and 'objectivity' likely serve different narrative functions. While this essay will not attempt to catalogue the various possibilities of reported speech in narrative, a few examples may help clarify my point.

Clifford Geertz (1988) has written extensively on the narrative device he calls 'being there'. Geertz argues that one of the most crucial aspects of good ethnography is the ability to convince the reader that the ethnographer was in fact 'there' in the village among the natives. Geertz argues that the personal narrative which relates the transition from the ordinary world to the exotic world of the native is an essential ethnographic device. Mary Louise Pratt (1986) elaborates on the manner in which personal narrative has become a convention of ethnographic writing, but while Pratt agrees that personal narrative may be a necessary rhetorical device, she points out that objective description is equally essential to the ethnographic genre, because personal narrative without objective description mimics the travel books and, therefore, appears to be unscientific. Geertz calls this textual move 'being here'. I believe that in 'Complex Visions' you can find this same juxtaposing of descriptive narrative and objective description although in an altered form.

Since 'Complex Visions' is a historical writing, and I, the author, had not actually 'been there' in Hamilton teaching school during the 1930s, it is impossible for me to write a personal narrative in the form that Geertz (1988) and Pratt (1986) have in mind. The purpose of personal narrative is to convince the reader that the teller of the story actually was there, and therefore, the tale is to be believed. In my case, the task was to convince the reader that the informants had in fact 'been there', so that their tale as retold in my text could be believed. This was partially accomplished by the following anecdote from 'Complex Visions.'

As children, Linda and her friends used to walk to elementary school together. They would laugh and talk on their way to school staying on the west side of the street and keeping one eye out for Miss K., their second grade teacher. Miss K., who usually walked the mile from her home to Taylor School on the east side of Pleasant Avenue, occasionally would start out on the west side. When she did, Linda and her friends crossed the street to the other side. That way they would not have to speak to her. 'We just admired her so', Linda said, 'we were afraid we'd say something we shouldn't.'

There is only a brief direct quotation. The rest is indirect reported speech. This technique helps to emphasize the particularity of Hamilton by elaborating the physical setting of children walking to school, and in doing so, helps convey the necessary sense that the informant was a concrete participant in the historical event, rather than just an abstract figure to be manipulated by the academic discourse of the historian. But to rely solely on such elaborated indirect reported speech might convey too much intrusion of the researcher into the story, and so most of the reported speech is direct quotation taken out of the particular physical environment of the past and placed within the abstract academic context of the historian's text. This use of direct reported speech confirms the 'objectivity' and the 'validity' of the historian's analysis. In shifting from the particular environmental context of the participants to the abstracted academic context of the historian, we can move from a rhetoric that makes the story believable by 'bringing it alive' to a rhetoric that makes the story believable by making it 'scientific'. In this way the article is able to claim 'scientific' authority and 'eye-witness' authority at the same time.

But, of course, oral history has a particular problem in establishing the 'objectivity' of the personal anecdotes even if they are written as direct reported speech. While the historian can avoid the charge of bias by relying primarily on direct reported speech, the informants' biases and mismemories still threaten the validity of the historian's conclusions. This problem is overcome in 'Complex Visions' by paying less attention to the content of the quotations, and concentrating instead on the metaphors used by the informants in telling their anecdotes. Consequently, I make a 'scientific' claim that whatever the 'real' world was like, it was through these shared metaphors that many of the teachers 'defined the situation'. By combining a form of indirect reported speech and direct reported speech, I was able to establish both the credibility of the informants as having 'been there', while legitimizing my own 'scientific' analysis of their speech. These rhetorical devices help make my own narrative convincing.

But merely presenting interpretive evidence is not enough. In the world of academic history we must place this reported speech of historical participants within the dialogue of historians. In this way, the reported speech, while pointing to concrete events, is abstracted out of the particular of past dialogues and placed within a particular dialogue of the present. In 'Complex Visions' this was accomplished by placing the interpreted culture of teachers of the 1930s into a 1980s dialogue about unionization. In this way, the particular culture of the past becomes abstracted out of the past and reconstituted as a particular culture of present academia. The article of the historian is itself an utterance in a dialogue; that dialogue is well removed from the dialogue of the original historical event. While this can be said for all forms of history, in oral history things are further complicated, because the utterance, that is to be used as evidence, is actually a part of a particular dialogue well removed from both the original historic event 'and the academic dialogues of the historian. The oral historian collects evidence by engaging in a dialogue with a historical participant, but in the present. Thus, oral evidence introduces another level of reported speech, and these utterances work to serve more than one dialogue. There are multiple contexts within which the utterance can be located: the original historical dialogue, the reported speech within the informant interview, and reported speech of the reported speech of the informant interview in the historical essay. These multiple contexts suggest that we need to pay more attention to rhetoric in historical writing than has been done in the past. Certainly we need to elaborate the place of rhetoric and grammar in our methods for conducting interpretive research and for writing up our investigations (See White, 1973).

I have spent considerable time in this essay reflecting on 'subjectivity' and 'objectivity' in historical research in order to elaborate an understanding of 'interpretive', which incorporates some of the insights of those who are associated with poststructural and postmodern discourse. By refocusing our understanding on the discursive aspects of historical evidence we will be able to participate in the best of present scholarly dialogue. Furthermore, I believe, if we build our discursive approach around the philosophy of the Bahktin Circle, as well as the work of poststructuralists and postmodernists, we will be able to avoid the intellectual and reactionary anarchy that is so often found in postmodern writing.

In 1987 my approach to interpretive history centered around a unified sense of consciousness and culture. Today I must acknowledge a multiple and fractured understanding of consciousness and culture. This is easily accomplished through a redefining of consciousness as 'behavioral ideology' and culture as a 'multivoiced dialogue'. Multivoiced dialogue is a concept which suggests that culture should be presented as conflictual dialogue located in historically constrained, asymmetrical power relations (see Quantz and O'Connor, 1988). If interpretive method in historical research attempts to describe the 'subjective forces in historical action' or 'in clarifying the part that human consciousness plays in the active formation of historical events', then we must understand that 'subjectivity' and 'consciousness' are euphemisms for discourse legitimated by particular, concrete discursive networks formed within asymmetrical social, economic, and political structures.

Ethnohistory and Interpretive Method

Interpretive history can be found in many approaches to history, principle among them are are psychohistory, oral history, and ethnohistory. But while these historical approaches often utilize interpretive method, we should not equate psychohistory, ethnohistory, and oral history with interpretive method, because each of these historical approaches can easily avoid interpretive method and they often do. Certainly much oral history is traditional in every aspect except in the initial evidence collection stage. Ethnohistory is often as traditional in its conception of historiography as any other approach (for example, see Grant, 1988). And while psychohistory does attempt to recognize the subject in history, most psychohistorians seem to use psychology in the study of history much the same way social historians use sociology, that is, they use modern psychological concepts and impose them on historical figures or societies. For example, Henderson (1975) sees psychohistory as the discovery and confirmation of archetypes of the Jungian collective unconscious. While it is true that historians who use interpretive method do, at some point, place their evidence in a modern discussion, what makes it interpretive is the attempt to clarify the meaning that participants in historical events constructed in order for their actions to make sense through the elaboration of consciousness or culture. Interpretive methods attempt to describe constructs which would be recognizable to the participants of the time period. The better psychohistorians use an interpretive approach to clarify the social meanings constructed by historical participants and eschew the popular use of Freudian or Jungian constructs to interpret past actors' psyches. In education, Finkelstein (1979, p. 2) explains the purpose of psychohistory as 'exploring the meaning of educational environments'. This is the spirit of interpretive history.

There has been much written on psychohistory (DeMause, 1982; Gilmore, 1984; Henderson, 1975; Kren and Rappoport, 1976; Prisco, 1980) and oral history (Allen and Montell, 1981; Curtis *et al.*, 1973; Davis *et al.*, 1977; Evans, 1975; Havlice, 1985; Hoopes, 1979; Sitton *et al.*, 1983; Thompson, 1978), but very little on ethnohistory, especially by historians (Evans-Pritchard, 1961; Finley, 1956; Lantis, 1970; Sapir, 1949; Wallace-Hadrill, 1962). There has been little use of ethnohistory among educational historians (Quantz, 1985 see chapter 10; Grant, 1988) and yet, I believe that ethnohistory could be helpful to interpretive historians.

Ethnohistory is a recent term for a practice which can be found as early as 1916 (Sapir, 1949). As with all new terminology, ethnohistory has not yet developed an agreed-upon definition. Herskovits (1955, p. 473) describes ethnohistory as the 'welding of ethnographic and historical methods.' Lantis (1970, p. 5) identifies two meanings of ethnohistory: (1) 'use of written historical materials in preparing an ethnography ... or use of historical materials to show culture change' and (2) 'use of a people's oral literature in reconstructing their own history'. But whatever the arguments over a precise definition, ethnohistory is a term used primarily by anthropologists to describe techniques used to discover the history of a group's culture. These techniques generally use some combination of archaeology, ethnography, and documentary history. As will become clear, I believe there needs to be a concept of ethnohistory more compatible to the interests of interpretive historians than anthropologists, and in that interest, I suggest that we define *ethnohistory as the interpretive description of cultures in time.*

When members of one culture place their own world view onto another culture, we call it ethnocentrism. When those of one period place their own value and conceptions onto those who lived in the past, they are engaged in what could be termed 'temperocentrism'. Historians attempt to overcome the bias of time by seeking 'objectivity' in their theory and method. Traditionally anthropologists have also sought to eliminate bias by pursuing 'objectivity'. In recent years, however, anthropologists have tried to combat ethnocentrism by presenting a 'subjective' interpretation. The 'subjective' approach attempts to describe the world from the perspective of the people being studied. The 'objective' approach has come to be called 'etic', while the 'subjective' method is known as 'emic'. Although some anthropologists still adhere to either one or the other, most would seem to favor a study which uses both an 'emic' and 'etic' perspective. Goodenough (1970, Ch. 4) seems to argue for an 'emic' method in the collection of evidence and an 'etic' approach in the interpretation of the evidence. As an interpretive method, I believe that ethnohistory should recognize that the division between 'emic' and 'etic' is more of a rhetorical than a logical division, but a rhetorical division which can be utilized effectively in the collection, presentation, and interpretation of evidence. Perhaps the major purpose of ethnohistory is the conscious effort of the ethnohistorian to present a concrete image of the world as defined by the group and placed within a discourse of interest to historians. Ethnohistory should seek to describe the fractured and contradictory cultures of historical participants and ought to do so through techniques which clarify the multivoiced dialogues which help constitute culture.

The idea that culture should be understood as multivoiced dialogues follows from the work of the Bakhtin Circle. A Bakhtinian concept of culture suggests that culture is a complex, multivoiced phenomenon inseparable from historical structures and ideology. The cultural constructions of historical participants, then, cannot be understood to be merely spontaneous and independent constructions of a group of autonomous subjects, but must be seen as representations of political and social consciousness. If culture is understood as the legitimated utterances of social encounters, then culture must be analyzed in terms of particular political relations. Ethnohistory being an interpretive description of cultures in time requires that this description not be isolated from the social, political, and economic structures of the period (Quantz and O'Connor, 1988; Quantz, in Press).

Arguing that culture and consciousness are inseparable from historical structures is not to argue that consciousness and culture are mechanical representations of historical forces. One of the important contributions of postmodern writing is to re-introduce human agency into culture and history. The rejection of a unified subject and culture should not be confused with a rejection of human agency. Far from rejecting agency, postmodern writing tends to celebrate it. In fact, in the hands of some there is a danger that the rejection of a foundation has led them to over-celebrate the openness of human choice. By concentrating on discourse, as defined by the sign, these writers often abstract the social out of the concrete, leaving the impression that meaning is anarchic and unlimited. The Bakhtin Circle, however, by focusing on the utterance in dialogue, never loses sight of material and structural forces even while recognizing the human agent in particular social dialogue. When dialogue is understood to be multivoiced, instead of dialectic or monologic, then the fractured and heteroglossic society requires an agent. Ethnohistory developed from a Bahktinian sense of culture and consciousness can help clarify the meaning that leads human agents to act as they do without separating the agent from historical structure.

Ethnohistory in Education

'Ethno' as a prefix can be used to refer to a study of any cultural group. In a like way ethnohistory is generally used to describe historical study of non-European cultures, but it does not have to be so limited (Finley, 1978; Wallace-Hadrill, 1962). If educational institutions are seen as cultural systems within a larger society, then they should be able to be studied from an ethnohistorical perspective. Ethnohistory generally concentrates on those groups not represented in traditional political histories. It tends to be interested in those groups of lower status which have less power in the present social order. Keeping within this spirit suggests that ethnohistory in education would concentrate on the culture of students, minority groups, parents, secretaries, and labor groups such as custodians and bus drivers. It might also pay attention to teachers and building administrators, as a low status group within the hierarchy, instead of considering teachers as mere extensions of school boards, politicians, and other social elites.

Ethnohistory, as applied to educational history, might seek a concrete image of the constructed world of these teachers, students, parents, secretaries, youth leaders, and school dropouts. It should try to recreate a complex world built on the personal visions of the participants. How did students talk about school? How did they view their teachers? What was it like to be young, female, and a school teacher? What was the classroom like? Is it talked about as cold and austere, or warm and friendly? What did different parents say was going on in the local schools? These kinds of questions do not seek the 'truth' but rather the discourse through which participants acted. It seeks multiple voices rather than one.

To accomplish this undertaking, ethnohistorians combine techniques of history and ethnography. From history, they take the methods developed for oral and documentary sources; from ethnography, they utilize techniques around informant interviewing and cultural analysis. The basic techniques of locating people to interview, of recording the interviews, and of gaining personal releases are basically the same, whether one is doing oral collection as part of a traditional or an interpretive history. The appropriate use of standard oral history methods are presented in several good, standard works (See especially Curtis *et al.*, 1973; Hoopes, 1979). But while traditional practices of oral history can be used in any interpretive approach, there are some methods particular to ethnohistory which can help clarify and elaborate cultural constructions. These methods differ from those of most oral history

approaches primarily in the interview procedures and the cultivation of informants. These two points, interview procedures and informants, need to be
further developed.

Interview Procedures

Perhaps the real contribution of ethnography to the interpretive historian is
the attitude which drives the interview. If one reads ethnography, one begins
to concentrate on the interpretive aspects of phenomena which provide meaning and value to participants. This 'emic' approach requires the interviewer to
eliminate as much as possible the urge to apply external structure to the
interview. Instead of a formal interview schedule which has all of the questions planned ahead of time, the interpretive interview must be a process
which is flexible enough to follow the lead of the interviewee while not losing
sight of the object. The typical interview might begin with what Spradley and
McCurdy (1972) call the 'grand tour' question. Such questions are designed to
be directive enough to require concrete and precise responses, yet open
enough to allow the interviewee to go in any direction. In my Hamilton oral
history project, after obtaining the preliminary demographic information
necessary, I often began with a 'grand tour' question like 'Lead me through a
typical day teaching fifth grade at Jefferson', or 'Tell me what it was like to be
a teacher in Hamilton during the Great Depression'. Such questions allow the
interviewees to go in any direction, to recall anything they think might be
important or amusing. On the basis of their usually very lengthy response to
this initial question, the interviewer should have a wealth of material to begin
more specific follow-up questioning. In this way, a typical interview has been
structured by the interviewee, but is clarified by the follow-up questioning of
the interviewer. Later, after exploring the world as the interviewee presents it,
the interviewer can introduce memory-jogs like pictures, or stories that others
have told, or events that historical documents have recorded. With the original conversation as the foundation for the discussion, these new explorations
are more likely to take on the perspective and language of the interviewee
than if the interview starts off with the interviewer setting the agenda and
organizing the discourse.

To conduct an interpretive interview successfully, the interviewer should
be careful not to assume understanding of anything. The interviewer should
assume (which should not imply 'pretend') he/she is ignorant of even the
simplest ideas and terms requiring the interviewee to explain meanings, relationships, and categories. While occasionally this naive approach to interviewing may be mildly embarrassing for the researcher, such techniques are
required if an insider's view is ever to be understood. When the interviewers
rely on their own understandings of concepts and ideas, they become likely to
either misinterpret an interviewee's statement or, even more damaging, influence the information volunteered because, like all story-tellers, the interviewees often try to tailor their stories to please their audience.

Informants

The pursuit of the social construction of an historical event requires an understanding of the culture of the participants. What is crucial to understanding any culture is to recognize that which is taken for granted by the members of the group and comes to organize their world. This world-taken-for-granted is usually very difficult for a member to recognize, because it is literally the assumed ordering of the world and is rarely consciously analyzed. In other words, what the ethnohistorian is interested in is so ordinary, that the interviewee often does not recognize that it is important, and that the researcher does not already know it. The member of the group assumes that everybody sees the world in this way and, consequently, will not point such ideas out. Since culture is understood as 'multivoiced dialogue', then the study of the rhetoric and grammar of the informants' anecdotes allows insight into the discursive patterning of the historical actions. While I am not claiming that the discursive patterning in the anecdotes of historical participants is sufficient to explain historical events, it can be a clue to the way in which historical actors constructed their consciousness and, therefore, chose to act.

Interpretive method in ethnohistory promises to provide historians with an approach to 'critique' or 'deconstruct' the 'discursive practices' of the past. It allows us to participate in the active dialogues of present-day social and cultural researchers. And it provides a mechanism for reconstructing the multiple, contradictory, and conflictual cultures of the past in such a manner as to reveal new stories of struggle and complacency, of resistance and acceptance, of domination and mindlessness that characterize the life of teachers, students, and other school participants in our past.

Notes

1 The Bakhtin Circle was a group of Russian intellectuals whose work was primarily although not solely produced during the Stalinist period in the Soviet Union. Because of the heavy censorship and real danger for intellectuals during this period, authorship of the work of these individuals is in dispute. Many scholars claim all of the work is largely that of M.M. Bakhtin. Others claim that other works are truly written by the named authors. Regardless of who the actual writers were the works of M.M. Bakhtin, P.N. Medvedev, and V.N. Volosinov can be collectively referred to as the Bakhtin Circle.
2 With the rapid political changes in Eastern Europe some conservatives have begun to talk about 'the end of history' in anticipation of some final capitalistic hegemony (see Giroux, in press). I am *not* using the phrase in this way.

Chapter 13

The History of Teaching:
A Social History of Schooling

Richard J. Altenbaugh

In the end, the quality of American education can be no greater than the dignity we assign to teaching.

Carnegie Foundation (1988)

Social history represents 'both a set of topics and an approach'. In the former, social history treats two broad subject areas that conventional history has largely ignored. 'First, it deals with ordinary people rather than the elite.' 'Common folk' possess a 'vibrant past and contribute to larger historical processes' (Stearns, 1983, p. 4). The beauty of social history therefore lies in how it alters the priorities of the historical record: 'The great and the famous cause less than we used to think, while ordinary people cause more.' (Stearns, 1983, p. 6). Until recently these people appeared to be 'relatively inarticulate', with few speaking or writing 'as a matter of public record'; they remained invisible. Second, social history uncovers and analyzes 'ordinary activities, institutions, and modes of thought' (Stearns, 1983, pp. 4, 5). In this regard, the American brand of social history, more than its French or British counterparts, has tapped sociological concepts like gender, race, class, and ethnicity (Zunz, 1985, p. 59). Thus, social history seeks to recapture the culture of the majority of the people, not just of leaders and aristocrats, studies how they created it, and investigates its impact.

As an approach, social history stresses the 'unfolding of a process' rather than emphasizing conventional events — unless, of course, an event represents the cause or effect of a profound change in the way people behave. Consequently, social history, unlike its conventional counterpart, usually follows no prescribed periodization, that is, it focuses solely on change, overlapping traditional chronological periods or defying them altogether. Social history also dwells on 'individuals as illustrations of large groupings or trends'. Finally, most social history efforts tend to concentrate on local or regional studies rather than national ones (Stearns, 1983, pp. 6, 7). This trait may invite criticism from historians who promote synthesis, but as the late Herbert G. Gutman asserted: 'Social history is local history but local history in a larger context that permits the careful examination of grand and sweeping hypotheses' (1977, pp. 258–259). This linkage to wider social phenomena enhances its significance and generalizability, allowing social history to avoid the label of 'antiquarianism' (Zunz, 1985, p. 60).

As a result, social history has deepened and enriched the context of American history. In some cases, its findings have challenged conventional generalizations while, in other cases, they have generated new interpretations. As Peter Stearns (1983, p. 13) concludes: 'At its best, and for those people for whom a historical approach aids understanding, social history's continuing victory depends above all on its contribution to some sense of why our lives and our society are the way they are.'

The social history approach could not be accommodated without novel research techniques. Quantitative methods have been usually associated with social history, but 'social history is not quantitative history, and vice versa' (Stearns, 1983, p. 8). Rather, social historians rely on a variety of techniques.

Every form of record became a legitimate source of evidence if it offered the potential for a fresh vantage point on the world. This approach to history from the bottom up was motivated by a real need to uncover the concerns of everyday life that had hitherto been neglected. The interest in new sources of evidence is also a reflection of the pronounced populist bias of new social history, the feeling that ordinary people are responsible for their own history. Men, women, and children replaced abstractions. (Zunz, 1985, p. 58)

The formerly inarticulate speak to us through their diaries, autobiographies, photographs, and oral histories. Life history, a derivative of oral history, facilitates an analysis of micro- and macro-level interaction: 'In studying a life-history one is forced to consider its historical context and the dialectical relationship between self and society.' (Sikes, Meason, and Woods, 1985, p. 14). Ivor Goodson (1980–81, p. 74) clarifies the relationship between method and social history: 'Through the life history, we gain insight into individuals coming to terms with imperatives in the social structure.... From the collection of life histories, we discern what is general within a range of individual studies; links are thereby made with macro theories but from a base that is clearly grounded within personal biography.' This leads us to the next logical step: What does this study of the social history of teaching tell us about the educational past? and, How does it provide insight into the way we view schooling today?

Although the Whig interpretation of education received sharp criticism some three decades ago (Bailyn, 1960; Cremin, 1965), few historians since have treated the experiences of those the schools did not serve: 'its dropouts rather than its valedictorian, its teachers rather than its superintendent' (Grumet, 1988, p. 59). This volume, a modest social history, represents only a beginning, a mere fragment of a much larger picture. Nevertheless, it reveals extreme complexity and thick texture. Teachers continuously coped with the interaction of at least two variables, gender and social class, and at times a third factor, race or ethnicity. Further, teachers' professional and personal lives varied greatly, depending on context. Where a teacher resided and taught, in a small town or large city, in the rural Southwest or the urban Northeast, shaped their realities and responses.

In order to break the grip of the institutional approach, different or new theoretical frameworks need to be considered, practiced, and debated. 'Theory', Bryan Palmer persuasively argues, 'is the *only* way to enhance a history of lived experience, extending understanding of the past in ways that can address human activity with an appreciation of the confinements that were not necessarily perceived and fully comprehended by men and women caught within them' (1990, p. 94). Educational historians must employ a cogent theory, whether Weberian, emphasizing status, or Marxian, focusing on class, or poststructuralism/postmodernism, relying on discourse.

The latter two offer great promise. A Marxist perspective, as Ozga and Lawn (1981) stress, certainly must be entertained. Teaching has become so proletarianized that to view it otherwise misses a potentially fruitful avenue of research. Teachers are workers, reflecting the social relation of production. During the nineteenth century, Marx (1869, p. 509) observed that the private 'schoolmaster' who 'has laid out his capital in a teaching factory, instead of a sausage factory, does not alter the relation'. Only now have sociologists and historians begun to extrapolate this idea to an analysis of public school teachers (Apple, 1986; Ozga and Lawn, 1981).

Quantz, in Chapter 12, points to postmodernism/poststructuralism, giving a new meaning to the teacher's voice. Grumet (1988) has juxtaposed this onto a feminist framework, reaping provocative results and promising potential. The teacher's voice is indeed powerful because it provides a valuable perspective; it translates the teacher's historical role and enriches the historical context of schooling and teaching. The teacher's voice reveals human agency, expressed in many, and at times seemingly contradictory, ways.

Yet we must not fall victim, as Palmer points out, to simply identifying the 'word' as power: 'In that analytic search for meaning historians have recently been drawn to literary theory, and poststructuralist thought' (1990, p. xii). He warns, however 'Critical theory is no substitute for historical materialism; language is not life' (1990, p. xiv). We must certainly recognize the significance of discourse, and as the debate continues it should prove to be thought-provoking, ground-breaking, and productive (see the debates in 'A Round Table', 1988, and *AHR* Forum, 1989): 'For before critical theory reaches the point of the reification of language, it contains insights and guides capable of opening new doors of understanding to historians committed to a materialism that recognizes the need for a rigorous reading of documents and texts/contexts' (Palmer, 1990, p. 189).

Theory is important because the social history approach and qualitative research methods often produce fractured realities, seemingly defying easy generalizations. In this study, gender, community, and the notion of work all contributed to many permutations, confronting conventional history as well as baffling policy makers. As David Tyack (1989, p. 419) comments on Elsbree's 1939 classic: 'Its coherence came from a unified but incomplete and problematic concept of professionalism. A multiplicity of voices are now heard where once [a] few spoke for the many. But it is not idle to hope that a new and complex history, focused on teachers and their work and their *own* needs and aspirations, could interpret their world, and inform policy.'

Recent reform reports have expressed alarm that teaching has slipped precipitously from the 'immortal profession', celebrating 'the joys of teaching and learning' (Highet, 1976), to the 'imperiled profession', bewailing its 'symptoms of sickness' (Duke, 1984). From the histories presented in this collection, such simplistic positive or negative generalizations appear not only inaccurate but inappropriate. Teaching is not, nor has it ever been, immortal or imperiled; the former represents the product of romantic folklore, while the latter reflects a shallow hysteria, rather than the result of in-depth historical analysis. We know that teaching has been (and can still be) liberating as well as inhibiting for women, men, and racial and ethnic minorities. The community has always intruded in the classroom, usually to the detriment of the instructor. The teaching occupation encompassed more than just the classroom, affecting teachers' personal lives and, in many cases, their families in profound ways. And teachers' work has experienced profound, dramatic, and historical change during this century. Through it all, teachers have responded in a variety of ways, helping to shape the schools, though not always asked to do so.

This has become patently clear in the current school reform movement. In 1988, after five years of reform efforts, the Carnegie Foundation conducted a nationwide survey of 13,500 teachers 'to find out how they feel about school reform' (p. 1). Twenty per cent of them awarded a 'D' or 'F' grade; in all, 70 per cent 'said the national push for school reform' deserves a 'C' or less (p. 1). The report puzzled over these disturbing findings: 'many teachers have remained despirited, confronted with working conditions that have left them more responsible, but less empowered. They are concerned about loss of status, bureaucratic pressures, negative public image, and the lack of recognition and rewards' (p. 11). Fifty per cent of them believed that morale declined substantially during that period. After noting the limitations, if not failures, of this school reform movement, the Carnegie report (p. 11) arrived at these startling conclusions:

> It's time to recognize that whatever is wrong with America's public schools cannot be fixed without the help of those already in the classroom. To talk about recruiting better students into teaching without examining the circumstances that discourage teachers is simply a diversion. . . . In the end, the quality of American education can be no greater than the dignity we assign to teaching.

The chapters in this volume instruct us that these conclusions should not be surprising.

References

ABBOTT, J. (1986) 'Accomplishing "a man's task": Rural women teachers, male culture, and the school inspectorate in turn-of-the-century Ontario", *Ontario History*, 77, 4, (December), pp. 313–30.

ADAMS, D.W. (1988) 'Fundamental considerations: The deep meaning of Native American schooling, 1880–1900', *Harvard Educational Review*, 58, 1, p. 27.

ALICE ROBERTSON COLLECTION, Oklahoma Historical Society, Oklahoma City, OK.

ALLEN, B. and MONTELL, W.L. (1981) *From Memory to History: Using Oral Sources in Local Historical Research*, Nashville, TN, The American Association for State and Local History.

'Allie Smith Collins: Wife, mother, teacher' (1982) *Amarillo Daily News*, 20 November 1982.

ALLMENDINGER, D.F., JR. (1979) 'Mount Holyoke students encounter the need for life-planning, 1837–1850', *History of Education Quarterly*, 4, Spring, pp. 27–46.

ALTENBAUGH, R.J. (1989) 'Teachers, their world, and their work: A review of the ideal of "professional excellence" in school reform reports', in SHEA, C.M., SOLA, P., and KAHANE, E. (Eds) *The New Servants of Power: A Critique of the School Reform Movement of the 1980s*, Westport, CT, Greenwood Press.

'A married teacher's ruse, expectant mother to stay at work to embarrass education board' (1914) *New York Times*, October 13, p. 18, col. 2.

AFT (1919) 'Areas assigned to vice-president, American Federation of Teachers. Miscellaneous' June 3, Charter of Local 89, Atlanta Public School Teachers' Association. Atlanta Education Association Collection (Box 8) Southern Labor Archives, Atlanta, GA, Georgia State University.

'AHR Forum' (1989) *American Historical Review*, 94, 1, pp. 581–653.

Annual Report of the Commissioner of Indian Affairs of the Department of the Interior for the Fiscal Year ended June 30, 1990, (1990) Washington, DC, Government Printing Office.

Annual Report of the Commissioner of Indian Affairs of the Department of the Interior for the Fiscal Year ended June 30, 1907, (1908) Washington, DC, Government Printing Office.

ANONYMOUS SOURCE (1981) Correspondence with Vaughn-Roberson (Summer).

APPLE, M.W. (1983) 'Interpreting teaching: Persons, politics and culture', *Educational Studies*, 14, pp. 112–35.

APPLE, M.W. (1986) *Teachers and Texts: A Political Economy of Class and Gender Relations in Education*, New York, Routledge and Kegan Paul.

APPLE, M.W. and WEIS, L. (Eds) (1983) *Ideology and Practice in Schooling*, Philadelphia, PA, Temple University.

References

'A round table' (1988) *Journal of American History*, **75**, pp. 115–62.

APSTA (1906–1921) 'Minutes of the Atlanta Public School Teachers' Association', Atlanta Education Association Collection (Box 10), Southern Labor Archives, Atlanta, GA, Georgia State University.

'Are there too many women teachers?' (1904, June) *Education Review*, **28**, pp. 98–105.

ARNOLD, F. (1915) 'The unit of supervision, cost and efficiency', *School and Society*, **2**, pp. 1–11.

ARTHUR vs. NYQUIST (1976) *United States District Court, Western-District of New York*, **415** F.Supp. 904 (W.D.N.Y.) 1976.

ASSOCIATION OF MEN TEACHERS AND PRINCIPALS OF NEW YORK CITY (1907) 'Arguments against the White Bill, some resolutions: The economic talley of equalization theory', (A political circular held by the New York City Public Library).

ATLANTA BOARD OF EDUCATION (1916–1922) 'Minutes of the Board', Atlanta, GA, Office of the Board.

ATLANTA CITY COUNCIL (1918) 'Evidence and proceedings before a special committee of five, appointed under a resolution of city council', Atlanta, GA, Office of the Clerk.

Atlanta City Directory (1874, 1877, 1889, 1921, 1922) Various publishers.

ATLANTA PUBLIC SCHOOLS (1891, 1899, 1907, 1909) *Personnel Directories*, Office of the School System Historian/Archivist.

BAGLEY, W.C. (1910) *Classroom Management*, New York, NY, MacMillian.

BAILEY, F.L. (1939) *A Planned Supply of Teachers for Vermont*, New York, NY, Teachers College, Bureau of Publications.

BAILYN, B. (1960) *Education in the Forming of American Society: Needs and Opportunities for Study*, Chapel Hill, NC, North Carolina University Press.

BAKHTIN, M.M. (1981) *The Dialogic Imagination: Four Essays*, Ed. HOLQUIST, M., trans. EMERSON, C., and HOLQUIST, M., Austin, TX, University of Texas.

BAKHTIN, M.M. (1984a) *Problems of Dostoyevsky's Poetics*, Ed. and trans. Emerson, C., v. 8 of *Theory and History of Literature*, Minneapolis, MN, University of Minnesota.

BAKHTIN, M.M. (1984b) *Rabelais and His World*, Trans. H. Iswolsky, Bloomington, IN, Indiana University.

BAKHTIN, M.M. and MEDVEDEV, P.N. (1985) *The Formal Method in Literary Scholarship: A Critical Introduction to Sociological Poetics*, Trans. A.J. Wehrle, Cambridge, MA, Harvard University.

BARDEEN, C.W. (1912) 'The monopolizing woman teacher', *Educational Review*, **43**, p. 19.

BARDWICK, J.M. and DOUVAN, E. (1972) 'Ambivalence: The socialization of women', in BARDWICK, J.M. (Ed.) *Readings on the Psychology of Women*, New York, NY, Harper and Row, pp. 52–8.

BARKER, M.C. (1921a) 'The Riordan case statement prepared by Mary C. Barker, chairman special committee', Mary Barker Papers (Box 4, Folder 'Atlanta Public School Teachers' Association Records, 1920–1921'), Special Collections, Atlanta, GA, Emory University.

BARKER, M.C. (1921b, 16 June) 'Letter to members and letter to president, Atlanta Board of Education', Mary Barker Papers (Box 3, Folder 'Correspondence, 1919–1921'), Special Collections, Atlanta, GA, Emory University.

BARKER, M.C. (1921c) 'The Atlanta Public School Teachers' Association as an agent of democracy', Mary Barker Papers (Box 4, Folder 'Atlanta Public School Teachers' Association Records, 1920–1921'), Special Collections, Atlanta, GA, Emory University.

BARKER, M.C. (1921d, 20 July) Memorial to executive council, Atlanta Federation of Trades, Mary Barker Papers (Box 3, Folder 'Correspondence, 1919–1921'), Special Collections, Atlanta, GA, Emory University.

'Bar out teachers with small babies' (1911) *New York Times*, Nov, 30, p. 13:1.

'Battle over teachers fought before board: Miss Riordan dropped' (1921) *Atlanta Constitution*, 11 June.

BEALE, H.K. (1936) *Are American Teachers Free? An Analysis of Restraints upon the Freedom of Teaching in American Schools*, New York, NY, Charles Scribner's Sons.

BECKER, H.S. (1957) *Role and Career Problems of the Chicago Public Schoolteacher*, New York, NY, Arno Press.

BEECHEL, E.E. (1946) 'The challenge of the future', March 23, (Box 1, no. FF11) Edith E. Beechel Collection, Western History Department, Denver, CO, Denver Public Library.

BEECHER, C.E. (1846) *The Evils Suffered by American Women and American Children: The Causes and Remedies*, New York, NY, Harper and Brothers.

BENNETT, J. (1983) 'Human values in oral history', *Oral History Review*, 11, pp. 1–15.

BERGER, P. and LUCKMANN, T. (1967) *The Social Construction of Reality*, Garden City, NY, Anchor.

Bergen, B.H. (1982) 'Only a schoolmaster: Gender, class and the effort to professionalize elementary teaching in England, 1870–1910', *History of Education Quarterly*, 22, pp. 1–22.

BERKELEY, K.C. (1984) 'The ladies want to bring about reform in the public schools: Public education and women's rights in the post-Civil War south', *History of Education*, 24, pp. 45–58.

BERMAN, B. (1983) 'Business efficiency, American schooling and the public school superintendency: A reconsideration of the Callahan thesis', *History of Education Quarterly*, 23, pp. 297–322.

BERNARD, R.M. and VINOVSKIS, M.A. (1977) 'The female school teacher in antebellum Massachusetts', *Journal of Social History*, 10, Spring, pp. 332–45.

BERROL, S. (1981) 'The open city: Jews, jobs and schools in New York City, 1880–1915', in RAVITCH, D. and GOODENOW, R.K. (Eds) *Educating an Urban People: The New York City Experience*, New York, NY, Teachers College Press, pp. 101–115.

BERTAUX, D. (1981) 'From the life-history approach to the transformation of sociological practice', in BERTAUX, D. (Ed.) *Biography and Society: The Life-history Approach in the Social Sciences*, Beverly Hills, CA, Sage Publications.

BIBBS, H. (July, 1853) *Voice of the Fugitive*, State University of New York at Buffalo, New York.

BIKLEN, S.K. (1978) 'The progressive education movement and the question of women', *Teachers' College Record*, 80.

BIKLEN, S.K. (1985) 'Can elementary schoolteaching be a career? A search for new ways of understanding women's work', *Issues in Education*, 3, pp. 215–31.

BLACK, P.F. (1972) Historical study of the structures and major functions of the Pittsburgh Board of Public Education. *Dissertation Abstracts International*, 33, 4139-A. (University Microfilms No. 73-4130).

BLACKWELL, A.S. (1910) 'Do women teachers need the ballot?', *Woman's Journal*, 72, p. 110.

BLACKWELL, H.B. (1905) 'Why teachers are underpaid', *Woman's Journal*, 36, p. 142.

BLAIR, K.J. (1980) *The Clubwoman as Feminist: True Womanhood Redefined, 1868–1914*, New York, NY, Holmes and Meier Publishers.

BLAKE, K.D. (1915) 'Signs of victory', *Woman Voter*, 6, p. 12.

BLANTON, A.W. (1923) *A Hand Book of Information*, Austin, TX, State Department of Education.

BLEDSTEIN, B.J. (1976) *The Culture of Professionalism: The Middle Class and the Development of Higher Education in America*, New York, NY, W.W. Norton.

References

BLODGETT, G. (1971) Alice Stone Blackwell, *Notable American Women, 1607–1950*: *A biographical Dictionary*, I, pp. 156–8.

BLUMER, H. (1969) *Symbolic Interaction: Perspective and Method*, Englewood Cliffs, NJ, Prentice-Hall.

'Board rules against the women teachers' (1906) *New York Times*, May 10, p. 9, col. 3.

BODNAR, J. (1982) *Workers' World: Kinship, Community, and Protest in an Industrial Society, 1900–1940*, Baltimore, MD, Johns Hopkins University.

BOGDAN, R.C. and BIKLEN, S.K. (1982) *Qualitative Research for Education: An Introduction to Theory and Methods*, Boston, MA, Allyn and Bacon.

BOSTON UNIVERSITY (1988) 'Schooling in the postmodern age', A special issue of the *Journal of Education*, **179**, p. 3.

BOYCE, A.C. (1915) *Methods for Measuring Teachers' Efficiency*, Chicago, IL, University of Chicago.

BOYER, E.L. (1983) *High School: A Report on Secondary Education in America*, New York, NY, Harper and Row.

BRAVERMAN, H. (1974) *Labor and Monopoly Capital: The Degradation of Work in the Twentieth Century*, New York, NY, Monthly Review Press.

BROWN, R.C. and WATSON, B. (1982) *Buffalo, Lake City in Niagara Land*, Woodland Hills, CA, Windsor Publication.

BUFFALO CITY DIRECTORIES (1828–1855) Buffalo, NY, Crary *et al*.

BUFFALO TEACHERS EXAMS (1892–1906) *Records of Buffalo Teachers Exams*.

BULLESEL, M. (1981) Correspondence with Vaughn-Roberson, Summer.

Bulletin of the Voters' League Concerning the Public School System of Pittsburgh (1911) Pittsburgh, PA, Voters' League.

BURSTYN, J.N. (1980) *Victorian Education and the Ideal of Womanhood*, New York, NY, Barnes and Noble Books.

BURSTYN, J.N. (1980) 'Historical perspectives on women in educational leadership', in S.K. BIKLEN and M.B. BRANNIGAN (Eds) *Women and Educational Leadership*, Lexington, MA, D.C. Heath, pp. 65–76.

BURSTYN, J.N. (1987) 'History as image: Changing the lens', *History of Education Quarterly*, **27**, 2, pp. 167–80.

BUTTON, H.W. (1979) *Creating More Useable Pasts: History in the Study of Education*, *Educational Researcher*, Washington, DC.

BUTTON, H.W. and PROVENZO, E.F., Jr. (1983) *History of Education and Culture in America*, Englewood Cliffs, NJ, Prentice-Hall.

CALLAHAN, R.D. (1962) *Education and the Cult of Efficiency: A Study of the Social Forces that Have Shaped the Administration of the Public Schools*, Chicago, IL, University of Chicago.

CAMPBELL, L. (1981) Correspondence with Vaughn-Roberson, Summer.

CARNEGIE FORUM ON EDUCATION AND THE ECOMONY (1986) *A Nation Prepared: Teachers for the 21st Century*, The Report of the Task Force on Teaching as a Profession of the Carnegie Forum on Education and the Economy. New York, NY, Carnegie Corporation.

CARNEGIE FOUNDATION FOR THE ADVANCEMENT OF TEACHING (1988) *Report Card on School Reform: The Teachers Speak*, Princeton, NJ, Carnegie Foundation.

CARTER, S.B. (1989) 'Incentives and rewards to teaching', in WARREN, D. (Ed.) *American Teachers: Histories of a Profession at Work*, New York, NY, Macmillan, pp. 49–62.

'Catholics and the public schools' (1921) *Atlanta Constitution*, August 19.

'Catholics reply to Sims' charge' (1921) *Atlanta Constitution*, August 19.

CATTELL, J.M. (1909) 'The school and the family', *Popular Science Monthly*, **74**, pp. 91–2.

'Celibate female teachers' (1903) *Independent*, **55**, August 6, pp. 188–93.

'Censure teachers for campaign work' (1911) *New York Times*, p. 20, col. 1.

CENSUS (1855) *Buffalo and Erie County Census*, Erie County Hall, Buffalo, NY.

Census Statistics of Teachers, Bulletin 23 (1905) Washington, DC, US Bureau of the Census.

CHADWICK, F.E. (1914) 'The woman peril in American education', *Educational Review*, 47, pp. 109–19.

CHAFE, W.H. (1972) *The American Woman: Her Changing Social, Economic, and Political Role*, New York, NY, Oxford University Press.

CHANCELLOR, W.E. (1906) 'Shall married women teach?', *School Journal*, 22, pp. 558–60.

CHANCELLOR, W.E. (1908) *Our Schools: Their Administration and Supervision*, Boston, MA, D.C. Heath.

CHERRYHOLMES, C. (1988) *Power and Criticism: Poststructural Investigations in Education*, New York, NY, Teachers College.

CHURCH, E.R. (1882) *Money-Making for Ladies*, New York, NY, Harper and Brothers.

'City's women teachers demand pay of men' (1906) *New York Times*, April 8, p. 22, col. 6.

CLARK, S.P. and BLYTHE, L. (1962) *Echo in my Soul*, New York, E.P. Dutton.

'Class teachers war over equality plan' (1905) *New York Times*, May 10, p. 9, col. 5.

CLIFFORD, G.J. (1975) 'Saints, sinners, and people: A position paper on the historiography of American education', *History of Education Quarterly*, 15, pp. 257–72.

CLIFFORD, G.J. (1978) 'Home and school in the 19th century America: Some personal-history reports from the United States', *History of Education Quarterly*, 18, pp. 3–34.

CLIFFORD, G.J. (1989) 'Man/woman/teacher: Gender, family and career in American educational history', in WARREN, D. (Ed.) *American Teachers: Histories of a Profession at Work*, New York, NY, Macmillan Publishing Co., pp. 293–343.

COFFMAN, L.D. (1911) *The Social Composition of the Teaching Profession*, New York, NY, Teachers College.

COLES, R. (1964a) 'How do teachers feel'? *Saturday Review*, May 16, pp. 72–3.

COLES, R. (1964b) *Children of Crisis*, Boston, MA, Atlantic Monthly.

COLLIER, M.D. (1904) 'Will permit women teachers to marry, *New York Times*, April 28, p. 16:3.

COLLIER-THOMAS, B. (1982) 'The impact of Black women in education: An historical overview', *Journal of Negro Education*, 51, 3, pp. 173–80.

COLLINS, C.W. (1976) 'Schoolmen, schoolma'ams and school boards: The struggle for power in urban school systems in the progressive era', Unpublished doctoral dissertation, Cambridge, MA, Harvard University.

COLLINS, R. (1975) *Conflict Sociology*, New York, NY, Academic Press.

'Compensation of male and female teachers' (1855) *'The New York Teacher IV*, pp. 94–5.

'Contents of McCalley's affidavits are bared' (1921) *Atlanta Constitution*, August 14.

CONWAY, J.K. (1974) 'Perspectives on the history of women's education in the United States', *History of Education Quarterly*, 14, Spring, pp. 1–12.

COOK, B.W. (1979) 'Female support networks and political activism: Lilliam Wald, Crystal Eastman, Emma Goldman', in COTT, N.F. and PLECK, E.H. (Eds) *A Heritage of Her Own*, New York, NY, Simon and Schuster, pp. 412–44.

COOK, E. (1854) *Eighteenth Annual Report of the Superintendents of Common Schools, Buffalo, New York*, Buffalo, NY, Clapp Matthews & Co.

CORDIER, M.H. (1988) 'Prairie schoolwomen, mid-1850s to 1920s, in Iowa, Kansas, and Nebraska', *Great Plains Quarterly*, 8, Spring, pp. 102–19.

COTT, N.F. (1977) *The Bonds of Womanhood: Woman's Sphere in New England, 1780–1835*, New Haven, CT, Yale University Press.

COTT, N.F. (1984) 'Feminist politics in the 1920s: The National Woman's Party', *Journal of American History*, 71, June, pp. 43–68.

COUNTS, G.S. (1972) *The Social Composition of Boards of Education*, New York, NY, Arno Press. (Original work published 1927).

CREMIN, L.A. (1965) *The Wonderful World of Ellwood Patterson Cubberley: An Essay on the Historiography of American Education*, New York, NY, Teachers College Press.

CREMIN, L.A. (1980) *American Education: The National Experience, 1783–1876*, New York, NY, Harper and Row.

'The crime of motherhood' (1913) *Literary Digest*, 47, p. 802.

CROSS, B.M. (Ed.) (1965) *The Educated Woman in America: Selected Writings of Catharine Beecher, Margaret Fuller, and M. Carey Thomas*, New York, NY, Teachers College Press.

CUBAN, L. (1984) *How Teachers Taught: Constancy and Change in American Classrooms, 1890–1980*, New York, NY, Longman Press.

CURTI, M. (1935) *The Social Ideas of American Educators*, Totowa, NJ, Littlefield-Adams and Co.

CURTIS, R.D., SHUMWAY, G.L. and STEPHENSON, S.E. (1973) *A Guide for Oral History Programs*, Fullerton, CA, California State University, Fullerton Oral History Program and Southern California Local History Council.

CUTLER, W.W. (1983) 'Asking for answers: oral history', in BEST, J.H. (Ed.) *Historical Inquiry in Education: A Research Agenda*, Washington, DC, American Educational Research Association.

DALL, C. (1914) *The College Market and the Court*, Boston, MA, Memorial Edition.

DAVIS, C., BACK, K. and MCLEAN, K. (1977) *Oral History: From Tape to Type*, Chicago, IL, American Library Association.

DAVIS, M.W. (Ed.) (1982) *Contributions of Black Women to America, v. II, Civil Rights, Politics and Government, Education, Medicine, Sciences*, Columbia, SC, Kenaday Press, pp. i–ix, 261–356.

DAVIS, S. (1843) *Minutes of the National Convention of Colored Citizens, Buffalo, N.Y.*, Buffalo, NY, Percy and Reed.

'The Davis salary schedule: Full text of the new law regulating the pay of teachers in New York City' (1900) *School Journal*, 60, pp. 518–19.

DEAN, D.M. (1979) *Defender of the Race, James T. Holly, Black Nationalist Bishop*, Boston, MA, Lambeth Press.

'Defeated by own sex: Women teachers feared Miss Goessling's agitation for equal pay' (1905) *New York Times*, May 18, p. 5, col. 2.

DEGLER, C.N. (1980) *At Odds: Women and the Family in America from the Revolution to the Present*, New York, NY, Oxford University Press.

DELTA KAPPA GAMMA SOCIETY (1967) *Torchbearers: Biographical Sketches of Colorado Women Educators*, Boulder, CO, Johnson Publishing Co.

DELTA KAPPA GAMMA (1979) *Our Golden Anniversary*, Austin, TX, Delta Kappa Gamma.

DELTA KAPPA GAMMA, IOTA CHAPTER (1980) *Personalities: IOTA Delta Kappa Gamma*, Denton, TX.

DEMAUSE, L. (1982) *Foundations of Psychohistory*, New York, NY, Creative Roots.

DERRIDA, J. (1973) *Speech and Phenomena*, Trans. D.B. Allison, Evanston, IL, Northwestern University.

DERRIDA, J. (1974) *Of Grammatology*, Trans. G.C. Spivak, Baltimore, MD, Johns Hopkins University.

DICKEY, I. (1980) 'Christine Kirkpatrick', in FULWILER, L.B. and KOBLER, T. (Eds) *Personalities: IOTA Delta Kappa Gamma*, Denton, TX, Delta Kappa Gamma, pp. 46–7.

'Did Miss Riordan get a square deal'? (1921) *Journal of Labor*, August 12.

'Directory of Women's Suffrage Headquarters in New York City' (1910) *Woman Voter*, 1, October, pp. 7–8.

DOHERTY, R.E. (1979) 'Tempest on the Hudson: The struggle for "equal pay for equal work" in the New York City public schools, 1907–1911', *History of Education Quarterly*, 19, pp. 413–34.

DONOVAN, F.R. (1938) *The Schoolma'am*, New York, NY, Frederick Stokes.

DUKE, D.L. (1984) *Teaching — The Imperiled Profession*, Albany, NY, State University of New York Press.

'Duties of teachers' (1908) Rules of the Education Department of the Board of Education of the City of Chicago, Unpublished document located at the Chicago Historical Society, p. 1, col. 1.

DYER, T. (Ed.) (1981) *To Raise Myself a Little: The Diaries and Letters of Jennie, a Georgia Teacher*, Athens, GA, University of Georgia Press.

DYER, T.G. (1978) 'The Klan on campus: C. Lewis Fowler and Lanier University', *South Atlantic Quarterly*, 77, pp. 453–69.

EATON, W.E. (1975) *The American Federation of Teachers, 1916–1961*, Carbondale, IL, Southern Illinois Press.

ECKE, M.W. (1972) *From Ivy Street to Kennedy Center: Centennial History of the Atlanta Public School System*, Atlanta, GA, Atlanta Board of Education.

'Education board refuses hearing to teacher' (1921) *Atlanta Constitution*, July 9.

EDWARDS, H. (1980) *The Struggle That Must Be*, New York, NY, Macmillan.

ELSBREE, W.S. (1939) *The American Teacher: Evolution of a Profession in a Democracy*, New York, NY, American Book Company.

EPSTEIN, C.F. (1970) *Woman's Place: Options and Limits in Professional Careers*, Berkeley, CA, University of California Press.

'The equal pay meeting' (1909) *School*, December 9, p. 136.

'Equal pay or equal work' (1906) *Woman's Journal*, 37, 51, p. 212.

'Equalization of salaries' (1907) *Outlook*, 85, March 16, p. 595.

ETZIONI, A. (1961) *Comparative Analysis of Complex Organizations: On Power, Involvement, and Their Correlates*, New York, NY, Free Press.

EVANS, C.E. (1955) *The Story of Texas Schools*, Austin, TX, The Steck Co.

EVANS, G.E. (1975) *The Days That we Have Seen*, London, UK, Faber and Faber.

EVANS, M.G. (1929) The history of the organized labor movement in Georgia. Unpublished doctoral dissertation, Chicago, IL, University of Chicago.

EVANS-PRITCHARD, E.E. (1961) *Anthropology and History*, Manchester, UK, Manchester University Press.

FAHERTY, W.B. (1956) 'Regional minorities and the woman suffrage struggle', *Colorado Magazine*, 33, July, pp. 212–17.

'A fair request: Why not a fair response'? (1921) *Atlanta Journal*, August 14.

FAIRBUSH, I. (1939) *Last Will and Testament*, Surrogate Court, Erie County, State of New York, Erie County, NY.

FAIRBUSH, I. (1897) *MacBee Report*, Buffalo Board of Education.

FARAGHER, J.M. (1979) *Women and Men on the Overland Trail*, New Haven, CT, Yale University Press.

FARRIS, Z. (1976) Correspondence, Oklahoma Historical Society, Oklahoma City, OK, Oklahoma Retired Teachers Collection.

FAULCONER, E. (1981) Correspondence with Vaughn-Roberson, Summer.

References

FEISTRITZER, C.E. (1983) *The Condition of Teaching: A State by State Report*, A Carnegie Foundation Technical Report, Princeton, NJ, Carnegie Foundation for the Advancement of Teaching.

FERREE, M.C. (1987) 'The struggles of superwoman', in BOSE, C. *et al.* (Eds) *Hidden Aspects of Women's Work*, New York, NY, Praeger.

FEULNER, P.N. (1979) *Women in the Professions: A Social Psychological Study*, Palo Alto, CA, R. and E. Research Associates.

FILENE, C. (1920) *Careers for Women*, Boston, MA, Houghton Mifflin Company.

FILLER, L. (1971) 'Lucy Stone', *Notable American Women, 1607–1950: A biographical dictionary*. *III*: 387–90.

FINKELSTEIN, B.J. (1970) 'Governing the young: Teacher behavior in American primary schools, 1920–1880', PhD dissertation, New York, NY, Bureau of Publications Teachers College, Columbia University.

FINKELSTEIN, B.J. (1974) 'Schooling and schoolteachers: Selected bibliography of autobiographies in the nineteenth century', *History of Education Quarterly*, **14**, pp. 293–301.

FINKELSTEIN, B.J. (1979) *Regulated Children/Liberated Children: Education in Psychohistorical Perspective*, New York, NY, Psychohistory Press.

FINKELSTEIN, B.J. (1989) *Governing the Young: Teacher Behavior in Popular Primary Schools in Nineteenth-Century United States*, London, UK, Falmer Press.

FINLEY, M.I. (1956) *The World of Odysseus*, London, UK, Chatto and Windus.

FINLEY, M.I. (1978) *The Word of Odysseus*, Rev. Ed., New York, NY: Viking Press.

FITTS, D. (1979) 'Una and the lion: The feminization of district school- teaching and its effects on the roles of students and teachers in nineteenth-century Massachusetts', in FINKELSTEIN, B. (Ed.) *Regulated Children Liberated Children: Education in Psychohistorical Perspective*, New York, NY, Psychohistory Press, pp. 140–57.

FITZPATRICK, F.A. (1908) 'Does teaching repel men?', *Education Review*, **35**, pp. 501–05.

'For opportunity classes' (1915) *New York Times*, June 20, p. 11, col. 4.

FORRESTER, E.H. (1907) 'A question of sex and justice', *The Bookman*, **25**, pp. 177–79.

FOSTER, H. (Ed.) (1983) *The Anti-Aesthetic: Essays on Postmodern Culture*, Port Townsend, WA, Bay Press.

FOUCAULT, M. (1980) *Power/Knowledge: Selected Interviews & Other Writings 1972– 1977*, in GORDON, C. (Ed.) New York, NY, Pantheon.

FOX, R.W. and LEAR, T.J.J. (1983) *The Culture of Consumption: Critical Essays in American History, 1880–1980*, New York, NY, Pantheon Press.

FRANK, K. (1974) Interview, November 2, Oklahoma Historical Society Living Legends Project, Oklahoma City, OK.

FRASER, J.W. (1989) 'Agents of democracy: Urban elementary-school teachers and the conditions of teaching', in WARREN, D. (Ed.) *American Teachers: Histories of a Profession at Work*, New York, MacMillan, pp. 118–157.

FREDERICK, E. (1981) Correspondence with Vaughn-Roberson, Summer.

FREDERICKSON, M.E. (1980) 'Barker, Mary Cornelia', in SICHERMAN, B. and GREEN, C.H. (Eds) *Notable American Women: The Modern Period. A Biographical Dictionary*, Vol. 4, Cambridge, MA: Belnap Press, pp. 50–2.

FREEDMAN, E.B. (1974) 'The New Woman: Changing views of women in the 1920s', *Journal of American History*, **61**, pp. 372–93.

FREEDMAN, E. (1979) 'Separatism as Strategy: Female institution building and American feminism, 1870–1930', *Feminist Studies*, **5**, Fall, pp. 512–29.

FRIEDAN, B. (1963) *The Feminine Mystique*, New York, Dell.

FRIEDLANDER, P. (1975) *The Emergence of a UAW Local*, Pittsburgh, PA, University of Pittsburgh Press.

FRISCH, M. (1979) 'Oral history and hard times', *Oral History Review*, pp. 70–9.

GARRETT, F.M. (1954) *Atlanta and Environs: A Chronicle of Its People and Events*, 2, New York, NY, Lewis Historical Publishing.

GEERTZ, C. (1964) 'Ideology as a cultural system', in APTER, D. (Ed.) *Ideology and Discontent*, New York, NY, Free Press of Glencoe.

GEERTZ, C. (1988) *Works and Lives: The Anthropologist as Author*, Stanford, CA, Stanford University.

GILLIS, J.G. (1977) 'Towards a social history of education', *History of Education Quarterly*, 17, pp. 89–92.

GILMAN, C.P. (1904) 'The married teacher', *Woman's Journal*, May 7, 35, 19: 146.

GILMAN, C.P. (1913) 'Education and Social Progress', *The Forerunner* 4, 3: 71–2.

GILMAN, C.P. (1915) 'Freedom of speech in public schools', *The Forerunner* 6, 3: 72–4.

GILMAN, C.P. (1916) 'Maternity benefits and reformers', *The Forerunner* 7, 3: 65–6.

GILMAN, C.P. (1966) *Women and Economics*, New York, NY, Harper Torchbooks (original work published in 1899).

GILMER, M.F. (1939) 'History, activities, and present status of the Atlanta Public School Teachers' Association', Unpublished MA thesis, Atlanta, GA, Emory University.

GILMORE, W.J. (1984) *Psychohistorical Inquiry: A Comprehensive Research Bibliography*, New York, NY, Garland.

GIROUX, H.A. (in press) *Border Crossings: Cultural Workers and the Politics of Education*, London: Routledge Press.

GITLIN, A. (1983) 'School structure and teachers' work', in APPLE, M.W. and WEIS, L. (Eds) *Ideology and Practice in Schooling*, Philadelphia, PA, Temple University Press.

GLUCK, S. (1977) 'Tropical guide for oral history interviews with women', *Frontiers*, 2, 2, pp. 110–113.

GOLDMAN, M.S. (1981) *Gold Diggers and Silver Miners: Prostitution and Social Life on the Comstock Lode*, Ann Arbor, MI, University of Michigan Press.

GOODENOUGH, W.H. (1970) *Description and Comparison in Cultural Anthropology*, Chicago, IL, Aldine.

GOODLAD, J.I. (1984) *A Place Called School: Prospects for the Future*, New York, NY, McGraw-Hill.

GOODSON, I. (1980–81) 'Life histories and the study of schooling', *Interchange*, 11, pp. 62–76.

GORDON, D.M., EDWARDS, R. and REICH, M. (1982) *Segmented Work, Divided Workers: The Historical Transformation of Labor in the United States*. New York, NY, Cambridge University.

GORDON, L. (1976) *Woman Body, Women's Right: A Social History of Birth Control in America*, New York, NY, Grossman.

GRAF, H.F. (1939) 'Abolition and Anti-Slavery in Buffalo and Erie County', unpublished masters thesis, Buffalo, NY, State University of New York at Buffalo.

GRAHAM, P.A. (1974) *Community and Class in American Education, 1865–1918*, New York, NY, John Wiley.

GREDEL, S. (1965) *Reminiscences of the Past of the Negroes of Buffalo*, unpublished, Buffalo, NY, Buffalo and Erie County Historical Society.

GREEN, E.A. (1979) *Mary Lyon and Mount Holyoke: Opening the Gates*, Hanover, NH, University Press of New England.

GRELE, R. (1975) *Envelopes of Sound: Six Practitioners Discuss the Method. Theory and Practice of Oral History and Oral Testimony*, Chicago, IL, Precedent.

GRENDON v. BOARD OF EDUCATION OF THE CITY OF NEW YORK (1906), 114 App. Div. 759.

References

GRENFELL, E.I. (1939) *A Brief Sketch of the Life and Works of Helen Thatcher Loring Grenfell*, Denver, CO, Smith-Brooks Printing Co.

GRUMET, M.R. (1988) *Bitter Milk: Women and Teaching*, Amherst, MA, University of Massachusetts Press.

GUILLIFORD, A. (1984) *America's Country Schools*, Washington, DC, The Preseveration Press.

GUTMAN, H.G. (1977) *Work, Culture, and Society in Industrializing America*, New York, NY, Vintage.

HAMILTON, A. (1981) Correspondence with Vaughn-Roberson, Summer.

HAMMACK, D.C. (1982) *Power and Society: New York at the Turn of the Century*, New York, NY, Russell Sage Foundation.

HAMNER, L.V. (1958) *Light n' Hitch: A Collection of Historical Writing Depicting Life on the High Plains*, Dallas, TX: American Guild Press.

HANSON, F.A. (1979) 'Does God have a body? Truth, reality, and cultural relativism', *Man*, **14**, 3, pp. 515–29.

HANSOT, E. and TYACK, D. (1988) 'Gender in American public schools: Thinking institutionally', *Signs: Journal of Women in Culture and Society*, **13**, 4, pp. 741–60.

HARAVEN, T.K. (1987) 'The Dynamics of Kin and Industrial Community', in GERSTEL, N., and ENGEL GROSS, H. (Eds) *Families and Work*, Philadelphia, PA, Temple University Press, pp. 55–83.

HARDIMAN, R. (1981) Interviewed by Vaughn-Roberson, Summer.

HARLAND, R. (1987) *Superstructuralism: The Philosophy of Structuralism and Post-Structuralism*, London, UK, Methuen.

HARLEY, S. (1982) 'Beyond the classroom: The organizational lives of Black female educators in the District of Columbia, 1890–1930', *Journal of Negro Education*, **51**, 3, pp. 254–65.

HARRIS, J.H. (1906) 'Everybody's paid but teacher', *The Woman's Journal*, **37**, February 3, p. 20.

HARTSHONE, C., WEISS, P. and BURKS, A. (Eds) (1933–58) *The Collected Papers of Charles Sanders Peirce*, Cambridge, MA, Harvard University.

HAVLICE, P.P. (1985) *Oral History: A Reference Guide and Annotated Bibliography*, Jefferson, NC, McFarland.

HAWLEY, E. (1842) *Eighth Annual Report of the Superintendent of Common Schools, Buffalo, NY*, Buffalo, NY, Steele Press.

HAWLEY, E. (1843) *7th Annual Report of the Superintendents of Common School, Buffalo, NY*, Buffalo, NY, Clapp and McCredic Press.

HAWLEY, E. (1844) *8th Annual Report of the Superintendents of Common School, Buffalo, NY*, Buffalo, NY, Clapp and McCredic Press.

HAYS, S.P. (1964) 'The politics of reform in municipal government in the Progressive Era', *Pacific Northwest Quarterly*, **55**, pp. 157–69.

HENDERSON, J.L. (1975) *A Bridge Across Time: An Assessment of Historical Archetypes*, London, UK, Turnstone Books.

HENSON, J. (1849) *The Life of Josiah Henson*, Boston, MA, Arthur D. Phelps.

HERSKOVITS, M.J. (1955) *Cultural Anthropology*, New York, NY, Alfred A. Knopf.

HIGHET, G. (1976) *The Immortal Profession: The Joys of Teaching and Learning*, New York, NY, Weybright and Taley.

HILL, F.M. (1976) Correspondence. Oklahoma Historical Society, Oklahoma City, OK, Retired Teachers Collection.

HOFFMAN, N. (1982) *Women's 'True' Profession: Voices from the History of Teaching*, Old Westbury, NY, Feminist Press.

HOFSTADTER, R. (1963) *Anti-Intellectualism in American Life*, New York, NY, Vintage Books.

HOLLER, L. (1981) Correspondence with Vaughn-Roberson, Summer.

HOLMES GROUP (1986) *Tomorrow's Teachers*, East Lansing, MI, Holmes Group, Inc.

HOMEL, M.W. (1984) *Down from Equality: Black Chicagoans and the Public Schools, 1920–41*, Urbana, IL, University of Illinois Press.

HOOPES, J. (1979) *Oral History: An Introduction for Students*, Chapel Hill, NC, The University of North Carolina Press.

HORNER, M. (1970) 'Femininity and successful achievement: A basic inconsistency', in BARDWICK, J., DOUVAN, E., HORNER, M. and EUTMANN, D. (Eds) *Feminine Personality and Conflict*, Belmont, CA, Brooks-Cole, pp. 45–74.

HOUSE OF REPRESENTATIVES, UNITED STATES, COMMITTEE ON RULES (1921) *The Ku Klux Klan: Hearings before the Committee on Rules, House of Representatives*, 67th Congress, 1st Session.

HUBBELL, J.W. (1982) 'Women in education', in THURMAN, M. (Ed.) *Women in Oklahoma: A Century of Change*, Oklahoma City, OK, Oklahoma Historical Society, pp. 140–61.

HUME, B.D. (1981) Correspondence with Vaughn-Roberson, Summer.

INGER, M. (1969) *Politics and Reality in an American City: The New Orleans School Crisis of 1960*, New York, NY, Center for Urban Education.

INGRAM, V. (1980a) 'Mary Curden', in FULWILER, L.B. and KOBLER, T. (Eds) *Personalities: IOTA Delta Kappa Gamma*, Denton, TX, Delta Kappa Gamma, pp. 8–9.

INGRAM, V. (1980b) 'Ruth Marshall', in FULWILER, L.B. and KOBLER, T. (Eds) *Personalities: IOTA Delta Kappa Gamma*, Denton, TX, Delta Kappa Gamma, p. 57.

ISSEL, W.H. (1967) 'Teachers and educational reform during the Progressive Era: A case study of the Pittsburgh Teachers Association', *History of Education Quarterly*, 7, pp. 220–33.

ISSEL, W.H. (1970) 'Modernization in Philadelphia school reform, 1882–1905', *Pennsylvania Magazine of History and Biographies*, 94, pp. 358–83.

JACKSON, K.T. (1967) *The Ku Klux Klan in the City*, New York, NY, Oxford University Press.

JAMES, L.B. (1982) 'Woman's Suffrage Oklahoma Style, 1890–1918', in THURMAN, M. (Ed.) *Women in Oklahoma: A Century of Change*, Oklahoma City, OK, Oklahoma Historical Society, pp. 182–98.

JAMES, L.B. (1979) 'The woman's suffrage issue in the Oklahoma Constitutional Convention', *Chronicles of Oklahoma*, 56, Winter, pp. 379–92.

JEANSONNE, G. (1977) *Leander Perez: Boss of the Delta*, Baton Rouge, LA, Louisiana State University Press.

JEFFREY, J.R. (1979) *Frontier Women: The Trans-Mississippi West, 1840–1880*, New York, NY, Hill and Wang.

JENSEN, B.B. (1964) 'Let the women vote', *Colorado Magazine*, 41, Winter, pp. 13–25.

JENSEN, B.B. (1973) 'Colorado woman suffrage campaigns of the 1870s', *Journal of the West*, 12, April, pp. 254–71.

'Jerome Jones' [OBITUARY] (1940) *Journal of Labor*, September 27.

'Jobs for teachers contingent on tax increase' (1921) *Atlanta Journal*, June 10.

JOHNSON, S.M. (1984) *Teacher Unions in Schools*, Philadelphia, PA, Temple University Press.

JONES, J. (1979) 'Women who were more than men: Sex and status in freedmen's teaching', *History of Education Quarterly*, 14, Spring, pp. 47–59.

JONES, J. (1980) *Soldiers of Light and Love: Northern Teachers and Georgia Blacks, 1865–1873*, Chapel Hill, NC, University of North Carolina Press.

JOY, A.C. (1981) Correspondence with Vaughn-Roberson, Summer.

References

'Justice to teachers' (1908) *Outlook 88*, p. 482.

KAESTLE, C.F. (1974) *The Evolution of an Urban School System: New York City, 1750–1850*, Cambridge, MA, Harvard University.

KAESTLE, C.F. and VINOVSKIS, M.A. (1980) *Education and Social Change in Nineteenth-Century Massachusetts*, New York, NY, Cambridge University.

KATZ, M.B. (1975) *Class, Bureaucracy, and the Schools: The Illusion of Educational Change in America*, New York, NY, Praeger.

KAUFMAN, P.W. (1984) *Women Teachers on the Frontier*, New Haven, CT, Yale University Press.

KELLEY, M. (1979) 'At war with herself: Harriet Beecher Stowe as woman in conflict within the home', in KELLEY, M. (Ed.) *Woman's Being, Woman's Place: Female Identity and Vocations in American History*, Boston, MA, G.K. Hall, pp. 201–19.

KELLY, M. (1931) *Little Citizens: The Humours of School Life*, New York, NY, Peter Smith.

KELLY, M. (1975) *Little Aliens*, New York, NY, Arno Press. Reprint.

KERBER, L. (1976) 'The republican mother: Women and the enlightenment — An American perspective', *American Quarterly*, **28**, 2, pp. 187–205.

KERBER, L.K. (1982) 'Daughters of Columbia: Educating women for the republic, 1787–1805', in FRIEDMAN, J.E. and SHADE, W.G. (Eds) *Our American Sisters: Women in American Life and Thought*, Lexington, MA, D.C. Heath, pp. 137–53.

KESSLER-HARRIS, A. (1982) *Out to Work: A History of Wage-Earning Women in the United States*, London, UK, Oxford University Press.

K.G. (1902) 'Disenfranchised teachers', *The Woman Journal*, **33**, pp. 22–3.

KINGSLEY, S. (1841) *Fourth Annual Report of the Superintendent of Common Schools, Buffalo, NY*, Buffalo, NY, Press of Thomas and Company.

KOEHLER, L. (1984) 'Women's rights, society and the schools: Feminist activities in Cincinnati, Ohio, 1864–1880', in Carter, PATRICIA, A. (Ed.) *Women in Cincinnati: Century of Achievement, 1870–1970, v. II*, Cincinnati, OH, Cincinnati Historical Society.

KRADITOR, A.S. (1981) *The Ideas of the Woman Suffrage Movement, 1890–1920*, New York, NY, W.W. Norton.

KREN, G.M. and RAPPOPORT, L.H. (1976) *Varieties of Psychohistory*, New York, NY, Springer.

KRIG, V. (1981) Correspondence with Vaughn-Roberson, Summer.

KUHN, T.S. (1970) *The Structure of Scientific Revolutions*, Chicago, IL, University of Chicago.

LABAREE, D.F. (1988) *The Making of an American High School: The Credentials Market and the Central High School of Philadelphia, 1838–1939*, New Haven, CT, Yale University.

'Labor is refused reasons of board in Riordan case' (1921) *Atlanta Constitution*, August 16.

'Labor will pass today on answer of school board' (1921) *Atlanta Constitution*, August 18.

LaCAPRA, D. (1983) *Rethinking Intellectual History: Texts, Contexts, Language*, Ithaca, NY, Cornell University.

LaCAPRA, D. (1985) *History and Criticism*, Ithaca, NY, Cornell University.

LaCAPRA, D. (1987) *History, Politics, and the Novel*, Ithaca, NY, Cornell University.

LAMBERT, G.H. and RANKIN, G.M. (1969) 'Oklahoma', in PEARSON, J. and FULLER, E. (Eds) *Education in the States: Historical Development and Outlook*, Washington, DC, National Education Association of the United States, pp. 976–91.

LANTIS, M. (Ed.) (1970) *Ethnohistory in Southwestern Alaska and the Southern Yukon: Method and Content*, Lexington, KY, University Press of Kentucky.

LATHROP, T. (1870) *Thirty-Third Annual Report of the Superintendents of Common Schools, Buffalo, NY*, Buffalo, NY, Haas and Kelly.

LATHROP, T. (1872) *Thirty-Fifth Annual Report of the Superintendents of Common Schools, Buffalo, NY*, Buffalo, NY, Buffalo Printing Co.

LEGGATT, T. (1970) 'Teaching as a profession', in JACKSON, J.A. (Ed.) *Professions and Professionalization*, London, UK, Cambridge University Press, pp. 155–77.

LERNER, G. (1977) *The Female Experience: An American Documentary*, Indianapolis, IN, Bobbs-Merrill, pp. 234–36.

LEVINSOHN, F. and WRIGHT, B. (1976) *School Integration: Shadow and Substance*, Chicago, IL, University of Chicago Press.

LITWACK, L.F. (1966) *North of Slavery: The Negro in the Free States, 1790–1860*, Chicago, IL, University of Chicago.

LOGAN, R.W. and WINSTON, M.R. (1982) *Dictionary of American Negro Biography*, New York, NY, W.W. Norton and Company, Inc.

LONG, S. (1981) Correspondence with Vaughn-Roberson, Summer.

LORTIE, D.C. (1975) *Schoolteacher: A Sociological Study*, Chicago, IL, University of Chicago Press.

'Lost job as teacher for bearing child, case of Mrs. Lily Weeks of Astoria very much like that of Mrs. Edgell, Brooklyn' (1913) *New York Times*, March 16, p. 10, col. 3.

LUCAS, M. (1980) 'Joe Johnson', in FULWILER, L.B. and KOBLER, T. (Eds) *Personalities: IOTA Delta Kappa Gamma*, Denton, TX, Delta Kappa Gamma, p. 43.

LYNN, R.L. (1960) 'The educational points of view and services of the Texas state superintendents of public instruction', MA thesis, TX, Baylor University.

McCoy, W.D. (1951) 'Public education in Pittsburgh, 1835–1950', *Western Pennsylvania History Magazine*, **34**, pp. 219–38.

McGINNIS, W.C. (1954) 'Mrs. Charlotte McGinnis: Salida, Colorado (May 17)', in Ruth Hardiman's home, Denver, Colorado.

McGOVERN, J.R. (1987) 'The American woman: Her changing social, economic, and political role', in FRIEDMAN, JEAN E. (Ed.) *Our American Sisters: Women in American Life and Thought*, Lexington, MA, D.C. Heath and Co.

McKENNA, R. (1981) Correspondence with Vaughn-Roberson, Summer.

MANN, H. (1840) Eleventh report, *The Common School Journal III*, pp. 96–7.

MANN, H. (1843) *Sixth Annual Report: Massachusetts Board of Education*, Boston, MA, Dutton and Wentworth.

MANN, T. (1860) 'The female teacher', *New York Teacher*, **9**, pp. 157–58.

'Marriage under bar' (1903) *New York Times*, January 15, p. 1, col. 1.

'Married teacher appeals to Finley' (1914) *New York Times*, October 5, p. 4, col. 7.

'Married teachers' (1918) *School and Society*, **18**, 8, pp. 226–27.

'A married teacher's ruse, expectant mother to stay at work to embarrass education board' (1914) *New York Times*, October 13, p. 18, col. 2.

'Married teachers victory' (1904) *New York Globe and Commercial Advertiser*, as printed in the *Woman's Journal*, **35**, 10, p. 73:2.

'Married women as teachers' (1903) *Education Review*, **25**, pp. 213–214.

'Married women as teachers' (1906) *Woman's Journal*, **37**, October 20, p. 168.

MARX, K. (1869) *The Eighteenth Brumaire of Louis Bonaparte*, in Feuer, L.S. (Ed.), *Marx and Engels: Basic Writings on Politics and Philosophy* (1959) New York, NY, Anchor Books.

MARX, K. (1967) *Capital: A Critique of Political Economy*, Vol. I, New York, NY, International Publishers.

MASON, O.C. (1979) Interview, 18 May, Fort Collins, CO, Colorado Oral History Project, Fort Collins Public Library.

References

'Maxwell submits report giving names of all teachers absent from school in order to bear children' (1913) *New York Times*, October 23, pp. 20, col. 1–2.

MAXWELL, W.H. (1903) 'Teachers' salaries in New York City', *Journal of Education*, **65**, pp. 255–57.

'May make it a test case: Woman school teacher who married and refused to resign to be tried' (1903) *New York Daily Tribune*, November 13, p. 6, col. 1.

'Mayor responsible for her discharge, Miss Riordan holds' (1921) *Atlanta Constitution*, August 12.

MELDER, K. (1972) 'Woman's high calling: The teaching profession in America, 1830–1860', *American Studies*, **13**, pp. 19–32.

MELDER, K. (1974) 'Mask of oppression: The female seminary movement in the United States', *New York History*, **55**, July, pp. 261–79.

MELOSH, B. (1982) *The Physician's Hand: Work Culture and Conflict in American Nursing*, Philadelphia, PA, Temple University Press.

'Men teachers reply, say women teachers erred in their resolution on salary dispute' (1909) *New York Times*, June 11, p. 5, col. 5.

MILKMAN, R. (1979) 'Women's work and the economic crisis: Some lessons from the Great Depression', in COTT, N. and PLECK, E. (Eds) *A Heritage of their Own*, New York, NY, Simon and Schuster, pp. 527–41.

MILLER, A.D. (1904) 'The ideal candidates', *The New York Tribune*, reprinted in Miller, Alice Druer (1915), *Are Women People? A Book of Rhymes for Suffrage Times*, New York, NY, George Doran Company, pp. 89–91.

MINUTES OF THE BOARD OF EDUCATION FOR NOVEMBER 11, 1914 (1914a) *Journal of the Board of Education of the City of New York*, p. 2354.

MINUTES OF THE BOARD OF EDUCATION FOR NOVEMBER 25, 1914 (1914b) *Journal of the Board of Education of the City of New York*, pp. 2373–74.

MINUTES OF THE BOARD OF EDUCATION FOR DECEMBER 30, 1914 (1914c) *Journal of the Board of Education of the City of New York*, p. 2649.

'Miss Strachan's Denial: Did not urge women teachers to join suffrage parade, she says' (1913) *New York Times*, April 30, p. 3, col. 1.

MONTGOMERY, D. (1979) *Workers' Control in America*, New York, NY, Cambridge University.

MONTGOMERY, D. (1981) 'History as human agency', *Monthly Review*, **33**, pp. 42–48.

MOORE, K. (1976) Correspondence. Oklahoma Historical Society, Oklahoma City, OK, Oklahoma Retired Teachers Collection.

MORAIN, T. (1980) 'The departure of males from the teaching profession in nineteenth-century Iowa', *Civil War History*, **26**, pp. 161–70.

MOSELEY, C.C. (1973) 'The political influence of the Ku Klux Klan in Georgia, 1915–1925', *Georgia Historical Quarterly*, **57**, pp. 235–55.

'Motherhood and teaching' (1913) *Outlook*, **105**, p. 462.

'Motherhood held as civic service, on the ground League of Women will insist on Mrs. Edgell's rights, agitation will be kept up' (1913) *New York Times*, June 28, p. 7, col. 3.

'Mrs. Gamse asks clubwomen's aid' (1914) *New York Times*, January 19, p. 7, col. 3.

'Mrs. Grace Strachan Forsythe' (1922) *School and Society*, **14**, p. 130.

MURPHY, M. (1981) 'From artisan to semi-professional: White collar unionism among Chicago public school teachers, 1870–1930', *Dissertation Abstracts International*, **42**, 3721-A. (University Microfilms No. 8200530).

MURPHY, M. (1986) 'The aristocracy of women's labor in America', *History Workshop*, **22**, pp. 56–69.

MURPHY, M. (1990) *Blackboard Unions: The NEA and The AFT*, 1900–1980, Ithaca, NY: Cornell University Press.

MURPHY v. MAXWELL, (1902) 39 Misc. 166.

NASH, J.E. (1940) *The Negro in the Early History of Buffalo*, Buffalo NY, Buffalo Star.

NATIONAL EDUCATION ASSOCIATION (1904) *Journal of Proceedings and Addresses*, Winona, MN, Author.

NEARING, S. (1917) 'Who's who on our boards of education', *School and Society*, 5, p. 90.

NELSON, M.K. (1988) 'The threat of sexual harassment: Rural Vermont school teachers, 1915–1950', *Educational Foundations*, 2, 2 (Summer), pp. 61–78.

'New fight to save teacher-mothers, Women's Civic League will ask public hearing' (1914) *New York Times*, October 1, p. 20, col. 1.

NEWMAN, J.W. (1978) A history of the Atlanta Public School Teachers' Association, local 89 of the American Federation of Teachers, 1919–1956. Unpublished doctoral dissertation, Atlanta, GA, Georgia State University.

NEWMAN, J.W. (1981a) 'Mary C. Barker and the Atlanta teachers' union', in REED, M.E., HOUGH, L.S. and FINK, G.M. (Eds) *Southern Workers and Their Unions, 1880–1975*, Westport, CT, Greenwood Press, pp. 60–79.

NEWMAN, J.W. (1981b) 'Teacher unionism and racial politics: The Atlanta Public School Teachers' Association', in GOODENOW, R.K. and WHITE, A.D. (Eds) *Education and the Rise of the New South*, Boston, MA, G.K. Hall, pp. 131–68.

NEWMAN, J.W. (1983) 'Barker, Mary Cornelia', in COLEMAN, K.D. and GURR, C.S. (Eds) *Dictionary of Georgia Biography*, Vol. 1, Athens, University of Georgia Press, pp. 53–5.

NEWMAN, L.M. (1985) *Men's Ideas/Women's Realities: Popular Science, 1870–1915*, New York, NY, Pergamon Press.

'New York women teachers' (1906) *Journal of Education*, 68, p. 479.

'New Turn in equal pay fight — men principals accused of hampering campaign of women teachers' (1908) *New York Times*, June 6, p. 4, col. 5.

NICHOLSON, L.J. (Ed.) (1990) *Feminism/Postmodernism*, New York, NY, Routledge.

'No big deal', *Pittsburgh Press*, 5 December 1981.

'No formal trial ever given her, states teacher' (1921) *Atlanta Constitution*, August 9.

NORTON, M.B. (1980) *Liberty's Daughters: The Revolutionary Experience of American Women, 1750–1800*, Boston, MA, Little, Brown.

'Not a crime to marry' (1903) *New York Tribune*, Dec. 4, p. 7:5.

'Not the most eligible' (1914) *New York Times*, October 28, p. 12, col. 3.

OLNECK, M.R. and LAZERSON, M. (1988) 'The school achievements of immigrant children: 1900–1930', in McCLELLAN, B.E. and REESE, W.J. (Eds) *The Social History of American Education*, Urbana, IL, University of Illinois Press, pp. 257–86.

O'NEILL, W.L. (1973) 'Divorce in the progressive era', in GORDON, MICHAEL (Ed.) *The American Family in Social-Historical Perspective*, New York, NY, St. Martin's Press.

'Organized labor sponsors Atlanta woman teacher's case' (1921) *Journal of Labor*, August 12.

OZGA, J.T. and LAWN, M.A. (1981) *Teachers, Professionalism and Class: A Study of Organized Teachers*, London, UK, Falmer Press.

PALMER, B.D. (1990) *Descent into Discourse: The Reification of Language and the Writing of Social History*, Philadelphia, PA, Temple University Press.

PATTERSON, H. (1915) 'Shall biological failures be our teachers'? *School and Society*, 2, pp. 297–301.

PAYNE, J. (1976) 'Black women in urban schools', in HILLER, D.V. and SHEETS, R.A. (Eds) *Women and Men: The Consequences of Power*, Cincinnati, OH, Office of Women's Studies, University of Cincinnati, pp. 196–211.

References

'Penalizing motherhood' (1913) *Independent*, March 20, pp. 605–6.

PERKINS, L.M. (1983) 'The impact of the "Cult of True Womanhood" on the education of Black women', *Journal of Social Issues*, **39**, Fall, pp. 17–28.

PERKINS, L.M. (1989) 'The history of Blacks in teaching: growth and decline within the profession', in WARREN, D. (Ed.) *American Teachers: Histories of a Profession at Work*, New York, NY, Macmillan.

PETERSON, J. (1981) Correspondence with Vaughn-Roberson, Summer.

PHILLIPS, C.E. (1921) 'Letter to Mary Barker, June 24', Mary Barker Papers (Box 3, Folder 'Correspondence, 1919–1921'), Special Collections, Atlanta, GA, Emory University.

Pittsburgh School Bulletin (later *Pittsburgh Teachers Bulletin*) (1911–1912), November 1911: pp. 2–7; March 1912: p. 14; April 1912.

PITTSBURGH BOARD OF EDUCATION HANDBOOK (1916) Pittsburgh, PA, Board of Public Education.

PITTSBURGH BOARD OF PUBLIC EDUCATION (1912) *Annual Report*, Pittsburgh, PA, Author.

PITTSBURGH BOARD OF PUBLIC EDUCATION (1913) *Annual Report*, Pittsburgh, PA, Author.

PITTSBURGH BOARD OF PUBLIC EDUCATION (1916) *Annual Report*, Pittsburgh, PA, Author.

PITTSBURGH BOARD OF PUBLIC EDUCATION (1925) *Annual Report*, Pittsburgh, PA, Author.

PITTSBURGH BOARD OF PUBLIC EDUCATION (1935–1936) *Annual Report*, Pittsburgh, PA, Author.

PITTSBURGH BOARD OF PUBLIC EDUCATION (1945–1946) *Annual Report*, Pittsburgh, PA, Author.

PITTSBURGH BOARD OF PUBLIC EDUCATION (1954–1955) *Annual Report*, Pittsburgh, PA, Author.

PITTSBURGH BOARD OF PUBLIC EDUCATION (1966–1967) *Annual Report*, Pittsburgh, PA, Author.

'Plan to condemn education board beaten by labor' (1921) *Atlanta Constitution*, August 25.

PLANK, D.N. and PETERSON, P.E. (1983) 'Does urban reform imply class conflict? The case of Atlanta's schools', *History of Education Quarterly*, **23**, pp. 151–74.

POLANYI, M. (1958) *Personal Knowledge*, Chicago, IL, University of Chicago.

PRATT, M.L. (1986) 'Fieldwork in common places', in CLIFFORD, G. and MARCUS, G.E. (Eds) *Writing Culture: The Poetics and Politics of Ethnography*, Berkeley, CA, University of California.

PRESTON, J.A. (1982) 'Feminization of an occupation: Teaching becomes women's work in nineteenth-century New England', *Dissertation Abstracts International*, **43**, 2115A. (University Microfilms No. 8220108).

PRISCO, S. (1980) *An Introduction to Psychohistory: Theories and Case Studies*, Washington, DC, University Press of America.

PROCTOR, M.R. (1934) *Vermont's System of Education*, Report of a Special Commission named by Governor Wilson with its Conclusion and Recommendations, Brattleboro, VT, The Vermont Printing Company.

PROCTOR, R. (1979) 'Racial discrimination against Black teachers and Black professionals in the Pittsburgh public school system, 1834–1973', *Dissertation Abstracts International*.

'Progressive Cincinnati' (1914) *Journal of Education*, **76**, p. 155.

PROJECT AT THE UNIVERSITY OF MICHIGAN (1977) 'Interview guide for the twentieth century trade union movement: Vehicle for social change', *Frontiers*, **2**, 2, pp. 114–118.

QUANTZ, R.A. (1983) '*Conceptual and methodological bases of oral history: The case of small-town, midwestern teachers during the Great Depression*. Paper presented at the annual meeting of the American Educational Research Association, Montreal, Canada.

QUANTZ, R.A. (1985) 'The Complex Visions of Female Teachers and the Failure of Unionization in the 1930s: An Oral History', (see Chapter 10).

QUANTZ, R.A. (1988) 'Culture: A critical perspective.' Paper presented at American Educational Studies Association Annual Meeting, Toronto, Canada, 3 November 1988.

QUANTZ, R.A. and O'CONNOR, T.W. (1988) 'Writing critical ethnography: Dialogue, multivoicedness, and carnival in cultural texts', *Educational Theory*, **38**, 1, pp. 95–109.

RACINE, P.N. (1973) 'The Ku Klux Klan, anti-Catholicism, and Atlanta's board of education', *Georgia Historical Quarterly*, **57**, pp. 63–75.

'Reasons for discharge of Miss Riordan denied labor by school board' (1921) *Atlanta Constitution*, August 9.

'Recommends equal pay' (1910) *Woman's Journal*, October 29, p. 184.

REID, R.L. (1968) 'The professionalization of public school teachers: The Chicago experience, 1895–1920', *Dissertation Abstracts International*, **29**, 2193-A. (University Microfilms No. 69-1918)

REID, R.L. (Ed.) (1982) *Battleground: The Autobiography of Margaret A. Haley*, Urbana, IL, University of Illinois Press.

RESER, E. (1976) Correspondence. Oklahoma Historical Society, Oklahoma City, OK, Oklahoma Retired Teachers Collection.

RINEHART, A.D. (1983) *Mortals in the Immortal Profession: An Oral History of Teaching*, New York, NY, Irvington Publishers.

RIORDAN, J.T. (1921) 'Letter to Lamar Jeter, September 2', Atlanta Education Association Collection (Box 22, Folder 'Pension, 1938'), Southern Labor Archives, Georgia State University.

RIORDAN, J.T. (1922) 'Open letter to Atlanta Public School Teachers' Association, January 31', Atlanta Education Association Collection (Box 22, Folder 'Pension, 1938'), Southern Labor Archives, Atlanta, GA, Georgia State University.

RIPLEY, C.P. (1986) *The Black Abolitionist Papers Vol. 11, Canada 1830–1865*, Chapel Hill, NC, University of North Carolina Press.

ROBERSON, M. (1981) Interview by Vaughn-Roberson, Spring.

ROGERS, S.L. (1915) *Indian Population in the United States and Alaska*, Washington, DC, Bureau of the Census.

ROOSEVELT, T. (1924) 'American problems', in HAGEDORN, H. (Ed.) *The Works of Theodore Roosevelt*, New York, NY, Scribner and Sons.

ROSENFELD, S.A. (1977) *Centralization or Decentralization? A Case Study of School and District Organization in Vermont*. EdD Thesis, Cambridge, MA, Harvard University.

ROSS, A. (Ed.) (1988) *Universal Abandon?: The Politics of Postmodernism, Minneapolis*, MN, University of Minnesota.

RURY, J.L. (1986) 'Gender, salaries, and career: American teachers, 1900–1910', *Issues in Education*, **4**, pp. 215–35.

RURY, J.L. (1989) 'Who became teachers? The social characteristics of teachers in American history', in WARREN, D. (Ed.) *American Teachers: Histories of a Profession at Work*, New York, NY, MacMillan, pp. 9–48.

RYAN, M.P. (1975) *Womanhood in America: From Colonial Times to the Present*, New York, NY, Franklin Watts Publishers.

RYAN, M.P. (1981) *Cradle of the Middle Class: The Family in Oneida County, New York, 1790–1865*, New York, NY, Cambridge University Press.

SACKETT, J.B. (1863) *Twenty-Seventh Annual Report of the Superintendents of Common Schools, Buffalo, N.Y.*, Buffalo, NY, Joseph Warren and Company.

References

SALOMONSON, E. (1981) Correspondence with Vaughn-Roberson, Summer.

SAPIR, E. (1949) 'Time perspective in aboriginal American culture: A study in method', in MANDELBAUM, D. (Ed.) *Edward Sapir, Selected Writings ... in Language, Culture and Personality*, Berkeley, CA, University of California Press.

SCALES, O. (1976) Correspondence. Oklahoma Historical Society, Oklahoma City, OK, Oklahoma Retired Teachers Collection.

SCHATZ, R.W. (1984) 'Labor historians, labor economics, and the question of synthesis', *Journal of American History*, **71**, pp. 93–100.

SCHLISSEL, L. (1982) *Women's Diaries of the Westward Journey*, New York, NY, Schocken Books.

'Schoolma'ams want men teachers' pay' (1905) *The New York Times*, April 30, p. 8, col. 1.

'Schoolteachers and suffrage' (1912) *Woman Voter*, March, p. 9.

'Schoolteachers issue statement' (1919) *Atlanta Constitution*, January 16.

SCOTT, A.F. (1978) 'What, then, is the American: This new woman', *Journal of American History*, **65**, 3, pp. 679–703.

SCOTT, A.F. (1979) 'The ever-widening circle: The diffusion of feminist values from the Troy Seminary, 1822–1827', *History of Education Quarterly*, **19**, 1, pp. 3–25.

SCOTT, C.W. (1934) *Indefinite Teacher Tenure: A Critical Study of the Historical, Legal, Operative, and Comparative Aspects*, New York, NY, Bureau of Publications, Teachers College, Columbia University.

SCOTT, W. (1981) Correspondence with Vaughn-Roberson, Summer.

SELLMAN, V. (1981) Correspondence with Vaughn-Roberson, Summer.

SEXTON, P.C. (1974) 'Schools are emasculating our boys', in STACEY, J., BÉREAUD, S. and DANIELS, J. (Eds) *And Jill Came Tumbling After: Sexism in American Education*, New York, NY, Dell, pp. 139–41.

SCHARF, L. (1980) *To Work or to Wed: Female Employment, Feminism and the Great Depression*, Contributions to Women's Studies, no. 15, Westport, CT: Greenwood Press.

'Should mothers teach?' (1913) *Journal of Education*, October 30, p. 432.

'Should the married woman teach?' (1909) *Independent*, **67**, August 12, pp. 363–64.

'Should women teachers have equal pay?' (1904) *Woman's Journal*, November 5, p. 356.

SIKES, P.J., MEASOR, L. and WOODS, P. (1985) *Teacher Careers: Crises and Continuities*, London, UK, Falmer Press.

SILVERMAN, E.L. (1975) 'Theodore Roosevelt and the education of women', *Journal of Education*, **9**, 3, pp. 176–82.

'Sims continues Catholic attack' (1921) *Atlanta Constitution*, August 28.

SITTON, T., MEHAFFY, G.L. and DAVIS, Jr. O.L. (1983) *Oral History: A Guide for Teachers (and Others)*, Austin, TX, University of Texas.

SIZER, T.R. (1984) *Horace's Compromise: The Dilemma of the American High School*, Boston, MA, Houghton-Mifflin.

SKLAR, K.K. (1973) *Catharine Beecher: A Study in American Domesticity*, New Haven, CT, Yale University Press.

SKLAR, K.K. (1987) 'Catharine Beecher: Transforming the teaching profession', in KERBER, L.K. and DeHART, J. (Eds) *Women's America: Refocusing the Past*, New York, NY, Oxford University Press, pp. 158–166.

SMALLWOOD, J. (1976) *And Gladly Teach*, Norman, OK, University of Oklahoma Press.

SMITH, J. (1981) Correspondence with Vaughn-Roberson, Summer.

SMITH-ROSENBERG, R. (1982) *Beyond Separate Spheres: Intellectual Roots of Modern Feminism*. New Haven, CT: Yale University Press.

SOCHEN, J. (1974) *Herstory: A Woman's View of American History*, New York, NY, Alfred Publishing.

SOLOMON, B.M. (1985) *In the Company of Educated Women: A History of Women in America*, New Haven, CT, Yale University Press.

SPAULDING, F.E. (1955) *School Superintendent in Action*, Ringe, NH: R.R. Smith.

SPENCER, H. (1899) *Study of Sociology*, NY: Appleton.

SPRADLEY, J. (1970) *You Owe Yourself a Drunk: An Ethnography of Urban Nomads*, Boston, MA, Little, Brown, and Co.

SPRADLEY, J.P. and McCURDY, D.W. (1972) *The Cultural Experience: Ethnography in Complex Society*, Chicago, IL, Science Research Associates.

SPRING, J.H. (1972) *Education and the Rise of the Corporate State*, Boston, MA, Beacon Press.

SPRINGER, I. (1981) Correspondence with Vaughn-Roberson, Summer.

STANLEY, R.M. (1967) 'Alice M. Robertson: Oklahoma's first congresswoman', *Chronicles of Oklahoma*, **45**, Autumn, pp. 259–89.

'Stanley will probe cost of living among teachers' (1919) *Atlanta Constitution*, January 15.

STANTON, T. and BLATCH, H.S. (1922) *Elizabeth Cady Stanton*, New York, NY, Harport Brothers.

STATE DEPARTMENT OF COLORADO (1943) *Thirty-Third Biennial Report of the State Superintendent of Public Instruction of the State of Colorado*, Denver, CO, State Department of Education.

STATE DEPARTMENT OF OKLAHOMA (1948) *Twenty-Second Biennial Report of the State Department of Education of Oklahoma*, Oklahoma City, OK, State Board of Education.

Statistics of Women at Work (1907) Washington, DC, Bureau of the Census.

STEARNS, P.N. (1983) 'The new social history: An overview', in GARDNER, J.B. and ADAMS, G.R. (Eds) *Ordinary People and Everyday Life: Perspectives on the New Social History*, Nashville, TN, American Association for State and Local History.

STEELE, O. (1839) *Third Annual Report of the Superintendent of Common Schools, Buffalo, New York*, Buffalo, NY, Steele Press.

STEELE, R.M. (1826) *A Study of Teacher Training in Vermont*, New York, NY, Teachers College, Bureau of Publications.

STINNETT, T.M. (1969) 'Teacher education, certification, and accreditation', in FULLER, E. and PEARSON, J. (Eds) *Education in the States, Nationwide Development Since 1900*, Washington, DC, National Education Association, pp. 383–437.

STRACHAN, G.C. (1910a) *Equal Pay for Equal Work: The Story of the Struggle for Justice Being Made by Women Teachers of the City of New York*, NY, B.F. Buck and Company.

STRACHAN, G.C. (1910b) 'Our fight for equal pay, New York women school-teachers object to men getting often twice as much for the same work, *The Delineator*, **75**, pp. 202 and 258.

STRACHAN, G.C. (1913) 'Miss Strachan not to march (Letter to the Editor), *New York Times*, April 13, section III, p. 6, col. 7.

STROBER, M.H. and BEST, L. (1979) 'The female/male salary differential in public schools: Some lessons from San Francisco, 1879', *Economic Inquiry*, **17**, pp. 218–36.

STROBER, M.H. and LANFORD, A.G. (1986) 'The feminization of public school teaching: Cross-sectional analysis, 1850–1880', *Signs: Journal of Women in Culture and Society*, **11**, p. 212–35.

STROBER, M.H. and TYACK, D. (1980) 'Why do women teach and men manage? A report on research on schools', *Signs: Journal of Women in Culture and Society*, **5**, pp. 494–503.

References

'Suffrage school well-attended (1913) *Everywoman*, **3**, September 25.

Survey on Salaries, Tenure of Office and Pension Provisions of Teachers (1905) Washington, DC, National Education Association.

SUTHERLAND, J.E. (1983) 'Of mills and memories: Labor-management interdependence in the Cheyney silk mills', *Oral History Review*, **11**, pp. 17–47.

TAX, M. (1980) *The Rising of Women: Feminist Solidarity, Class Conflict, 1880–1917*, New York, NY, Monthly Review Press.

TAYLOR, F.W. (1911) *Principles of Scientific Management*, New York, NY, Norton.

TAYLOR, E. (1951) 'The woman suffrage movement in Texas', *Journal of Southern History*, **17**, May, pp. 194–215.

'Teacher becomes mother, child born to Mrs. Wagner soon after she quits classroom' (1914) *New York Times*, November 1, section II, p. 13.

'Teacher plans to make demand for affidavits' (1921) *Atlanta Constitution*, July 10.

'Teacher suffragists organize' (1915) *New York Times*, April 11, p. 6, col. 3.

'Teacher-mother appeal to mayor' (1914) *New York Times*, November 5, p. 14, col. 5.

'Teacher-mother to mayor' (1914) *New York Times*, November 6, p. 11, col. 4.

'Teacher-mothers case at Albany' (1914) *New York Times*, December 15, p. 6, col. 1.

'Teacher-mothers win final verdict' (1915) *New York Times*, January 12, p. 5, col. 3.

'Teachers ask equal pay' (1907) *The Woman's Journal*, March 9, p. 1.

'Teacher's election fight' (1905) *New York Times*, May 7, p. 12, col. 2.

'Teacher's equal pay bill' (1907) *Woman's Journal*, May 25, p. 82.

'Teachers may marry' (1904) *Independent*, 51, May 5, p. 1044.

'Teachers of city to ask showdown at meeting today' (1919) *Atlanta Constitution*, June 23.

'Teachers oppose salary reduction' (1921) *Atlanta Journal*, May 17.

'Teachers ready to present plan' (1919) *Atlanta Constitution*, January 23.

Teacher's Salaries and the Cost of Living (1913) Ann Arbor, MI, National Education Association.

'Teachers to enter soapbox campaign' (1915) *New York Times*, June 2, p. 13, col. 3.

'Teachers to get maternity leave' (1914) *New York Times*, November 13, p. 8, col. 4.

'Teachers to the front' (1915) *Woman Voter*, **6**, July, p. 23.

'Tell men teachers they shan't meddle — women in the schools flatly inform them that their aid isn't wanted — equal pay question' (1909) *New York Times*, June 10, p. 16, col. 5.

'10 Minutes will be devoted daily to Bible reading' (1920) *Atlanta Constitution*, August 10.

TENTLER, L.W. (1979) *Wage-Earning Women: Industrial Work and Family Life in the US, 1900–1930*, Oxford, UK, Oxford University Press.

TERKEL, S. (1970) *Hardtimes: An Oral History of the Great Depression*, New York, NY, Washington Square Press.

THOMAS, W.I. and THOMAS, D.S. (1928) *The Child in America: Behavior Problems and Programs*, New York, NY, Knopf.

THOMPSON, E.P. (1963) *The Making of the English Working Class*, Middlesex, UK, Penguin Books.

THOMPSON, P. (1978) *The Voice of the Past: Oral History*, New York, NY, Oxford University Press.

'To all lovers of law and order peace and justice, and to all the people of the United States', (1921) *Atlanta Constitution*, 9 August.

'To try another married teacher' (1913) *New York Times*, November 3, p. 7, cols. 1–2.

TYACK, D. (1967a) 'Bureaucracy and the common school: The example of Portland, Oregon, 1851–1913', *American Quarterly*, **19**, pp. 474–98.

TYACK, D. (1967b) *Turning Points in American Educational History*, New York, NY, John Wiley.

TYACK, D.B. (1974) *One Best System: A History of American Urban Education*, Cambridge, MA, Harvard University Press.

TYACK, D.B. (1989) 'The future of the past: What do we need to know about the history of teaching'? in WARREN, D. (Ed.) *American Teachers: Histories of a Profession at Work*. New York, NY, MacMillan.

TYACK, D.B. and HANSOT, E. (1982) *Managers of Virtue: Public School Leadership in America, 1820–1980*, New York, NY, Basic Books.

TYACK, D.B., and STROBER, M.H. (1981) 'Jobs and gender: A history of the structuring of educational employment by sex', in SCHMUCK, P.A., CHARTERS, W.W., Jr., and CARLSON, R.O. (Eds) *Educational Policy and Management: Sex Differentials*, New York, NY, Academic Press, pp. 131–52.

TYACK, D.B., LOWE, R. and HANSOT, E. (1984) *Public Schools in Hard Times: The Great Depression and Recent Years*, Cambridge, MA, Harvard University Press.

UNDERWOOD, K. (1986) 'The pace of their own lives: Teacher training and the life course of western women', *Pacific Historical Rewiew*, **55**, November, pp. 513–30.

US BUREAU OF THE CENSUS (1910) *13th Census of the United States*, Volume III, Population, and *Abstract of the Census with Supplement for the State of Vermont*, Washington, DC, Government Printing Office.

US BUREAU OF THE CENSUS (1930) *15th Census of the United States*, Volume III, Part 2, Population, Washington, DC, Government Printing Office.

US BUREAU OF THE CENSUS (1950) *Census of Population*: 1950, *Volume I*, and Volume II, Part 45 — Vermont, Washington, DC, Government Printing Office.

US DEPARTMENT OF EDUCATION (1983) *A Nation at Risk: The Imperative for Reform*, Washington, DC, Government Printing Office.

URBAN, W.J. (1977) 'Progressive education in the urban South: The reform of the Atlanta schools', in EBNER, M.H. and TOBIN, E.M. (Eds) *The Age of Urban Reform: New Perspectives on the Progressive Era*, Port Washington, NY, Kennikat Press, pp. 131–41.

URBAN, W.J. (1982) *Why Teachers Organized*, Detroit, MI, Wayne State University Press.

VAN HOOVE, D. (1981) Correspondence with Vaughn-Roberson, Summer.

VAUGHN-ROBERSON, C.A. (1984) 'Sometimes independent but never equal — Women teachers, 1900–1950: The Oklahoma example', *Pacific Historical Review*, **53**, February, pp. 39–58.

VERMONT STATE BOARD OF EDUCATION (1910–1950) *Vermont School Reports*, Rutland, VT, Tutle Company.

VIOLAS, P.C. (1971) 'Academic freedom and the public school teacher, 1930–1960', *Educational Theory*, **21**, pp. 70–80.

VOLOSINOV, V.N. (1973) *Marxism and the Philosophy of Language*, Trans. MATEJKA, L. and TITUNIK, I.R., New York, NY, Seminar Press.

VOLOSINOV, V.N. (1976) *Freudianism: A Marxist Critique*, Trans. TITUNIK, I.R., New York, NY, Academic Press.

WALLACE-HADRILL, J.M. (1962) *The Long-Haired Kings and Other Studies in Frankish History*, London, UK, Methuen.

WALLER, W. (1932) *Sociology of Teaching*, New York, NY, Russell and Russell.

WARREN, D.R. (1978) *History, Education, and Public Policy*, Berkeley, CA, McCutchan Publishing.

WARREN, D.R. (Ed.) (1989) *American Teachers: Histories of a Profession at Work*, New York, NY, Macmillan.

WATKINS, F. (1981) Correspondence with Vaughn-Roberson, Summer.

WEIN, R. (1974) 'Women's colleges and domesticity, 1875–1918', *History of Education Quarterly*, **14**, Spring, pp. 31–47.

References

WEINBERG, M. (1981) *The Education of Poor and Minority Students*, Westport, CT, Greenwood Press.

WEINER, L.Y. (1985) *From Working Girl to Working Mother: The Female Labor Force in the US, 1820–1980*, Chapel Hill, NC, University of North Carolina Press.

WELTER, B. (1966) 'The cult of true womanhood: 1820–1860', *American Quarterly*, **18**, Summer, pp. 151–74.

WHEELER, F. and G. (1978) 'Colorado Oral History Project No. 1894 (Spring), Steamboat Springs, CO, Steamboat Springs High School.

WHITE, H. (1973) *Metahistory: The Historical Imagination in Nineteenth-Century Europe*, Baltimore, MD, Johns Hopkins.

WIEDER, A. (1986) 'A principal and desegregation', *Equity and Excellence*, **22**, pp. 125–129.

WIEDER, A. (1988) 'The Whites Who Stayed', *Vitae Scholasticae*, **5**, pp. 169–189.

'Will permit women teachers to marry' (1904) *New York Times*, April 28, p. 16, col. 3.

WILLIAMS, M. (1981) Correspondence with Vaughn-Roberson, Summer.

WILSON, J.D. and STORTZ, P.J. (1988) '"May the Lord have mercy on you": The rural school problem in British Columbia in the 1920s,' *British Columbia Studies*, **79**, (Autumn) pp. 24–58.

WINSHIP, A.E. (1906) 'Should married women teach?', *Journal of Education*, **68**, p. 581.

WITEVER, N. (1981) Correspondence with Vaughn-Roberson, Summer.

'Women teachers begin higher salary fight' (1906) *New York Times*, November 4, p. 3, col. 3.

'Women teachers challenge — they call men in schools to debate equal pay question' (1908) *New York Times*, March 1, p. 1, col. 2.

'Won't act against teachers, notice of her marriage forthwith elastic' (1913) *New York Times*, March 20, p. 22, col. 2.

WOODY, T. (1980) *A History of Women's Education in the United States*, *1*, New York, NY, Octagon Books.

YOUNG, B. (1981) Correspondence with Vaughn-Roberson, Summer.

YOUNG, R. (1914) 'Guilty of motherhood', *Good Housekeeping*, **58**, pp. 27–33.

ZITKALA-SA (GERTRUDE BONNIN) (1921) *American Indian Stories*, Washington, DC, Hayworth Publishing House, pp. 7–108.

ZUNZ, O. (1985) 'The synthesis of social change: Reflections on American social history', in ZUNZ, O. (Ed.) *Reliving the Past: The Worlds of Social History*, Chapel Hill, NC, University of North Carolina Press.

Notes on Contributors

Richard J. Altenbaugh (PhD, University of Pittsburgh, 1980), an Associate Professor in the Department of History at Northern Illinois University, has taught at Indiana University, the University of Louisville, and the University of Pittsburgh. His articles and reviews have appeared in *History of Education Quarterly, Urban Education, Theatre Journal, Journal of American History*, among others. He has also published essays in several anthologies, and has authored *Education for Struggle: The American Labor Colleges of the 1920s and 1930s* (Temple University Press, 1990).

Phyllis McGruder Chase is a graduate student in the Department of Sociological, Philosophical and Historical Foundations at the State University of New York at Buffalo. In 1960, she began teaching in the Buffalo school system, and later served as Project Director of the community based Jefferson Education Center. She also worked with the Training of Teachers Program and taught courses in the Sociology of Education for the Social Foundations Department and for the Department of Black Studies at State University of New York at Buffalo. For the past decade she has coordinated cultural services for the Buffalo Public School System.

Patricia Carter (EdD 1985, MCP 1986, University of Cincinnati) teaches and serves as Associate Director of Women's Studies at the University of Connecticut. She is the executive producer of two nationally distributed historical video documentaries, 'Women Working Through Ohio's History' (1986) and 'The Women of Rookwood' (1987). Her articles have appeared in the *Journal of Midwest History of Education Society, The Women's Studies Forum, Educational Studies*, and the *National Association of Arts Educators Quarterly*.

Margaret K. Nelson (PhD, Sociology, Columbia University) teaches at Middlebury College, where she is Professor of Sociology and Director of the Women's Studies Program. She is the editor (with Emily K. Abel) of *Circles of Care: Work and Identity in Women's Lives* (State University of New York Press, 1990) and author of *Negotiated Care: The Experience of Family Day Care Providers* (Temple University Press, 1990).

Joseph W. Newman (PhD, Educational Foundations, Georgia State University, 1978) is Professor of Educational Foundations at the University of South Alabama, where he was named Outstanding Professor in 1986. Having published articles, reviews, and essays in such journals as *History of Education Quarterly, Educational Studies*, and *Phi Delta Kappan*, Newman is the author of *America's Teachers: An Introduction to Education* (Longman, Inc., 1990).

Richard A. Quantz received three degrees from the University of Virginia and taught elementary school both in Virginia and Mississippi. He is, at present, a Professor of Educational Studies in the Department of Educational Leadership and Associate Director of the Center for Education and Cultural Studies at Miami University, Ohio. His articles have been published in *History of Education Quarterly, Educational Theory, Educational Studies*, and other journals.

Courtney Vaughn-Roberson (EdD, Oklahoma State University, 1980) is Professor in the Department of Educational Leadership at the University of Oklahoma. She has published in *Pacific Historical Review, History of Higher Education Annual, The Journal of Research in Childbood Education, Issues in Education*, and *The Journal of Negro Education*, produced two co-authored books, and, with colleagues Michael Langenbach and Lola Aagaard, is currently under contract with Allan and Bacon Press to write *An Important Introduction to Educational Research*.

Alan Wieder studied with Bernard Mehl and completed his doctorate in Social Foundations of Education at Ohio State University in 1977. Since that time, he has taught in Oklahoma, Ohio, Louisiana, and Wisconsin. He is presently an Associate Professor at the University of South Carolina. He has written extensively about school integration in New Orleans. This work has been published in the *Journal of Negro Education, Phylon, Louisiana History, Equity and Excellence*, and *Vitae Scholasticae*. He also published methodological essays on oral history and visual sociological essays on race, class, and education.

Index

TEIKYO WESTMAR UNIV. LIBRARY

LB 1775.2 .T44 1991

The Teacher's voice
        (92-1225)

DEMCO